Rockin' in the Ivory Tower

Ceres
RUTGERS
STUDIES
IN HISTORY

Lucia McMahon and Christopher T. Fisher, Series Editors

New Jersey holds a unique place in the American story. One of the thirteen colonies in British North America and the original states of the United States, New Jersey plays a central, yet underappreciated, place in America's economic, political, and social development. New Jersey's axial position as the nation's financial, intellectual, and political corridor has become something of a signature, evident in quips about the Turnpike and punchlines that end with its many exits. Yet, New Jersey is more than a crossroad or an interstitial "elsewhere." Far from being ancillary to the nation, New Jersey is an axis around which America's story has turned, and within its borders gathers a rich collection of ideas, innovations, people, and politics. The region's historical development makes it a microcosm of the challenges and possibilities of the nation, and it also reflects the complexities of the modern, cosmopolitan world. Yet, far too little of the literature recognizes New Jersey's significance to the national story, and despite promising scholarship done at the local level, New Jersey history often remains hidden in plain sight. Ceres books represent new, rigorously peer-reviewed scholarship on New Jersey and the surrounding region. Named for the Roman goddess of prosperity portrayed on the New Jersey State Seal, Ceres provides a platform for cultivating and disseminating the next generation of scholarship. It features the work of both established historians and a new generation of scholars across disciplines. Ceres aims to be field-shaping, providing a home for the newest and best empirical, archival, and theoretical work on the region's past. We are also dedicated to fostering diverse and inclusive scholarship and hope to feature works addressing issues of social justice and activism.

James M. Carter, *Rockin' in the Ivory Tower: Rock Music on Campus in the Sixties*
Jordan P. Howell, *Garbage in the Garden State*
Maxine N. Lurie, *Taking Sides in Revolutionary New Jersey: Caught in the Crossfire*
Jean R. Soderlund, *Separate Paths: Lenapes and Colonists in West New Jersey*

Rockin' in the Ivory Tower

· ·

Rock Music on Campus in the Sixties

JAMES M. CARTER

Rutgers University Press

New Brunswick, Camden, and Newark, New Jersey

London and Oxford

Rutgers University Press is a department of Rutgers, The State University of New Jersey, one of the leading public research universities in the nation. By publishing worldwide, it furthers the University's mission of dedication to excellence in teaching, scholarship, research, and clinical care.

Library of Congress Cataloging-in-Publication Data
Names: Carter, James M., 1968– author.
Title: Rockin' in the ivory tower: rock music on campus in the sixties / James M. Carter.
Description: New Brunswick: Rutgers University Press, 2023. | Includes bibliographical references and index.
Identifiers: LCCN 2022041175 | ISBN 9781978829381 (paperback) | ISBN 9781978829398 (hardback) | ISBN 9781978829404 (epub) | ISBN 9781978829411 (pdf)
Subjects: LCSH: Rock music—Social aspects—United States—History—20th century. | College campuses—Social aspects—United States—History—20th century. | Rock music—United States—1961–1970—History and criticism.
Classification: LCC ML3918.R63 C38 2023 | DDC 781.6609/046—dc23/eng/20220826
LC record available at https://lccn.loc.gov/2022041175

A British Cataloging-in-Publication record for this book is available from the British Library.

References to internet websites (URLs) were accurate at the time of writing. Neither the author nor Rutgers University Press is responsible for URLs that may have expired or changed since the manuscript was prepared.

♾ The paper used in this publication meets the requirements of the American National Standard for Information Sciences—Permanence of Paper for Printed Library Materials, ANSI Z39.48-1992.

rutgersuniversitypress.org

Contents

Preface and Acknowledgments

The research for this book began several years ago as merely preparation for a class on the history of rock and roll. I found more than I bargained for and found most of it in my own proverbial backyard. I teach at one of the college campuses highlighted herein, Drew University in Madison, New Jersey. What I discovered in poking around in campus archives quickly went from interesting curiosities to something much more significant. The dozens of now iconic musicians and bands associated with the sixties who performed on the small campus in Madison weren't just one-offs. Those performances were at the very core of the development of rock music culture. Born around mid-decade, rock music's live performance was an ad hoc affair. More often than not, concerts took place in warehouses, outdoor parks, tiny, run-down clubs in the sketchier part of towns, and, of course, colleges. Owing to the postwar boom in higher education, the number of campuses in the United States ballooned by more than 500 in just the five years after 1960. And, not all that surprisingly in retrospect, those campuses quickly became welcoming hosts to the emerging rock music, with all its irreverence, amateurishness, and eclecticism. At both Drew University and Stony Brook University on Long Island, New York, a literal who's who of rock and roll, rock, R & B/soul, folk, and pop vocals routinely performed. I found the same pattern across the country. By the late sixties, college campuses made up a kind of ad hoc circuit for rock music's live performance.

One of the most fascinating components of this organic circuit was the role played by the students.

I had the good fortune to talk with a number of them, and I wish to thank them for their contribution to this work. At Drew, Greg Granquist, Glenn Redbord, Dave Marsden, Barry Fenstermacher, David Hinckley, Harry Litwack, Bob Smartt, Jeff King, Ken Schulman, Don Orlando, Tom McMullen, and Bob Johnson all were generous with their time and invaluable in getting a close-up sense of the experience of these years on the campus. In particular, Greg Granquist, David Hinckley, and Jeff King suffered me the most, engaging in numerous follow-up conversations and providing all sorts of unsolicited details and insights. They were immensely helpful. At Stony Brook, Howie Klein, Norm Prusslin, Charles Backfish, Nancy Malagold, Moyssi, and Mary Beth Medley (nee Olbrych) likewise provided so much more insight than would have otherwise been possible. I continue to routinely talk with Howie and Mary Beth. Other key participants in the events that fill out this book and who I was fortunate enough to interview are Bob Courboin, Tom Wetzler, Doug Chapman, and Barbara North. Bob was at the center of the so-called hippie house in Madison and, without him, I would simply not have been able to tell this story. He has been enormously generous with his time in our many conversations. Likewise, Doug, as a resident there and the son of a Drew professor, had unique insight. Barbara, a frequent visitor at the infamous house on Main Street in Madison, shared her experiences living communally in the late sixties in this small town and attending the many concerts at the campus across the street. Indeed, these contributions have added immeasurably to this fascinating and important story. Finally, I wish to thank Ed Ochs, a Billboard editor assigned to cover the new rock music in 1967. His editorials in the pages of the magazine prompted me to reach out to him on the outside chance he would talk with me. Happily, he did, and I thank him for his unique insight into the thinking of the leading industry publication at a time of so much swift change in popular music.

I also grasped about for expertise from a number of colleagues to make sure I was actually onto something. These include Reebee Garofalo, Patrick Burke, Michael Kramer, and Jeremy Varon. All were generous in answering my questions and gentle in pushing me in directions I had not realized the work needed to go. For that, thank you all! I would also like to thank Peter Mickulas, my editor at Rutgers University Press. Thanks as well to the outside readers, in particular Dewar McLeod for his time and attention to the manuscript. His comments and suggestions have made this a better book.

Finally, I need to thank the person who has indulged me the most by far, Angie Calder. My partner in every way, she is always there for me. Much like me, she has lived with this project from its incubation through the various twists and turns to this final point. She has read too many versions of too many versions, and she has always been willing to talk about them honestly and to challenge my thinking in ways not always expected. Being able to rely on her perspective and feedback has been tremendously helpful, even necessary. These words do not begin to account for her role in the work and in my life.

Rockin' in the Ivory Tower

Introduction

· ·

When, in 1960, Grinnell College president Howard Bowen interviewed Georgia Dentel for the new position of social coordinator, he told her, "I need activities. I need things happening for the students to do"—especially important for the rural Iowa liberal arts college with a growing student body. Dentel accepted the position and served for the next four decades as social coordinator, advising the Student Union in the management of the campus entertainment calendar and budget. "It emerged gradually that the only thing students wanted were concerts," she said recently. "They wanted rock and roll." Given that she had no background in the music industry and little knowledge of specific bands and artists, she just started calling people. Because she was aware of the rock music in San Francisco, she managed to get promoter Bill Graham on the phone. She asked if he had any bands that would make the trip to Iowa to play at the college "for the amount of money we could offer—it was very small—I can't believe I had the nerve to ask him. He said, 'No, I really don't. . . . I don't have anybody right now, but there's a band I'm thinking of bringing into the Fillmore. They're playing in a club.' . . . Just as we were about to hang up, I said 'Oh, by the way, what's their name?'" That band, barely a year old, turned out to be Jefferson Airplane. They played the homecoming dance at Grinnell in 1966.

Jefferson Airplane's manager Bill Thompson later recalled playing that early gig at the midwestern college campus, barely a week after Grace Slick had replaced Signe Anderson on vocals, her first performance outside of California:

> We flew to Grinnell College for the Homecoming. You should have seen it when we came out to play. We had a light show. But all the girls were in ruffled dresses all the way down to the ankles with corsages, and their *families* were there. We started the light show and we had three sets to do that night. The first set, it was like we were from Mars. Guys with their hair cut like Dobie Gillis were standing there and staring at us. The parents were all farmers. They were looking at one another and saying, "what the hell *is* this stuff? Too loud for me, Maude. Time to go home and milk the goat." So they all left.[1]

While the audience was no doubt ill-prepared for the show, the booking of one of the earliest psychedelic rock bands at the rural college is a landmark historical event. And while Dentel's name is not likely to grace the walls and halls of the Rock and Roll Hall of Fame anytime soon, her role in nurturing rock music during the second half of the sixties is important.

Rock Music, Counterculture, and the Sixties

Rock music, as distinct from rock and roll of a decade earlier, was in its infancy as a cultural phenomenon in 1966. Its emergence is typically marked from 1964 and the so-called British invasion, owing to the massive popularity of The Beatles, The Rolling Stones, and too many other British bands to list here. Additionally, American bands such as Jefferson Airplane, The Grateful Dead on the West Coast, and The Velvet Underground and The MC5 on the East Coast were just forming around 1965. They and others performed a brand of music different from what had come before—predominantly guitar-driven, lyrically provocative music combining psychedelic, blues, and folk elements, among other influences. Identified by several names, the music and its attendant culture soon came to be termed simply "rock." Most of the bands associated with it performed in obscure, out-of-the-way places, and none could be heard on AM radio. All that changed within a couple years.

From mid-decade, rock music culture quickly grew in the United States, and on college campuses in particular. In 1967, *Billboard* magazine proclaimed, based on its own extensive research, rock music had "attacked, stormed and conquered" the ivory tower. The industry magazine urged record labels to get their product into campus bookstores, which many immediately did. All this was well before the opening of the more famous private clubs hosting rock music, such as the Fillmores, East and West (in spring/summer 1968), and even before the Monterey Pop Festival (June 1967) and certainly prior to Woodstock (August 1969). By 1967, rock music surpassed all other music on college campuses in popularity, coming from dead last two years earlier.[2]

Rock music's arrival tracked with the other key phenomenon of the era: the dramatic expansion of higher education across the United States. Well documented by historians, this growth resulted from the war's end, specific legislative efforts such as the G.I. Bill, the massive "baby boom," and unprecedented prosperity during the following fifteen years. Total college enrollment expanded by 49 percent in the 1950s, and by 120 percent in the 1960s.[3] *Billboard* spotted the growth, along with its potential for the music industry, and began publishing its annual special issue "Music on Campus" in spring 1964, opening with an editorial on the scope and importance of the college campus as a market for popular music. Its author pointed out over 4.5 million students had enrolled in 2,140 colleges and universities around the nation, and that number was growing. The college campus became a place, if not *the* place, for the flourishing of a broad range of music from classical and chamber to pop vocals and folk music.[4]

Given this cocktail, it should come as little surprise to learn that rock music culture soon found the college campus, with its more or less captive audience of eighteen-to-twenty-two-year-olds. Or perhaps they found rock music. Nonetheless, it is surprising to many who hear of it now. To hear that Janis Joplin performed at Worcester Polytechnic Institute or that The Velvet Underground's first paying gig was Summit High School in New Jersey comes as something of a shock today. Many of rock's early bands played county fairs, high school dances, nearly empty warehouses, and run-down private clubs too small for more than a couple dozen people to crowd into spaces that were likely condemnable. All of this was more typical than not, at least for a short time. Amid this reality, many bands were drawn to the nation's rapidly growing colleges. Enterprising students sought entertainment at the head of student committees charged with spending considerable sums of money for that express purpose. With budgets running well into five figures, they found they could afford this latest "underground" music, with its popularity rising rapidly among precisely this demographic.[5]

We know a great deal about activism on college campuses during the sixties, about a dynamic student life, about protests, marches, walkouts, and occupations. However, we know much less about that same environment and its relationship to the growth and development of rock culture within the broader sixties culture. Of course, rock culture of the late sixties wasn't merely the hazy, drug-fueled trip of aimless rebellion and noise of subsequent popular culture fantasy. Nor was it limited to Woodstock or Altamont, or San Francisco's Haight-Ashbury for that matter. While each of those matters, rock culture was also happening in not-so-visible places and spaces, and its participants, shapers, and innovators could be and were quite earnest and sober. Rock music took shape in virtually every region of the country where it could gain some traction, find an audience, and sell enough tickets to pay for travel to the next gig. Its emergence after 1965–1966 paralleled the development of an accompanying and accommodating infrastructure and culture.

Moving away from these broadly accepted late-sixties historical tropes and hot spots, the picture becomes more complicated and richer, and a lot less the dreams or nightmares of sixties culture admirers or detractors, respectively. Mapping rock and roll and pop music of these years shows much more variation, less intentionality, more randomness, and more of the chaos, uncertainty, and conditionality of the period. For instance, otherwise disparate performers, bands, and artists appeared on the same bill—even Monterey, Woodstock, and Altamont. So too at hundreds of universities that have not become household names. Almost by accident, the nation's growing college campuses turned into an ad hoc circuit for developing popular music at the precise moment of so much diversity and growth for each. College students, enjoying much freedom, became, in effect, concert promoters. The view from the college campus highlights the organic nature of these social/cultural developments.

The story of college concert promotion likewise highlights and explains what Keir Keightley has called rock music culture's "stylistic eclecticism." I believe the college campus, with its built-in diversity of musical performance/taste, its unique relationship with the surrounding communities, and its reliably rotating student population, was one of the origin points of this noted eclecticism. Michael Kramer has added to rock's eclecticism the idea that the counterculture and its accompanying soundtrack, rock music, "fostered an efflorescence of civic engagement . . . to invent modes of citizenship" appropriate for difficult and changing times.[6] At the same time, the recent work of David Farber and Joshua Davis, and their ideas about "right livelihoods" and "activist entrepreneurs," respectively, has contributed to a historiographical trend away from the movement leaders, marches, and mass protests of the counterculture narrative and toward a focus on "the countercultural project," in Farber's apt words. This study continues that effort by placing relatively typical college students at the center of the earnest exploration of the rapidly changing world of the mid- to late sixties, the advent of rock music culture, and the counterculture.[7] More particularly, we should take notice of how, informed by the milieu of student activism in the civil rights movement and making the most of new ideals of freedom in higher education institutions, an organic entrepreneurialism functioned outside the hierarchical corporate structures of business culture to embrace a "do it yourself" style of music promotion and activity.

The "counterculture" is a notoriously difficult thing to define. The 1960s phenomenon known by that name is complicated, and the label often describes something too narrow. In moving away from the inherent limitations of a single definition or linear trajectory to frame the late-sixties counterculture experience, this study seeks to "historicize the countercultural project," in Farber's words. This project centers on the struggle to establish and live within space that allowed for personal liberation, to be "less complicit in practices and beliefs" viewed as destructive. Farber goes on to argue, "The counterculture [was] an on-going project of self-conscious cultural producers who tried to build more autonomy into their lives. . . . A necessary, sustaining and contentious aspect of their practice was figuring out who was part of the project and who was not: it was a precarious business of pattern creation, deployment and recognition in a cultural flux made dangerous by powerful antagonists, inept adoptees, rip-off artists of every description. To call this high-stakes game of cultural production normatively the 'counterculture' is to mistake a word for a set of actions that never achieved equilibrium or homeostasis."[8] Farber's argument for the counterculture as a high-stakes way of life is especially relevant in my research. He, Andrew Hunt, Alice Echols, John McMillian, Kimbrew McLeod, and others have done insightful work in recent years which encourages a reassessment and even a reframing of the sixties and the counterculture. Each has contributed in specific ways to decentering the history of these years and also in rethinking its temporal, geographical, and topical boundaries.[9]

The college campus provides an ideal opportunity for just this sort of examination, particularly given the intrinsic entrepreneurialism among students in developing an autonomous, organic cultural life. The campus provided an ideal space for this entrepreneurialism—a culturally and politically savvy enterprising spirit. With little to no faculty or administrative involvement or direction, students were free to make their own choices and to take lead roles in shaping campus life, and to use the campus as a vehicle to engage the rapidly changing world beyond its walls. At both campuses highlighted in the chapters that follow, entrepreneurialism on the campus flourished in between the existing music industry and the precorporate, artisanal music experience, especially regarding rock music culture.[10] This in-between space is crucial to understanding how rock culture and the counterculture emerged during the 1960s.

Taking organizing and promoting rock music on campus seriously broadens our understanding of what it meant to be an activist during this era. Student concert promoters were driven by an entrepreneurial spirit to assert independence and to reinforce and perpetuate those values and experiences they found worthwhile, while avoiding or rejecting those they did not. To engage, to organize and attend concerts, to play the music is activism; to do so on a large scale, to invite thousands of others, to spread the culture's influence through live performance is very much so. While never intending to turn rock into an industry, the student promoters played their part. Although they were unaware of or had not intended to play a particular role in the formation of rock culture, college campus impresarios did so as part of the simultaneously developing rock music industry and counterculture. These impresarios engaged with the world around them, giving rise to the wonderfully eclectic culture of rock music.

Histories of rock music, the counterculture, and higher education have missed the significant role the college campus played in shaping rock music culture as it developed following 1966. Specifically, the college campus experience gave rise to "rock culture," an unstable and eclectic mix of genres encompassing folk, rock and roll, R & B, gospel, pop vocalists, country and western, blues, and even jazz. Only later, in the 1970s, did rock music become a consolidated sound and genre. Likewise, only later did the counterculture, in which rock music played a key part and in turn helped to shape, turn into a more static social symbol and style.

This book places the college campus at the center of an emerging rock music culture. As private clubs and other hosting venues were only slowly emerging, the performance of rock music thrived on campuses, where a built-in audience, a tradition of music performance, and a student body enjoying remarkable autonomy (and a budget) in planning activities already existed. Of course, this did not occur in a vacuum; it was a key component of related movements and phenomena that we have come to think of as "the sixties," including civil rights, free speech, and antiwar movements, the counterculture, and the growth and spread of the underground press. Not simply coincidentally, rock music culture emerged with, and as a part of, the counterculture. One of the major themes of this book is how these multiple cultural, political, and social phenomena, often treated separately, were actually bound together and evolved in relation to each other in important ways. We have not sufficiently understood or taken stock of these developments, nor have historians adequately explained the origins of the culture of rock music that emerged in the United States after 1965. This book moves away from the conventional historical narrative and its key actors and places/ spaces to explore a dynamic, sometimes counterintuitive, and often unexpected story of the period.

Two Case Studies: Stony Brook and Drew Universities

Subsequent chapters focus much attention on two specific campuses that serve as case studies: Stony Brook University in Long Island, New York, and Drew University in Madison, New Jersey. These two campuses are especially insightful for several reasons. Geographically, they lie due east and west, respectively, of lower Manhattan's East Village, an acknowledged sixties site in its own right. Each campus also drew its students from the region around New York, bringing to campus many first-generation college students from the region's middle- and working-class families. At the same time, those students had come of age amid a postwar America enjoying unprecedented economic growth, particularly among those very groups, and fighting a Cold War that placed much emphasis on the righteousness of the struggle and the importance of the buy-in of its citizens. This combination made for a particularly engaged and earnest student population.[11]

Stony Brook University opened in the early part of the decade and immediately experienced exponential growth in student enrollment common to this period in higher education in general. From an initial student population of under one thousand, the campus teemed with several thousand undergraduates within two years. Students struggled through construction equipment, workers, and mud to get to and from classes. The mud, in fact, became one of the enduring, if not endearing, elements of the college experience for most of them. Most also hailed from the region's high schools, all brought together amid tremendous change to a campus that was then relatively isolated on the north shore of Long Island. A vibrant and rapidly growing student body found itself with near-total autonomy to determine campus life. As will become apparent in subsequent chapters, they did precisely that, exerting a great deal of control over their individual and collective destinies on campus, much to the chagrin of campus authorities and local law enforcement.

Lying due west, Drew University's heavily wooded campus of a little more than 186 acres is ensconced in the small, sleepy northern New Jersey town of Madison, with its major artery, Main Street, running straight through the middle of town and in front of the campus. The walk from the center of town to the campus takes about three minutes. The student population of around 1,200 made the private liberal arts college among the smallest in the area. While the student body did not expand nearly so dramatically as that at Stony Brook, the campus was nonetheless remarkably dynamic, and the students enjoyed much autonomy to engage and determine the course of campus life and culture. Indeed, in both cases, the individual and collective freedom and power of the students stand out. Though technically created with administrative or faculty supervision, in practice, the students set up their governing bodies and committees and then ran them with little to no input from either.

This, then, is a study of sixties counterculture and rock music as both grew up in and around the area surrounding New York City. A number of colleges and universities, large and small, quickly became hothouses for the era's cultural developments. Ballooning in number from a few hundred to more than two thousand during the mid-sixties, campuses played an outsized role in nurturing the growth of rock music culture in the absence of any infrastructure or venues for it. A relatively small number of campuses ended up being strategically located to become key spots in an organically developing ad hoc cultural infrastructure within a very short time. The chapters that follow explore how college campuses became the key hubs of the emerging ad hoc rock music circuit, propelling hundreds of artists and bands to iconic status, while nurturing rock music culture's rise to national prominence and ensuring its cultural permanence. Ironically, this success quickly led to changes in the infrastructure for rock music culture, and its relationship to the broader music industry. One of the consequences of these changes was that small venues such as colleges could no longer afford to play the role they had only a few years earlier in nurturing and sustaining rock music, and were supplanted by the large-scale performances of "arena rock" by the early 1970s.

One of the benefits in using relatively unknown college campuses as a point of departure lies in moving away from a traditional narrative arc that serves to sequester the various elements of sixties history. Most of the literature on the sixties, rock music, and counterculture centers on familiar places, such as Berkeley and San Francisco, or particular events like Monterey, Woodstock, or Altamont. The result is a conventional narrative that is reductive and siloing—elements of this history are too often cut off from one another. Much has gotten lost in these well-known narratives. This is certainly true of the important role played by colleges and universities. This study places them, and two campuses in particular, at the center of these developments and yields the kinds of insights that force a fundamental reassessment of what we think we know of 1960s political culture, rock music, and the counterculture.

Not only did campuses prove a welcoming environment but, owing to the vast expansion in enrollments over the previous decade, students were well positioned to nurture and shape not simply the music but the key features of the culture around it. My research shows a fascinating entrepreneurial spirit and near-complete autonomy for students to do as they wished. This cocktail of factors goes a long way toward explaining what others have identified as rock music culture's pronounced eclecticism. The historian of higher education John Thelin has argued in his book on going to college in the sixties that "music's diversification was *driven* by the appreciation of college student audiences."[12] For instance, otherwise disparate performers, bands, and artists routinely appeared on the same bill as part of rock's performance. This was often a product of student choice. A student committee sought out and booked available bands and artists based on their own tastes and available funds. More often than not, that meant a new rock music act got paired with an R & B group, an "oldie" such as Chuck Berry, or a folk singer. That diversity, which had organically become commonplace for small colleges well before the industry took notice, later became a key element, if not *the* key element, in the formation of rock music culture during the counterculture sixties.

Alongside nurturing rock music on the campus, students were active and engaged with the movements of the era, such as free speech and civil rights, through the campus newspaper and various forms of student activism. The campus newspapers at both Stony Brook (*The Statesman*) and Drew University (*The Acorn*) were entirely student-run, and the editorial staffs reflected a notable diversity of race, class, and gender at otherwise fairly homogenous campuses. In both cases, the editorial leadership made the decision to join the national syndicate for the underground press, the Liberation News Service. Subsequently, both papers' content quickly came to reflect the rapid changes sweeping the nation in the late sixties. Coverage included the subversive "comix" of R. Crumb, the latest rock concert and album reviews, reviews of radical publications, detailed instructions on how to avoid the draft, radical critiques of the military-industrial complex, the state of race relations on the campus and across the nation, and included syndicated selections from such well-known figures as Dick Gregory, Abbie Hoffman, Tom Hayden, Ralph Nader, and Huey Newton. The students also brought to campus a veritable who's who of speakers and activists of the period, on par with the diversity and eclecticism of their rock music bookings (see appendix A). Additionally, students picketed, marched across town and on the city governments of neighboring towns, held a Vietnam War moratorium, engaged activists at area high schools, occupied administration buildings, secretly recorded faculty meetings (then published it all in the campus paper!), and protested and marched on behalf of local "hippies" after police and the courts violently threw them out of their home across the street from the campus.

Like many current students, I learned of this rich and furtive history at Drew University, where I teach, through the replica concert posters hanging here and there around campus. Those smaller versions typically don't get much notice, but if one takes a minute to look, they are quite remarkable. They advertise, for instance, concert performances by The Lovin' Spoonful, The Animals, Judy Collins, The Four Tops, The Who, Jefferson Airplane, Jethro Tull, and Chuck Berry, all performing on the campus between 1967 and 1970. As an historian, this seemed odd to me. I had no place to put these concerts within what I already knew of the sixties. Why on earth had these bands and artists come to this tiny, out-of-the-way campus to perform? These were iconic acts, drawing huge crowds, and money! I soon learned the replica posters only reflected a small fraction of campus entertainment and furtive activity during the late sixties. There were actually others that had been forgotten; no one knew anything about most of this. There was no manifest record of it—that is to say, this rich history had not been told and told in a way that would make it an important, commonly recognized, and rearticulated facet of institutional history. There was evidently no tale to tell. I soon discovered a similar, but substantially more voluminous, pattern far away on the other side of New York City, on Long Island. Stony Brook had played host to far more of the era's iconic rock artists, hosting literally hundreds of concerts! Additionally, an intriguing pattern emerged: nearly every artist who performed at Drew also performed at Stony Brook and at around the same time. And, again similarly, beyond former students, no one knew anything about this.

As it turned out, there is very much a tale to tell here. While most of the student impresarios organizing, booking, and paying for the concerts did not know it at the time, this was happening at numerous campuses. These same bands and artists performed at dozens of colleges in the region around New York as part of the ad hoc, regional rock circuit on the East Coast. Around late 1966 and early 1967, colleges quickly emerged as receptive and enthusiastic audiences as no other venues or circuits existed. Private clubs, such as Fillmore East, did not open until well into 1968, and, even then, owner Bill Graham required bands not perform anywhere within a fifty-mile radius of his club during the period they performed there. Critically, the one exception was the college campus. Relatively new to the New York scene, Graham likely did not view the students there as actual promoters and, thus, his competition. Therefore, bands and artists could play gigs at area colleges when in and around New York, and one of the clear patterns that emerges is that when they performed at Fillmore East, they nearly always played college dates before and after. So, logically, the same bands performed at the same colleges and universities around the same time for several years until around 1968–1971. At the same time, by the time Graham decided to open the iconic East Village venue, the college campus rock music phenomenon was already a few years old. He and his much more famous club were actually tapping into a pre-existing system, and, even if Graham was loath to recognize it, his own ventures depended heavily on area colleges and their students.

Rockin' in the Ivory Tower

I believe the college campus became the hothouse for the development and nurturing of rock music culture in the late sixties. To be clear, rock culture, as distinct from simply "rock," includes its unstable, amorphous, and eclectic nature. As others then and now have noted, "rock" as a cultural phenomenon is famously broad and inclusive. Its participants included many bands and artists that today seem quite disparate and go by such divergent labels as "folk," or "blues," or "R & B," or the innumerable sublabels for rock and roll, "hard," "heavy," "progressive," "folk," and so on. Acknowledging that so much about these terms and their usage is a function of a capitalist marketplace, they are also insightful on their own terms. For instance, as a cultural phenomenon, these various terms comingled in the late-sixties rock culture. As will become clear in the chapters that follow, a surprisingly diverse range of performers routinely took the stage together, and this often reflected popular tastes, especially on college campuses. That is, they did so not in spite of their differences but because of them. The broad range of performers on campus reflected two realities: these were the bands and artists available and affordable, and their selection was most of the time an effort on the part of student impresarios to satisfy diverse campus elements.

I add one more element to the culture in suggesting its participants included more than just the bands. The culture's participants included college students and others whose role in shaping it proved formative. Students in general, and especially those at Stony Brook and Drew, enjoyed very direct roles in shaping the culture, the performances; they often built relationships with bands, artists, club owners, and each other in a process that shaped rock music. Although not intending to or even giving much thought to it, these participants frequently took on roles as promoters, agents, stage managers, drivers, sound engineers, salespersons, musicians, roadies, critics/writers, and friends. Precisely because rock music culture emerged so quickly around mid-decade and developed rapidly over the next two years in the absence of an industry infrastructure for guidance (or limitations), most of its roles were fluid. Few of its participants knew what they were doing or where it was all headed. This element is arguably the basis for so much of the excitement and dynamism experienced by them, carried dearly for decades, and shared with me in hours of conversation. Their important historic role demands inclusion and an accounting.

Rock music culture in what is sometimes referred to as the rock era was decidedly short-lived. An expansive view of it places it around 1965–1970.[13] This study takes a similar view, accepting these parameters for the rapid rise and development of rock music culture as part of the counterculture. Just as quick as this rise was its decline. As will become clear, by 1970 or so, the performance of rock on campus waned very quickly. Even acknowledging the varying degrees or pace of decline from place to place, the pattern is nonetheless clear: colleges simply no longer played the formative role after 1971 they had in the few years to that point. This remarkably furtive atmosphere provides an opportunity to explore and to re-examine the period. This, then, is a case study of the emergence and evolution of rock music culture during the late sixties, focusing on the college campus as the key space/place nurturing its development.

1

Postwar America, the Revolution in Higher Education, and Popular Music

● ●

In 1970, the venerable *Chronicle of Higher Education* sent its readers this stark warning: "Colleges Weigh Banning Rock's 'Super Groups.'" As the article explained, a number of colleges and universities were then contending with growing drug use, rowdy crowds, and a general "atmosphere of illegality" occasioned by the hosting of rock music concerts on campus. Because fans viewed rock music as "the people's music," the article went on, crowds were increasingly aggressive and confrontational, crashing the gates, and insisting the concerts be free. Compounding the problem, rock's so-called super groups actively encouraged the behavior, recreating what the article's author called "the Woodstock insanity," a reference to the landmark outdoor three-day rock concert in upstate New York a year earlier. Woodstock became instantly famous for, among other things, overwhelming crowds, shortages of everything, and lots of rain and mud. University administrators now feared many of the same problems. *The Chronicle* covered this evidently troubling trend in a series of articles during the early seventies.

With headlines like that above and "Rock Music Drowning Out the Classics in Campus Concert Halls" and "Rock Superstars on the Campuses," the coverage played to the same themes: increasing violence, property damage, and other illegalities, alongside rock music's debasing the college music listening experience.[1]

Whether aware of it or not, these and other chroniclers were marking a significant period of transition for rock music from the late sixties into the early seventies. Rock music, having emerged fewer than six years earlier, had grown up by achieving enormous commercial success and becoming increasingly mainstream for millions of Americans. Rock music was now commonly broadcast on FM radio, on television, and made up the soundtracks of many of the most notable films of these years. Dozens of rock concerts filled arenas and open outdoor spaces across the nation and attracted tens and even hundreds of thousands of fans.[2] Somewhat ironically, particularly in light of the dire warnings from some quarters, this very success also drove rock music from college campuses to a great extent. Only select campuses with large venues and even larger budgets could possibly host rock music, especially super groups. As one article explained, from a financial viewpoint, rock music on college campuses simply was no longer sustainable, and certainly not under the management of the students, who were mocked as "amateurish."[3]

The point here is to draw attention to the rapid rise of rock music culture, from mid-sixties outlier to global, billion-dollar business thoroughly ensconced within the American mainstream by decade's end.[4] I particularly want to highlight the unique role played by colleges and universities in this meteoric rise of a cultural phenomenon that many thought (and hoped) would be short-lived. Rock music had taken over the college campus a few years before 1970. In 1967, the entertainment industry magazine *Billboard* took careful note of the musical phenomenon and boldly declared "the aloofness of the Ivory Tower was attacked, stormed, and conquered . . . by rock and roll."[5] During the late sixties, the nation's colleges and universities formed a kind of de facto circuit for rock music, in the absence of an actual one. As difficult as it is to imagine now, few venues existed that welcomed rock music. Bill Graham only opened his famous Fillmores (both East and West) well into 1968. By then, rock music routinely called the college campus home. Thousands of performances across hundreds of campuses in nearly every corner of the country had become, for better or worse, normal. Importantly, rock music culture's emergence as a staple of college life dovetailed with the rapid rise of enrollment in higher education in the years following World War II.

Growth in Higher Ed in the 1950s and '60s

The growth of education in general, and of higher education in particular, constitutes one of the most significant changes of the post–World War II period in the United States. Well documented by historians, this growth resulted from the war's end, specific legislative efforts such as the G.I. Bill, the massive "baby boom," and unprecedented prosperity during the decade or so that followed. The G.I. Bill of Rights, passed in 1944, more than reversed educational trends from years earlier, providing assistance for housing, loans, and education for returning veterans, totaling $14.5 billion in the first decade. By the mid-1950s, around half of all those who had served in the war had taken advantage of the bill. The legislation's contribution to the expansion of higher education soon became clear. Nearly 500,000 Americans received college degrees in 1949–1950, more than doubling the figure for 1940. Dozens of colleges and universities raced to add buildings, faculty, staff, and other resources as more students poured in during the "baby boom" years.[6] Total college enrollment expanded by 49 percent in the 1950s, and by 120 percent in the 1960s.[7] This dramatic growth both benefited from and assisted a similarly expanding economy; the GNP soared by 37 percent during the fifties to $487 billion, and then grew another 35 percent during the first half of the sixties to $658 billion. The new postwar economy privileged college graduates as they became what historian James Patterson termed a "relatively scarce and prized commodity."[8] In numerous ways, the nation now seemed to grow virtually without limits as it emerged from years of depression and war, and millions of high school graduates now entered higher education to fill out the rapidly growing ranks of the middle-class, white-collar workforce.

Referring to that tumultuous decade following the fifties, historian Helen Horowitz wrote some years later, "No one surveying the campus scene in 1959 could have predicted the 1960s." College students, both male and female, were thoroughly ensconced as what she termed "the student wing of the establishment."[9] With an abiding belief in the promise of liberal America following World War II, young people now entered the genteel and heady context of the university, many of them the first in their family to do so. A college education was surely the path to success, especially for those making up and aspiring to the growing middle and upper middle class. That same year, 1959, *Life* magazine covered the explosion of the teen population, many of whom would be off to college over the next few years. In sharp contrast to their "Depression-bred parents," the essay read, "today's teenagers surround themselves with a fantastic array of garish and often expensive baubles and amusements." These parents were spending $10 billion every year on their offspring, $1 billion more than the total profits of General Motors. Businesses scrambled to meet the wants and demands of this evidently insatiable market for all sorts of consumables.[10] Hyperbole aside, the abundance characterizing the growing middle class and the affluent seemed to position the teenager not as likely to rebel but thoroughly invested in and dependent upon the rapidly expanding economy.

College administrators, faculty, and other observers simultaneously confirmed this new cohort of students as docile, even apathetic, and likely to "be dutifully responsive towards government," according to writer Philip Jacob. In his book *Changing Values in College* published in 1957, Jacob continues: "They expect to obey its laws, pay its taxes, serve in its armed forces—without complaint but without enthusiasm. They will discharge the obligations demanded of them though they will not voluntarily contribute to the public welfare. Nor do they particularly desire an influential voice in public policy. Except for the ritual of voting, they are content to abdicate the citizen's role in the political process and to leave to others the effective power of governmental decision. They are politically irresponsible, and often politically illiterate as well."

Famously, and utterly mistakenly, University of California president Clark Kerr declared, "Employers will love this generation, they aren't going to press many grievances. They are going to be easy to handle. There aren't going to be any riots."[11] Similarly, an extensive survey in the weekly *Nation* solicited the views of sixteen college professors on the state of the undergraduate. The results, perhaps expectedly, varied, but familiar themes emerged. Students were quiet, circumspect, cautious, in search of security, but ultimately elusive, with one contributor writing, "it would be hard to be more eclectic than the undergraduates I know," while another added, "the first thing that distinguishes this generation of students is the way they whisper their hopes."[12] By decade's end, young people had come under an intense spotlight of curious scrutiny and national inquiry as a distinct group or class.

The following academic year, 1960, nearly 4 million students enrolled in higher education, doubling the figure from 1950. The United States had become the first nation in the world whose college students outnumbered its farmers; by decade's end, that population had nearly doubled again to three times the number of farmers. By the mid-sixties, close to half of all high school graduates attended college—up from around 15 percent in 1940—while the number of universities with greater than 20,000 students had ballooned from two in 1940 to thirty-one by the late fifties. From 1960 to 1965, the number of colleges grew by more than 500, from 2,040 to 2,551.[13] Precisely because of the *quantitative* change, college students were uniquely positioned to affect *qualitative* change both on campus and beyond. Further, this was precisely the point of an intentional effort to expand higher education in the postwar years. As the director of the Center for Higher Education at the State University of New York at Buffalo wrote in 1970, "The emergence of students as an influential bloc, both in the academy and in society generally, rests significantly on (a) a national policy that has steadily and rapidly enlarged the accessibility of higher education and on (b) various components of the college experience itself." All told, the national "higher education ecosystem" expanded by around 400 percent.[14] In retrospect it seems all too clear that this kind of growth would inevitably reshape the college experience.

Growing Up Absurd

In his classic treatise on the disenchantment of youth in the fifties, *Growing Up Absurd* (1957), sociologist Paul Goodman wrote of "missed and compromised revolutions," those moments in the nation's history when genuine progress was made, but simultaneously something was sacrificed—democracy, class struggle, liberalism, free speech, fraternity, and so on. He concluded, "The accumulation of missed and compromised revolutions of modern times, with their consequent ambiguities and social imbalances, has fallen, and must fall, most heavily on the young, making it hard to grow up."[15] The premise of the book, echoing the large volume of essays and books devoted to the topic during the late fifties, centered on the anomie of youth in modern America. Because of the system of educating youth toward a career that, while perhaps safe financially, lacked real meaning, young people matured amid an absurd set of circumstances. Goodman highlighted an important tension not unique to but more significant for young people. As we now know, the students of the sixties were anything but quiet and circumspect. While many no doubt were, these are just not the adjectives that spring to mind when thinking about the sixties on the college campus. Rather, we know and take for granted that colleges were often the sites of greatest change, political, social, and cultural. So swiftly did experts of all sorts go from complaining of the lethargy and apathy of young people to complaining of precisely the opposite that the turnaround leaves one puzzling over the seeming disconnect.

Historians have thoroughly documented the ferment on college campuses in the sixties, and the most notable, from Berkeley in 1964 to Columbia in 1968, have made their way into popular culture and are indelibly marked on our popular consciousness. Those and scores of other campuses have become the sites for the iconic images and events of the era in walkouts, sit-ins, moratoria, marches, and occupations. Thousands of students moved against systemic racism, the Vietnam War, their own university's complicity in Cold War research, the overbearing dictates of in loco parentis, and the limits on free speech.[16] Rather than view this as a paradox of seemingly disconnected behaviors/actions on the part of college students, we would do well to focus on the paradox pointed to by Goodman and others; students grew up in a particular way, with a particular set of values, only to confront a world that undermined and/or did not conform to those values. Thus, they grew up amid an absurdity. In important ways, the sixties college campus became the site for many to encounter and contend with this absurdity.

The college experience and its social meaning in the 1950s–1960s shifted significantly relative to earlier in the twentieth century. The "contract" that had existed between parents and university administrators became one between student and university administrators as the needs of modern society shifted alongside expanded access to higher education and technological change. And although university or college life was not without politics and rebellion in the early twentieth century, the tumult of the sixties stands out. In the post–World War II years, expanding professional jobs and Cold War imperatives (Sputnik!) continued to reinforce the seriousness of obtaining a college education. And students reflected this reality. At the same time, as Helen Horowitz has written, "suspicion was growing that adherents of college life might be missing the real value of higher education."[17] A comprehensive survey of more than 5,100 students across twenty-nine diverse campuses in the 1960s found the typical activist to be, well, not all that typical. While acknowledging certain class realities in students, along with issues of privilege, the survey found activist students were not really outliers. Rather, they were leaders, good students in high school, they had been socialized to believe in doing good and steeped in taking life seriously, they were "intellectual but not academic." They were in search of community with a noted sense of morality in mind.[18] This observation dovetails with historian John Thelin's own notion that the sixties college experience was not all political activism all the time. But that is also a key piece of the story. The changing campus culture encompassed a good deal more than explicit political activism or protest. Engaging in explicitly political activism was merely one element of the changes in students and campus culture. At the same time, though often in the minority, student activists often led the changes for the "passive majority." As Thelin argues, whether the colleges were "source or recipient" of new ideas, they nonetheless served as the "staging site."[19]

The growth of colleges in the late fifties into the sixties resulted in more sites and places wherein this sort of culture formed. While a few campuses are now famous for this, the same campus culture developed in other obscure and out-of-the-way spots and at colleges large and small, public and private. Because so many colleges began turning away larger numbers of applicants as demand for admittance skyrocketed, students were forced to find other options. One student recalled, "High school graduates from the metropolitan Atlantic coast . . . were forced to find college in an unexpected place, namely at William Penn College, in Iowa." These "refugee" students brought in much-needed financial resources, saving the college, and also "diversified and energized campus life."[20] As out of the way as Iowa may seem for rock music in the sixties, numerous sites there and in surrounding states in the Midwest became nodes in an emerging rock circuit. During 1967–1970, Coe College, the University of Iowa, Iowa State University, and Loras College played host to more than fifteen rock and folk concerts. A similar pattern emerged in nearly every state from the East Coast to the West. Although certainly clustered on the coasts and the upper Midwest, thousands of popular music concerts happened at hundreds of colleges in every region of the country in the late sixties, with rock music making up the largest portion. Of all of the bands that took the stage at the famous late-sixties outdoor rock festival, the Monterey Pop Festival, all of them played numerous college dates during the late sixties.[21]

College students played the critical role in making this happen, and they enjoyed a remarkable degree of autonomy in decision-making of this kind. From student government, campus newspapers, various student committees, and an array of campus activities, students ran things with little to no faculty or administrative oversight. This autonomy was, I believe, a critical element in the formation of the campus culture that proved especially fertile ground not only for political activism but for rock music performance in particular. Students coordinated concerts, dances, festivals, and appearances from public figures, celebrities, activists, and intellectuals. They also dealt with relatively large budgets and negotiated with a broad range of agents, representatives, artists/celebrities, and companies beyond the campus. Additionally, because students cut their teeth as organizers and promoters of all sorts while in college, many found themselves well positioned to transition into related careers. Of those I've interviewed for this book, most went on to careers in entertainment journalism, concert promotion, artist management, and music performance, and some even became presidents of record labels. Not only did the college campus serve as one of the key sites for rock music culture performance, but it also served as a training ground for industry professionals for several years. This peculiar cocktail formed the basis for the evolution of a college campus culture that is at the center of this study.

In the New York area, the regional focus of this study, changes in higher education transformed the educational landscape. The exploding demand captured the attention of state legislators, the governor, academics, and other experts. This increased attention led to numerous studies and commissions and massive increases in financial resources aimed at expanding colleges (and engineering and tech, in particular), thus opening the doors of higher education to far more people than had ever been possible. Perhaps not surprisingly, years of depression and war had impacted the nation's educational infrastructure in ways that now needed urgent solutions. According to a Department of Labor estimate at the end of the fifties, the state of New York needed to educate more than one million workers over the fifteen years from 1960 just to satisfy existing needs of the changing economy. "The increased demand for college and university admittance will not be evidenced in its full magnitude, however, in one year, five years, or even ten," a state report concluded, "it will begin to grow within a year and will skyrocket shortly thereafter continuing upward for ten, twenty, twenty-five years, and, in fact, as far as we can see in the future."[22] The report's authors minced no words regarding the urgency of addressing the massive problem facing higher education, and not just in New York "but also . . . Pennsylvania, California, Massachusetts, and every other industrial state in the country. [The problem is] being recklessly underestimated by many who are too timid to look the long-run college admissions problem in the eye. The fact is that going to college is rapidly becoming as important to many individuals, and as necessary for the welfare of our country, as going to high school became during the period between the two World Wars."[23] In short, the state was not at all prepared for the tsunami fast approaching. And, if officials genuinely wanted to change higher education in New York from the "limping and apologetic enterprise" it was, a decades-long, thoroughly reimagined, publicly funded effort was needed. The report recommended that "state responsibilities for higher education should be realigned, private education should be strengthened, and the State University system should be expanded—all to the end that educational facilities and well-trained faculties are made available to every type of student, at every income level, and to meet all reasonable academic and technical needs." The results were transformative: the creation of the CUNY system, dramatic expansion of SUNY, a seismic shift in the relative share of the education burden between public and private schools, and massive increases in public funding for colleges and universities, community colleges, and medical and other vocational schools.[24]

"The Mud People" and the "University in the Forest"

In subsequent chapters of this book, I will draw attention to two specific universities in the greater New York area: Stony Brook University and Drew University. Combined, these two serve as an insightful and useful case study. Both experienced change in the postwar period that characterized so much of higher education and youth culture during these years. Though different in important ways, the similarities in the experiences at each are remarkable and demonstrative of the very cultural developments that have been overlooked or insufficiently explored. The complex interplay between sixties culture and politics, for instance, which evolved organically on these campuses is at odds with the often narrow or siloed narratives of the sixties that have erected walls between such things as the counterculture, protest movements, and rock music.

Stony Brook University on Long Island, New York, became the hallmark site for these developments. Anticipating exponentially increasing demand for decades beyond 1960, New York's governor oversaw the creation of a "major new university" on Long Island that became the Stony Brook campus and opened in September 1962 with 780 students. By the end of the decade, Stony Brook University enrolled more than 8,000 students, and topped 11,000 two years after that.[25] Students began referring to themselves as the "mud people" owing to the mess created by constant construction of buildings and facilities and lack of proper sidewalks to navigate the ever-changing campus grounds. While students routinely groused about the mud that evidently covered the campus, the 1967 yearbook also pointed out "it's mud with a purpose." That year, students staged a "mud-in," carrying buckets of mud directly to the administration in protest of it all.[26] In spite of the mud, the new university was fast becoming the flagship of the state system. Governor Nelson Rockefeller visited the campus in 1966 for a ribbon-cutting on major new construction plans. Later speaking to the students, he responded to a sign held aloft by a student that read "Rocky for tax collector" by saying, "I already have the job." In what the campus newspaper characterized as a nonpolitical speech, he told his listeners, "The money from the taxes has been used to add 19 new campuses to the State University system, bringing the total number of campuses to 61, and raising the number of students from 38,000 8 years ago, to the present number of 120,000."[27] The frenetic changes on the campus, from facilities to the student body, are a constant theme in both the annual yearbook and the student-run newspaper, *The Statesman*. With so many students arriving and matriculating amid the flurry of activity of all kinds, the campus atmosphere was filled with new possibilities and, at the same time, bewildering and fascinating.[28]

Students coming to the campus that year, whether they were aware of it or not, experienced the previous years' efforts by the state to expand higher education. The campus not only teemed with the sights and sounds of construction activity but welcomed students from a broad area around New York, many of them the first in their families to attend college. The inaugural class in 1964 also got busy organizing itself, creating a student body structure, establishing and filling out committees, and explaining all to their classmates in the pages of the *Statesman*, itself not yet a decade old.[29] One of the early committees created was the Student Activities Board (SAB), responsible for bringing entertainment to campus. Within a year, the fifteen students making up that committee had subsidized and brought to campus the top talent in folk, jazz, and pop vocals.[30]

About a year earlier, Glenn Redbord, a Long Island high school student, took a summer job booking musical acts for local beach clubs. He made arrangements for such popular music acts as The Platters, The Shirelles, and Little Anthony and the Imperials, all popular entertainment sure to sell tickets. Without realizing it, he was gaining valuable experience that he carried with him to a small, private liberal arts college in neighboring New Jersey, Drew University, as an entering freshman in fall 1964. By 1966, he had become chair of the student Social Committee. Much like the SAB at Stony Brook and student committees at many colleges across the country, the Social Committee at Drew enjoyed two distinct privileges: a large budget and near-total autonomy.

Drew is often referred to as the "university in the forest," owing to its heavily wooded 186-acre campus located in the small suburban town of Madison, New Jersey, about twenty-five miles west of Lower Manhattan. Like most colleges and universities during the immediate postwar years, Drew experienced rapid change. A large influx of veterans during the late forties expanded the student body significantly, accounting for nearly half of the total college enrollment. Having opened enrollment for women as well during the war years, the university made the institution permanently coed in 1947, and a female student had already become editor of the college newspaper, *The Acorn*, in 1945. By the mid-1950s, expanded (and coed) enrollments, coupled with broader cultural changes, compelled the institution to embrace change by retooling itself the "College of Liberal Arts," jettisoning "Brothers College."[31] In contrast to a state school such as Stony Brook, Drew's student body remained small at under 1,500. However, the campus experienced a similar dynamism and change that shaped the culture of student life. Some students, for instance, ultimately chose to attend the small, private liberal arts college after not getting into other schools owing to the deluge of applicants, much like the aforementioned Iowa anecdote. However, most students arriving at Drew were local, and several had also applied to schools such as Stony Brook, Syracuse, and Columbia. This same trend diversified student bodies everywhere. Likewise, the campus newspaper, numerous committees, and the broader atmosphere around the campus provided students with ample autonomy to engage with the wider world in ways not anticipated by administrators. One former student, Bob Johnson, looked back on his arrival on campus in the early sixties fondly, recalling hearing rock music drifting through open windows and out onto the campus. Others also noticed the prevalence of music generally, and rock music in particular upon first stepping on campus. Many, if not most, came from New Jersey and New York and had heard lots of music on the radio and fondly recalled area disk jockeys and their irreverent style. They had familiarity with lots of bands, artists, and LP records. At least one had also applied to Stony Brook, knowing well, as he told me recently, its reputation for radical students.[32]

I have chosen to emphasize Stony Brook University on Long Island and Drew University in Madison, New Jersey, due to the heavy volume of live music, and rock in particular, at each during the late sixties. These two campuses stand out for the sheer number of concerts they held, which also makes them important examples of the sort of cultural links I wish to highlight. Both also hosted the era's leading public intellectuals, artists, and activists in an ongoing process of interaction between the campuses and the wider, and changing, world. The two campuses are also geographically unique to the story—Stony Brook lies approximately fifty miles due east and Drew approximately twenty-five miles due west from New York City's East Village. This geography took on added import following the opening of the Fillmore East in 1968. For instance, campuses in and around New York no doubt benefited by their proximity to what quickly became the premier club for hosting rock music. At the same time, these two had already been doing so for at least two years by the time Bill Graham opened his famous East Village venue, suggesting some of the groundwork had already been laid and prompting him to open a club in the first place. Additionally, when the Fillmore East did open, the caveat Graham insisted on when booking bands was that they not book a show anywhere within a fifty-mile radius of his club for the week before and after the gig.

At the same time, this is not to suggest these two constitute the whole of the story. Indeed, among the many colleges and universities in the region around New York City that also played host to rock concerts were Brooklyn College, Suffolk County Community College, Farmingdale State College, C. W. Post College, Nassau Community College, St. John's University, Queens College, Iona College, Fordham University, Columbia University, Hunter College, Community College of New York, College of Staten Island, Fairleigh Dickinson University, William Paterson University, Montclair State University, Bloomfield College, Seton Hall University, Newark State College, Middlesex Community College, Upsala College, and Rutgers University. This partial list is illustrative of the scale and scope of campus involvement in playing host to, and thus nurturing, the performance of popular music.[33] It also suggests the ad hoc nature of an emerging circuit. The story of each of them is unique; that is, no two campuses came to play host to rock music in quite the same way. Rather, the process for doing so unfolded organically, in the absence of administrative guidance and/or oversight, and in the absence of a set of rules or even recognized precedent. These are just a few examples of a wider pattern which I want to highlight.

Growing Up Rock and Roll

Meanwhile, rock and roll was busy growing up alongside young people. While the music existed well before it was called that, its consumers were few and more or less siloed from each other. The music also went by other names such as "race" and "hillbilly." Assumptions regarding race and class still prevailed among the gatekeepers of popular culture and that included the broadcasting and dissemination of popular music. "Sales were localized in ghetto markets," said Atlantic Records vice president Jerry Wexler; "there was no white sale, and no white radio play" for "race" records. Following WWII this landscape changed with remarkable swiftness. In 1949, the old musical categories of "race" and "hillbilly" no longer seemed appropriate and were jettisoned in favor of "rhythm and blues" and "country and western," respectively. A couple years later, Wexler noticed something happening: "We became aware that Southern whites were buying our records, white kids in high school and college."[34] In part, this change reflected an effort on the part of record companies to assert control over and expand the market for records from something with regional appeal to something with national appeal. But this is only part of the explanation. The fact was, young people, many of them white teenagers, were listening to and buying up R & B records faster than anyone had anticipated.[35]

Technological changes also had unforeseen and profound impacts on popular music culture. The number of radio stations across the country expanded from 1,000 in 1946 to 2,000 two years later. Most of these played to regional audiences and operated independently of the big networks, the latter having been crushed with the advent of TV. The national radio network system had imposed radio programming on the nation as though it were a single audience—and, of course, that meant the audience was going to hear what executives thought white, middle-class people wanted to hear. By the early fifties, all this had changed. As one industry history has pointed out, "as radio suffered from the threat of television, local stations sought cheaper forms of programming. Records with top talent provided just such a resource. By the early fifties, record programming was the rule for radio, and the disk jockey had replaced live entertainment personalities that had dominated network radio in the 1930s and 40s."[36] Djs now ruled the airwaves, providing listeners access to a diverse world of musical culture, without regard to racial and other barriers. The rise of the disc jockey (dj), with his imposing personality, high jinks, unique voice, and independent mindedness, made local radio the primary vehicle for promoting music regionally. By the 1950s, radio programming included the "Top Forty" format in which radio played the top forty most played songs for the week—determined not by radio play alone but also by jukebox play. Some half million independently operated jukeboxes around the country filled beer halls, diners, and soda hops with a broad range of popular music—selected by listeners and astutely observed by jukebox operators responsible for shuffling their content. Consequently, the Top Forty, at least early on, was by far more diverse than anything that had come before.[37] One of the djs making up this rapidly developing infrastructure was Alan Freed, a Cleveland disc jockey who brought the term rock and roll to the airways—and then later claimed to have invented it! While that claim is dubious, he did more than anyone to promote the new form as rock and roll. Local radio operating independently of the big networks not only served to promote more and better local music but also broke down racial barriers in ways not foreseen at the time. Precisely because it was so decentralized, radio really couldn't discriminate.

Another technological innovation came with the transistor radio. From its commercial introduction in the fifties, improvements in reliability and lowered pricing made this handheld device indispensable for the dissemination of diverse popular music. Portability allowed young people to listen anywhere and to anything they liked. Sales climbed well into the millions by 1960.[38] Coupled with the greater availability of Vinylite following WWII, 45s became popular for the jukebox market, and the LP became the preferred form for full-length albums. The stage was set for what came next: the explosion of rock and roll nationally. As historian Reebee Garofalo writes in his widely used history of rock and roll, "The music that came to be called rock and roll began in the 1950s as diverse and seldom heard segments of the population achieved a dominant voice in mainstream culture and transformed the very concept of what was popular music."[39]

Rock and roll consisted of a tremendous diversity of people, history, and contexts that is difficult to reduce to simple language. Race, class, and gender issues abound. Rock and roll brought together an impossibly broad range of these issues into a seemingly single thing. As such, it was wild, raucous, and a hybrid of nearly every musical tradition in the country. The music and accompanying culture also sprang from African American traditions and practices. Sun Records, as a small independent label in Memphis, Tennessee, famously capitalized on this when its founder, Sam Philips, signed Elvis Presley—along with Carl Perkins (who wrote "Blue Suede Shoes," among others), Johnny Cash, and Jerry Lee Lewis. Lewis was famously shocking and outrageous for more than his sexually suggestive songs and performance. Similarly, Little Richard, once obscure and signed to small labels (Peacock, Specialty), erupted onto the scene with a flamboyant performance style. When only fourteen years of age, none other than Rosetta Tharpe overheard him singing prior to one of her shows in Atlanta. So impressed, she invited him to sing a song to open her show. He quickly fell in love with performing, jumped onto the vaudeville circuit (the "Chitlin' Circuit"), and earned a reputation as a drag performer with a very flamboyant presentation. Crowds loved him. His breakout song was "Tutti Frutti," a rendition of a song he used to perform on the circuit, with the sexually suggestive lyrics removed, of course. Still, he and a number of others were the source of significant cultural disruption.[40]

Within a few years, rock and roll dominated radio play and caused shock and alarm across the country—particularly among those whose interests were directly challenged by the new, chaotic, working-class, racially ambiguous noise. Late-night radio began bringing it to more and more homes as well as those portable radios. Record companies, jukebox owners, and radio station managers took notice of the trends as listeners demanded more of what was commonly called rhythm and blues, and, as rock music historian Ed Ward has written, "as odd as it may have seemed to some, not a few of those [listeners] were . . . high school- and college-age white kids, who loved the extroverted DJs and the music they played."[41] The increasing popularity of rock and roll music played out amid the swift and often contradictory changes of these years.

Among the many contradictions of the period, there was the tension between a faith in youth as the embodiment of the nation's hopes and future and a fear of youth as violent, out of control, and a danger to the nation's present. As historian Ronald Cohen writes, "Adults poured their love, faith, and resources into the young . . . but also dreaded their corruptibility and fragility, perhaps harboring the seeds of moral and social decay."[42] The great fear during that generally stultifying decade, as one outlier wrote at the time, was that parents had lost a degree of control as their children were now influenced by each other and outside sources such as television more than ever. Not surprisingly, rock and roll music served as a convenient target for the anxiety.[43]

Rock and roll was not new in terms of music, after all. That had existed for many years with varying degrees of regional popularity, and it had often been marketed to urban and African American communities. Rather, its newness resided in the creation, nourishment, and wider dissemination of rock and roll culture. That culture, as disc jockey Alan Freed's interracial Moondog Coronation Ball in March 1952 highlighted, flew in the face of contemporary social strictures. Freed organized a rhythm and blues concert that drew some twenty thousand young people, Black and white, for an evening of music and dancing. The show was abruptly ended after one song, with authorities citing the overflow crowd (more than double the venue capacity). As music historian David Hajdu has written of the event, while the music wasn't all that different, "the audience was changing, becoming more integrated as well as younger and more defiant and that transformed the way it was taken." The aborted dance quickly became a controversial symbol of growing tension over rock and roll and young people, with Alan Freed achieving a kind of infamy as he became the whipping boy for numerous vested interests from the American Society of Composers Authors and Publishers (ASCAP) and record companies to the FBI and the church. Some viewed the whole campaign as a strategy for the industry to assert control over rapidly changing developments in popular music. Established industry interests went after radio and DJs using payola, successfully turning "song plugging," which had been standard industry practice for many years, into something scandalous and subversive cast alongside the Black and subversive nature of the music itself. Following public hearings in 1959, Freed was ultimately convicted of bribery for accepting money from record promoters to play their records. This "payola scandal" saw him "ruined, humiliated and drunk," according to one music industry history.[44] Of course, all the scandal and visibility failed to end payola, and certainly failed to crush rock and roll. In January 1960, *Billboard* gloated, "Even after the payola scandals and the attempt to link all payola with rock and roll recordings, the music with a beat still dominates over 60 per cent of *The Billboard's* 'Hot 100' chart."[45]

Nor had the pace of change in popular music been slowed. Rock and roll's specific class, gender, and racial characteristics, combined with new technologies for its dissemination, continued to make the music available to far more people. Even amid the payola scandal, most stations refused to submit to what one industry insider called "musical McCarthyism," and continued to play rock and roll records.[46] The music remained wildly popular among the young, many of whom continued to listen clandestinely, as they had for years, to late-night radio shows such as Freed's. Though well outside the mainstream, numerous DJs had been doing precisely the same thing for years before Freed was made famous and brought down amid scandal. At the same time, it is worth noting that rock and roll was not the most popular music in the United States owing to growing popularity of other forms. From the early to mid-sixties, pop vocals, R & B, country, jazz, and folk each routinely topped the charts. An editorial in *Billboard* at the end of 1963 concluded, "Summing up the entire American musical scene, one must conclude that it is, beyond doubt, more diversified and richer than ever." Pop vocals, folk, and country dominated the top-selling singles that year.[47] Of course, from the music industry's viewpoint, this was all great news and tied to a soaring economy that allowed more spending on music: "All economic barometers point to a healthy fourth quarter 1963 and also indicated a healthy 1964." This end-of-year editorial went on to cite "other factors," such as "a slight increase in the number of teen-agers and the number of college students, both being highly significant to greater audience for records and in general the over-all expected rise in the economy and standard of living."[48]

Billboard's assessment of the diverse popular music landscape in the United States reflected the scene on college campuses as well. In the opening few years of the 1960s, classical, chamber, folk, and various forms of popular music flourished on campus. With more than two thousand rapidly growing colleges, many of them newly established, a robust economy driving more and more young people to pursue higher education, and an evolving campus culture manifesting broader national change, college students seemed perfectly positioned to be a leading national influence on cultural, if not also political, change in the years to come.

Conclusion: Colleges, Concerts, and the Academic Calendar

At the moment college students around New York City began to play the part of music promoters, the relationship between folk, rock and roll, and the popular music industry was in a state of flux, as it had been for several years. Unknown to many of them, the networks, managerial and custodial infrastructure, and concert circuit for rock acts either did not exist or were in their infancy. Though the student promoters and committees likely did not know it, these limitations were to their advantage. Students found themselves well positioned as not only the key demographic group for popular and rock and roll music but also able to take advantage of the lack of established practices determined and enforced by the music business. Additionally, college administrators paid little attention to these developments, until, as *The Chronicle of Higher Education* articles above suggest, rock concerts got their attention for all the wrong reasons. Over the several years from around 1964, these circumstances served as the parameters within which rock music culture developed, and the college campus became a key feature of and site for that development.

There are a number of important distinctions between college concerts and concerts in private clubs and other venues that need highlighting. By around mid-May each year, most college campuses went quiet. Following final exams, students packed up their dorm rooms and headed home for the summer. Activities around campuses shrank to nearly none, and that included live music performances. So while colleges, now dramatically expanded, served as venues for musical performance from the fifties forward, this was not true year-round. The academic calendar dictated the ebb and flow of live music performance. While private clubs often hosted live shows year-round and several nights a week, colleges typically did not. College concerts nearly always fell within the fall and spring terms, as most students left campus at the end of the spring term to go home, only returning in the fall. Additionally, campuses often could not host music every weekday for a variety of reasons, with cost being a serious consideration. With private clubs open for shows not only year-round but also every day of the week, hosting multiple shows per night, they obviously had the heaviest volume of live performances. However, considering the limitations of the academic calendar, the volume of concerts really stands out and needs to be understood on its own terms.

During the academic year, fall and spring terms, students were reliably on or within walking distance of campus. For live performances, that meant thousands of students attended concerts without parking a single car. In sharp contrast to private clubs that needed the audience brought to them, campuses merely needed the music brought to the audience. And that audience, especially during these years at four-year institutions when "traditional" students (eighteen- to twenty-four-year-olds) prevailed, was a captive one consisting of the most important demographic for rock music. When students at Stony Brook and Drew did advertise with posters and the like, they did so in shops in nearby towns, looking to draw from the communities, not the student body. In most cases, students also paid little to nothing for the concerts, while the public paid the advertised fee, typically in the two- to five-dollar range. Moreover, when bands and artists did perform at colleges, the opening acts were often local bands, sometimes even made up of the students or nearby residents. This relationship between locals, students, and touring bands and artists constituted what industry magazine *Cashbox* characterized as "the built-in audience."[49]

2

"The Sound of the Sixties"

• • • • • • • • • • • • • • • • • • •

Popular Music and College Campuses

In the early 1960s, folk music was at the height of its popularity on college campuses. A number of them even hosted annual folk festivals, and Swarthmore's 10th Annual Folk Festival in 1964 drew Doc Watson, Joan Baez, The New Lost City Ramblers, Danny Kalb, and Phil Ochs. A review in the student newspaper, *The Swarthmore Phoenix*, heaped praise on "left-wing political" singer Ochs's performance, citing "The Ballad of William Worthy" and "Vietnam" as "forceful" and "serious statements." Alongside numerous coffeehouse performances and the Newport Folk Festival, Ochs also performed at Union and Bryn Mawr Colleges during the year.[1] The folk scene on college campuses and its attendant seriousness contrasted sharply with contemporary popular music. In early 1964, as Phil Ochs's biographer writes, "the British invasion was in full swing and the American airwaves were clogged with the kind of pop music hooks that enabled a nation to distance itself from its recent troubles."[2] So, while The Beatles thrilled the nation's youth on *The Ed Sullivan Show*, the folk scene on college campuses teemed with a different energy.

The "folk revival" of the fifties and sixties sprang from left-wing roots of the thirties and forties. Woody Guthrie, Burl Ives, Pete Seeger, and numerous others and their groups carried forward a tradition of serious songwriting and politics that caught the searching ear of young people in these years.[3] In the postwar years, many young people were drawn to folk's exaltation of the poor, the marginalized, and the workers and their history of struggle. In that, many recognized a degree of honor, nobility, and purpose. These histories, rendered as they often were in clear, accessible, and unambiguous terms, dovetailed with the contemporary sensibilities on the college campuses which conveyed a defiant and inextinguishable earnestness. Folk tradition valorized honesty, hard work, loyalty, perseverance in adversity, and paying one's dues. There was respectability in the fact that "very few folk singers kicking around the streets of Lower Manhattan had shine on their shoes," as one author described the sixties folk scene.[4] As folk gained broader appeal, scores of groups achieved commercial success, often with the politics either muted or stripped entirely from otherwise traditional-sounding music. A *Time* magazine cover story from 1962 conveyed the broad appeal: "As a cultural fad folk singing appeals to genuine intellectuals, fake intellectuals, sing-it-yourself types, and rootless root seekers who discern in folk songs the fine basic values of American life." The article, centered on one of folk's approachable "gods," Joan Baez, pointed out the college-aged, devoted fan base, and the fact that "most of her concerts are given on college campuses."[5]

The folk revival on college campus was only one element of a dynamic music culture on dozens of campuses around the country. For years, classical and jazz reigned supreme, only eclipsed by folk, pop vocalists, and rock and roll during the sixties. Larry Bennet and Bert Block noticed the success of jazz musicians like Dave Brubeck, but believed students weren't "hip" enough for jazz to really resonate widely. Seeing much potential for growth around popular music, the two fifteen-year veteran booking agents left jobs at another company to create International Talent Associates (ITA) in 1960, focusing exclusively on college bookings. The two believed "simple, and melodic" music with "the overtones of protest" was just what collegians wanted. "There was no question that folk music fitted the bill," according to one industry view.[6] Over the next several years, ITA worked to ingratiate itself into the college scene, attending the Association of College Unions annual conference, carefully studying local college customs and patterns and making relationships with key students on campus in charge of the relevant committees and overseeing the relevant budgets. They learned some important things about college: when an artist played a campus, sales of the music spiked in the broad area around the college; and schools drawing their student body from around the nation were better for weekend gigs than so-called suitcase schools, where students typically went home on Friday and returned Sunday evening. For the latter, weekday gigs sold better. And, importantly, smoking was strictly forbidden at Brigham Young University, so no artists should be seen smoking.[7]

Booking agents, artists, and bands referred to the "college circuit" by the early 1960s. That circuit, diverse, ever changing, and evolving, consisted of hundreds of colleges from coast to coast and north to south whose student populations rotated more or less reliably every four years, while growing by leaps and bounds as both existing campuses expanded and new campuses were founded. A variety of entertainment thrived side by side. Big bands, crooners, pop vocalists, novelty acts, and comedians all made the rounds. From The Kingston Trio, Peter, Paul & Mary, and Judy Collins to Homer & Jethro, Dick Gregory, and Woody Allen, colleges welcomed a remarkably wide variety of talent. An artist could earn in a single college appearance what usually took a week of club performances. Some of these acts, like Peter, Paul & Mary, The Lettermen, and The Chad Mitchell Trio, performed 150–200 college dates each year. And, from the viewpoint of the booking agents, college students seemed to care less about money and more about the event, since they were not running a business but instead doing the work of a committee whose charge was providing entertainment to the student body.

Perhaps not surprisingly, as music tastes shifted and folk and then rock and roll became increasingly popular among the college demographic, marketers, agents, and others shifted along with them; they ramped up the resources poured into folk, pop, rock and roll, and folk-rock. They were reacting to what they saw happening on the college campus, and what they saw was a student body shifting each year as one class graduated and another entered as freshmen during years of swift change in the country. The college student body was necessarily and expectedly diverse. Its tastes determined the outlines of the campus culture to a great extent. So, not surprisingly, folk, pop, soul/R & B, and later folk-rock, hard rock, and psychedelic/acid rock were welcomed on the college campus during the sixties, precisely the period of significant change in popular music. This is the cocktail which makes up rock music culture.

"Collegians Shape the Nation's Musical Tastes"

Well before the students at Drew, Stony Brook, and numerous others began booking iconic rock bands, the music industry noticed the growth and potential at the nation's colleges.[8] Leading music industry magazine *Billboard* began publishing its annual special issue "Music on Campus" in the spring of 1964, precisely to promote and exploit this potential. The inaugural issue opened with an editorial comment on the scope and importance of the college campus as a market for popular music. Its author pointed out that over 4.5 million students had enrolled in 2,140 colleges and universities around the nation the previous year, and that number was growing. Marketers of various kinds scrambled to figure out who they were. And while there was no single type, research of 2,000 students at forty-two campuses yielded some intriguing data. Their musical tastes were quite diverse, with 15 percent preferring folk, followed closely (at 12 percent each) by classical, jazz, and rock and roll. They each purchased on average over five albums and three singles each year, or 18,000,000 albums and 6,000,000 singles collectively, with over 65 percent of those purchases coming from an off-campus record store. They had much more spending money than the previous generation of collegians, with 46 percent holding jobs. And nearly 70 percent of college students owned their own phonograph while at school. All of this directly impacted the growth and spread, and sales, of the music. An artist performing on a college campus could expect increased radio play and a spike in record sales in the area. Perhaps more important than this data though, the college campus had become a kind of hothouse for the development of all facets of popular music. From radio djs, program directors, and concert promoters to managers and the artists themselves, the college campus "was turning out the tradesters of the future." Playing the role of facilitator, this special issue included a "College Market Directory" listing dozens of colleges and every imaginable detail that might be useful for agents, promoters, and bands.[9] A few enterprising young people had already taken the plunge and begun to work directly with colleges booking musical talent.

A couple twentysomethings, Ken Kragen and Tom Carroll, started the College Concert Series in 1963, which focused entirely on a twenty-four-college circuit stretching coast to coast. The two booked everything from folk artists The New Christy Minstrels and Josh White to comedic acts Dick Gregory and The Smothers Brothers and even an improvisational act called The Committee. Kragen, son of the University of California chancellor, began his career as a promoter booking The Kingston Trio in an auditorium near the campus at the age of twenty-one. He had also begun a concert series at the UC Davis campus. By 1961, he took over the management of The Limeliters and began booking acts such as The Smothers Brothers, Louis Armstrong, Carroll Channing, and Peter Nero. Carroll worked as a dj at Emerson College and earned a master's degree there. He taught radio and television at Emerson and chaired the broadcast department at Endicott Junior College. Both had extensive experience with concerts on campuses as well as providing marketing and publicity. In their relatively short time working with colleges, they had traveled to nearly every major city in the country and learned a great deal about campus life. Both understood well the particulars of booking talent on campus and had learned "the key man in booking college dates is the director of student activities."[10]

Kenyon College, a small liberal arts college in rural Ohio, is a good example of how the process worked on campus. A committee of seven students managed everything under the umbrella of entertainment for the college. They divided up duties planning, booking, budgeting, and overseeing various concerts, dances, and other activities. A fee students paid as part of tuition supplied the committee's budget, which amounted to $7,000 each year. With that, this student-run social committee could pay for top talent and compel bands and artists to come to an otherwise out-of-the-way place. In spring 1963, they brought Josh White and Bo Diddley to campus. Later in the fall, the committee brought Bob Dylan to campus, who drew the largest crowd in the history of the concert series. Nina Simone followed in early spring. She, too, sold out the 600-seat campus hall as students came in from Denison, Lake Erie, and Ohio Wesleyan Colleges. Plans were underway to book folk artists Buffy Sainte-Marie and Dave Van Ronk later in the year. Ticket prices for the shows ran from $1.50 to $2.50, with most shows selling out well ahead of time. As the prices might suggest, the concerts routinely lost money, but that mattered little because, as *Billboard* announced excitedly to its business-oriented readership, "they're supposed to lose money."[11] For students, making a profit was beside the point. More importantly, they selected their own entertainment from the nation's talent and presided over the process from start to finish with complete autonomy.

A similar pattern prevailed at colleges large and small, public and private, new and old, and in every region of the country. The 1965 Music on Campus special issue cited "the revolution in higher education" for the "creation of some bustling institutions" such as Virginia's Old Dominion College. With a student body of 7,000 and growing, the student committee at this new college had already brought Bo Diddley, Nina Simone, Dave Brubeck, Peter, Paul & Mary, The Chad Mitchell Trio, and The Coasters to campus. Across the country at Oregon State, the well-oiled student-run committee dubbed Encore ran a tight ship, with twenty ushers in matching blue blouses and shirts, two student organizers keeping tabs via walkie-talkie, student security checking tickets at the door, and a "cheery gal" providing assistance to the talent in the dressing room. The students even hired a professional to design, build, and operate the sound system in the 6,000-seat auditorium. The 10,000-student campus likely reflected the pinnacle of student organization in the concert business, alongside University of California at Los Angeles, already known for its annual folk festival. But others weren't far behind. Even West Point cadets at the United States Military Academy enjoyed a broad range of entertainment courtesy of a student committee using a similar process. One profile of a southern and relatively obscure campus opened, "Due to the sharp increase in student enrollment in recent years, Eastern Kentucky State College is a promising showcase for recording talent." The student body there had grown by 1,000 in a single academic year to a total of 5,433. And, as the campus was twenty-six miles from the University of Kentucky and only fourteen miles from Berea College, "a concert at any one of these colleges attracts a large number of students from the others." When Peter, Paul & Mary performed there, an audience of nearly 5,000 showered the folk trio with adoring applause. Meanwhile, sales of their records spiked in local record shops the week they were in town. The student council organized this and other concerts, while the Young Democrats Club sponsored one, the Young Republicans another. This pattern could be found at the University of Missouri and West Virginia University in the South as well as Boston University and the Universities of North Dakota and Buffalo in the north and many points in between.[12] An ad hoc circuit was developing organically, with little to no communication between the various campuses, and certainly nothing approaching national coordination. Indeed, even the booking companies and agencies were caught on their heels and just trying to stay current.

Students were not in it for the industry and that is the key point. The degree of student involvement and autonomy in the creation of this pattern on college campuses had not been usurped from the industry while no one was watching. Nor had it been wrested away from unwilling college administrators once in control. Since the immediate postwar years, students had enjoyed much autonomy, only enhanced by the rapidity with which colleges expanded. Increased student autonomy coupled with the fact that the realm of popular music was left to the young yielded a now predictable result. From the start, around the late 1950s into the early 1960s, students, without necessarily intending to do so, began laying the groundwork for a rich musical/cultural experience on the nation's college campuses that would endure through the following decade, and beyond in some cases.

To take a single example from a concert cited above, the two students who organized the Bob Dylan concert at Kenyon College chaperoned the folk singer around all day, watching him pace nervously and gulp red wine right up until the show that evening. The two had picked him up at the airport (along with Victor, his assistant), and, at Dylan's insistence, stopped and bought him some wine before driving him to campus. They walked him around the facility where the concert would be held, then drove him to his hotel seven miles away, picked up dinner for him, came back to the room and watched TV with him (he was "completely absorbed" watching Steve McQueen in *The Magnificent Seven*), drove him to the campus for the show, ushered him through the crowd, managed the crowd, drove him back to the hotel after the show, drove him back to the airport, and watched him board the plane. One of the students then wrote a lengthy narrative of the whole day in the student newspaper, the *Kenyon Collegian*, spread over four pages of a nine-page issue. At no point is there any mention of Dylan, nor the students, coming into contact with a single administrator or faculty member. The elaborate story in the campus paper shared with readers some of the takeaway from the concert. The audience loved the performance, and "applauded at every derogatory mention of prejudice, injustice, segregation or nuclear warfare." The concert had been organized into two sets. Dylan returned for the second to rousing applause as some seventy-five students had left their seats and were seated in front of the stage. He walked off the stage after finishing the second set to thunderous applause. The two students then persuaded a sheepish and half-drunk Dylan to return for an encore.[13] This pronounced student presence in the process was typical.

These were the pivotal years for an organically developing musical infrastructure national in scope and situated on campuses. Popular music on campus also continued its development or evolution. The "British invasion" had just stormed ashore in February, and Dylan himself moved on to broader musical adventures the following year with the release of his fifth studio album, *Bringing It All Back Home* early in 1965. These changes brought much more visibility to rock and roll. The campus infrastructure, well established as rock and roll shifted to "rock" in the mid-sixties, became key for that transition, helping to mold and shape rock music and its attendant culture.

From Rock and Roll to Rock

No sooner had folk become thoroughly ensconced on campus than it, and all others, were eclipsed by rock and roll. Famously, even Bob Dylan had moved in that direction by 1965, leading the emergence of "folk-rock." During that year, and with the college student population swelled to nearly 6,000,000, *Billboard* still characterized the relationship between the music industry and the campuses as "erratic at best." Lamenting that record companies had made only "perfunctory moves" in the direction of properly exploiting the college market and sounding not a little insistent, the editorial opening the 1966 Music on Campus issue began, "It is with the intention of strengthening these lines of communication that *Billboard* publishes its third annual edition of Music on Campus."[14] The issue went on to list 145 colleges with a student body of over 1.2 million along with the particulars important to the industry: lighting and audio facilities, the name of the college newspaper editor, the name of the college bookstore and its manager, and the names of record shops in the area.[15] The magazine published these details in an effort to improve the "lines of communication" between the industry and what was fast becoming not only the major market for sales but the major site influencing pop music trends. In that year, and following clear trend lines, its own research found that while "the musical tastes of collegians don't fit into convenient patterns. . . . The cold statistics say that rock and roll leads all other classifications," findings that highlighted the value for the industry in establishing a better relationship with the nation's campuses. Citing expanded spending power on campus, the editorial pointed out that, on average, most students owned a phonograph, they had music libraries of seventy-nine singles and forty albums, and purchased thirteen singles and eight albums each year, "figures the record companies would do well to examine carefully." And, as enrollments continued to grow, so too did the budgets of the student committees booking entertainment.[16]

As might be expected on college campuses, the reality was appropriately complicated. While a plurality polled preferred rock and roll (18.8 percent), by the mid-sixties, a slightly smaller percentage preferred pop vocalists (17.7 percent), then pop instrumentalists (16.6 percent), then folk (16.6 percent), while classical and jazz had slipped to around 11.5 percent. The shifting tastes in music on campus mirrored shifting tastes in the country generally—the sample for these findings derived from 2,300 students across forty-four campuses, after all. These collegians chose as their favorite vocal group, for instance, The Beatles and The Rolling Stones, as numbers one and two, respectively. At the same time, *Billboard*'s list of hits for the year reflected the same trends: The Beatles and The Rolling Stones at or near the top of the charts, while pop vocalists and folk combined to fill out the typical top ten. The British invasion, usually marked around February 1964 with the arrival of The Beatles, certainly raised the profile of rock and roll music as the band shot up and totally dominated the American music charts. The leading music business magazine editorialized, "Everyone is tired of the Beatles—except the listening and buying public."[17] However, as others have argued, the phenomenon was less about an "invasion" than about British artists interacting with American artists in collaborative ways, which Keir Keightley calls "cross-fertilization," that brought a broader range of music to the attention of a wider American audience.[18]

The period marks a significant moment of change in popular music generally, and in rock and roll in particular. In the year following the "invasion," rock and roll experienced a big revival, and the "big beat," as some national media termed it, was now more mainstream than ever—in part the result of The Beatles and others from London and Liverpool, no doubt, but also the result of an almost meaninglessly broad categorization into which everything from The Rolling Stones and The Kinks to The Supremes and The Righteous Brothers now fit more or less comfortably. The national weekly magazine *Time*, in a 1965 cover story, explained to readers: "The big beat is everywhere. It resounds over TV and radio, in saloons and soda shops, fraternity houses and dance halls. It has become, in fact, the international anthem of a new and restless generation, the pulse beat for new modes of dress, dance, language, art and morality."[19]

Common categorizations, whether pop or rock and roll, proved increasingly misleading and fluid amid swift musical/cultural change. Even The Beatles were scarcely recognizable by 1966's release, *Revolver*. In short, in the brief two years from 1964, and alongside the mainstream embrace of popular forms of rock and roll, the music shifted culturally toward "rock" as it grew up, embraced adult themes, became increasingly sophisticated, and was taken more seriously by fans and a small but devoted number of music writers. Not merely coincidence, many of the most famous rock music critics emerged as early adopters who took rock seriously. Paul Williams, a seventeen-year-old student at Swarthmore College, began self-publishing a mimeographed magazine in 1966 he named *Crawdaddy!* In the debut issue in February, he explained its purpose: "This is not a service magazine.... We are trying to appeal to people interested in rock and roll, both professionally and casually. If we could predict the exact amount of sales of each record we heard, it would not interest us to do so. If we could somehow pat every single pop artist on the back in a manner calculated to please him and his fans, we would not bother. What we do want to do is write reviews and articles that you will not want to put down."[20] Williams's reference to "service" magazines was a self-conscious effort to draw the important distinction between *Crawdaddy!* and magazines designed explicitly for, and thus "servicing," the music business such as *Billboard, Cashbox, Record World,* and *Variety,* among others. The commitment to music for the music's sake was the key difference, and the college-age magazine founder making it explicit is a reflection of the emergence of "rock," as opposed to "rock and roll."

Joining Williams in the enterprise were Richard Meltzer and Sandy Pearlman, both from Stony Brook. Jon Landau also joined in the early days, producing "amateurish but convincing" reviews of rock, as he recalled, while also a student at Brandeis University and writing rock reviews and letters to the editors for the student newspaper, *The Justice,* complaining of a lack of rock music on campus.[21] Others taking the music seriously were Robert Cristgau, writing first for *Esquire,* then *The Village Voice;* Nat Hentoff, like Cristgau initially a jazz critic, writing for *Commonweal, The Village Voice,* and *Esquire,* among others; Ralph Gleason, cofounder of *Rolling Stone* (1967) with Jann Wenner; and Dave Marsh, cofounder of *Creem* (1969). Various bulletins and newsletters making up the underground press played a role as well, regularly contributing analyses and reviews of rock. These and a few other organs provided the space for some of the most influential rock music writers. Collectively, these served as the key means of spreading the word of the "sounds of the American cultural revolution," in the words of Oberlin undergraduate and later editor of *Commonweal* Johnathan Eisen.[22]

Many of the iconic bands of the rock era were also founded in the two years following 1964: Jefferson Airplane, Big Brother & the Holding

Company, Canned Heat, The Grateful Dead, The Lovin' Spoonful, Iron Butterfly, Blood, Sweat & Tears, Jethro Tull, The Jimi Hendrix Experience, The Doors, and too many others to list. While these are universally identified as "rock," they mingled with and performed alongside a wide range of others identified as folk or pop vocals or "oldies" in a rapidly evolving musical/cultural landscape. A folk act, for instance, routinely opened for a "psychedelic" band; a pop vocal act routinely opened for an "oldie." At Stony Brook in 1967, folk artist Tim Buckley opened for The Doors. At Drew University in 1969, Chuck Berry opened for Blood, Sweat & Tears. All these bands played college campuses consistently during the late sixties as rock swiftly dominated popular music, causing the lament in *Billboard*, "Where have all the folkies gone?" To answer her own question, *Billboard* staff writer Kristin White wrote, "Younger artists who a couple of years ago might have essayed the coffeehouse route are instead organizing rock groups and storming the bastions of pop music." They were becoming "serious professional musicians," like Bob Dylan, who now used "intricate imagery and surrealist narratives."[23]

In spite of what appears to be a growing attentiveness to and coverage of rock music, the industry (and the rest of the country) was actually slow to its embrace. Most in the business viewed rock as a distraction, and one that wouldn't be around for long. The music, amateurish as it was, just wasn't to be taken all that seriously. One of those insiders who did take it seriously was Frank Barsalona. Barsalona, who grew up on Staten Island, went to work for GAC Talent in New York booking rock bands, or at least attempting to. He soon found himself working in an industry that not only did not take the new rock music seriously but, like the people at GAC, didn't even understand it. Like many other talent agencies, GAC placed more emphasis on TV. Even its anemic-sounding name, General Artists Corporation, suggests that the agency wasn't exactly positioned at the cutting edge of rock music developments. The company, and the music business in general, believed rock music "was this bastardized part of show business that was going to be over in a couple of years. There was no future"; "it was the asshole of showbusiness, lower than the rodeo," said Barsalona.[24]

Fired from GAC in 1964, and coinciding with the British invasion, Barsalona started his own talent agency in New York, Premier Talent, specializing in rock acts. In these early days, the rock music industry was in its infancy and something of a mess. Not only was rock music not taken seriously, little if any managerial talent or infrastructure existed to promote it.

The Lovin' Spoonful concert poster announcement, Drew University.

Bands and artists came and went, as did agents and other impresarios bent on making a quick buck. Almost no one thought rock worth any long-term investment.[25] Very few venues catered specifically to rock music, or to what became known as "progressive rock" in the late sixties. Those few, however, proved crucial for the development of rock culture and the building of the relationship between the rock industry, such as it was, and the college campus amid the growing influence of pop music generally. Barsalona, at only

The Animals concert poster announcement, Drew University.

twenty-six years old, understood that unless the college circuit could be developed, the new rock would likely die out as a live form of music.[26]

Barsalona quickly developed a reputation for honesty and integrity, qualities often in short supply in the music business. Considered something of an anomaly, he genuinely liked rock music and sought to develop artists' careers for the long term rather than simply exploit them for quick profit.

Blood, Sweat & Tears, Chuck Berry concert poster announcement, Drew University.

In a tribute decades later, rock music writer Dave Marsh called him "idealistic to the point of recklessness" due to his commitment to developing the careers of bands and artists and not insisting on such details as a written contract. The famous music writer went on to describe the business before Barsalona: "Not only was there little respect or planning forth-coming from the talent agencies, there were few experienced managers capable of

Appearing one week from tomorrow night, in a Baldwin gym concert, will be Straight artist Tim Buckey and his guitar. Tickets will be $3.00 for Drew students, and are available at the information desk.

Buckley has released four albums, the latest of which was called "a truly satisfying musical experience" by the New York Times.

Folk singer-songwriter Tim Buckley performing in the campus gymnasium at Drew University, *The Acorn*, Drew University (where the university misspelled Buckley's name).

regarding musical success as a long-term proposition. There was no national network of promoters."[27] Barsalona soon changed all that. He began by identifying "underground" rock scenes around several major cities and those scenes' local, and unknown, promoters. Working closely with these young promoters, he soon established a network stretching from Bill Graham's Fillmore West in San Francisco to Larry Magid's Electric Factory in Philadelphia, to Don Law's Boston Tea Party ballroom and Russ Gibb's Grande Ballroom in Detroit, back to Aaron Russo's Kinetic Playground in Chicago. Whether in spite of or owing to his integrity, his Premier Talent became the go-to agency for many, while he was "the man who many feel invented the music business," according to one later tribute.[28] Of course, all this lay several years in the future.

Meanwhile, all indices suggested continued growth for popular music across the country. Sales of music and musical instruments grew by 7 percent in 1967, topping $6 billion. Sales of guitars alone climbed to more than 2 million units. "Americans will play, listen to and spend more money for music in 1967 than ever before in their history," according to the president of the National Association of Music Merchants.[29] Business boomed across a wide variety of pop music. One of every five dollars spent on recreation was spent on music—more per capita than the rest of the world combined.[30] The growing enthusiasm for music among Americans reflected both the diversity of and rapid changes in popular music. And while the industry enthusiastically embraced the newfound musicality across the country in terms of sales, its leaders did not necessarily comprehend the changes then taking place.

Rock and roll was itself undergoing significant change. From its origins in the mid-fifties, rock and roll was a cultural form predicated on change and novelty, emphasizing raucousness and rebellion through its lyrics, guitar-dominated music, and performance. By mid-decade, rock and roll combined these forms into a performance that was much more readily available, and to a wider audience than ever before. Wildly popular, especially among younger Americans, rock and roll's early stars such as Chuck Berry, Little Richard, Jerry Lee Lewis, Fats Domino, Bill Haley & His Comets, and, perhaps especially, Elvis Presley screamed, shouted, shook, gyrated, provoked, shocked, and seduced on radio and the new medium of television. But within only a few years, the phenomenon had ended, sort of.

By the end of the decade, and with Elvis in the army, Chuck Berry in prison, Little Richard retired, Jerry Lee Lewis's career ended through the scandalous marriage to his thirteen-year-old cousin, and with Buddy Holly and Ritchie Valens having perished in a plane crash, rock and roll experienced what some commentators term a "near-death experience." This initial period of rock and roll was then followed by a general flourishing of pop rock, the so-called girl groups such as The Ronettes, and the famous "Brill Building" sound, 1959–1963. The "British invasion" of 1964–1965 soon followed, most famously with The Beatles and The Rolling Stones. "Rock" finally emerged around 1966–1967. Historians, musicologists, and other chroniclers of rock and roll's storied past have identified this transitional period from the end of the fifties into the early to mid-sixties, during which "rock and roll" died and "rock" was born.[31]

Of course, the relationship between the two is more complicated, and the transition from rock and roll to rock was and is characterized by at least as much continuity as rupture. Nonetheless, the distinctions remain. For instance, "rock" is grown up, something to be taken seriously—it is even expressed in masculine language to reinforce its seriousness, "rock," as opposed to "rock and roll," which is a bit sillier, associated with the teeny-bopper. Even the word "teen," seen as inadequate in capturing the cultural shift, was replaced with "youth," a term more suggestively serious ("teen" is a clearly delineated stage of life; "youth" is a state of mind akin to being "hip"). The very format of pop music changed as well. While 45s and singles dominated fifties pop and rock and roll, the album came to characterize rock, again suggesting a higher degree of seriousness and adulthood, especially through thematic organization of making each single contribute to a larger whole. These "Long Play" (LP) records were cerebral, thoughtful, more artistic expressions of musicians, songwriters, and the bands themselves. They quickly became mainstays of rock music. And this is the music that characterized much of that era after 1966. Through the late sixties and well into the next decade, concept and themed albums became ubiquitous.[32] By 1969, albums accounted for 80 percent of all popular music sales, and a band could enjoy commercial success without having a hit in the Top 40 (and many did).[33]

Rock also borrowed from the teen music sensibilities and conventions of earlier years a particular understanding of successful popular music, and it varied a great deal, from folk, country and western, and gospel to R & B, blues, and "hard" rock. This "stylistic eclecticism," as historian Keir Keightley has termed it, was a holdover from the Top 40 and Hit Parade fashions of earlier years and continued to influence rock in the late sixties. Contemporaries also recognized this eclecticism. Jonathan Eisen wrote in the introduction to his 1969 anthology *The Age of Rock*, "Rock music is as varied—perhaps more so—as any other. There are even several journals such as *Crawdaddy!* which devote full time to exploring the nuances of the music while nobody even attempts to define it anymore." While still an undergraduate at Stony Brook, Richard Meltzer wrote of "the eclecticism of rock" while contextualizing it in other intellectual and art movements of the period in his famous, if also rarely read, *The Aesthetics of Rock*.[34] No one sound or band or performer determined what "rock" was. Consequently, it was many things, depending on a variety of factors, popular tastes being the most important among them. This eclecticism in part helps explain the continued presence and popularity of folk artists such as Judy Collins or Phil Ochs, alongside (and often performing with) rock acts such as Jefferson Airplane or Country Joe & the Fish. Considering all this, it might be more accurate or more to the point to refer to the advent of "rock culture," rather than simply "rock music."

One of the most cited events signaling this cultural shift to a more adult rock music came with the release of a single album in June 1967, The Beatles's *Sgt. Pepper's Lonely Hearts Club Band*. The product of a juggernaut of production and marketing, *Sgt. Pepper's* caused a sensation in the world of popular music, and, for many, crystallized the arrival of a genuine, youth-oriented counterculture. Some saw in it "a decisive moment in the history of Western civilization,"[35] while for others, the album contained basic truths of a religious, spiritual, and mystical nature. The underground rock press, itself just emerging, also embraced the band's latest offering. A writer for *International Times* wrote, "Tripping with this record is a mind-blowing experience. The record is a continuum of fantastic sound."[36] The album happened at a crucial moment in the formation of a counterculture of national scope. From serious or committed activists such as Abbie Hoffman—who later spoke of the "incredible impact" the album had on "activists, organizers, and counterculture people around the world"—to a great many more with little explicit involvement in day-to-day activism, *Sgt. Pepper's* rippled across the nation, seemingly bringing together a number of disparate strands of transcendent import.[37]

Two weeks after The Beatles released *Sgt. Pepper's*, some fifty thousand (police at the time suggested ninety thousand) pop music fans gathered for the now famous Monterey International Pop Festival in Monterey, California. As one reviewer rendered it, "They came 10 to a jeep, 60 to a bus, four to a hitch." The festival showcased the emergent counterculture in all its "flamboyant finery," including denim jackets, rhinestone-studded collages of feathers, bell-bottomed jeans, curly hair and long sideburns, flowers, and hashish brownies.[38] The performers during the three-day event included Jefferson Airplane, Eric Burdon & the Animals, Canned Heat, Big Brother & the Holding Company, Country Joe & the Fish, Buffalo Springfield, The Jimi Hendrix Experience, The Who, and The Grateful Dead. Aside from the particulars, one critic noted, "The thing about the Festival was simply its occurrence. We are witnessing something strangely dazzling in American youth culture. The birth of the flower child. Not the product of disc jockey hype or the denizens of the underground, but a new kind of hip homunculus."[39] Both events are often highlighted as key, even transformative, in the evolution of rock music culture of the era. By most accounts, as of summer 1967, the "summer of love," the counterculture had arrived and rock music was its vehicle.[40]

This more or less linear narrative on the rise of rock and counterculture in the late sixties elides some important contradictions. Rock music did not simply or suddenly emerge fully formed and universally popular. While growing numbers of young people and the underground press, especially conspicuous elements of the nascent rock music press such as *Crawdaddy!*, embraced rock, others remained skeptical or unconvinced. Mainstream press accounts often swung pendulum-like between the celebratory embrace of rock music and snarky condescension. That *Time* cover story from 1965 mentioned earlier reflected the ambivalence and suspicion of rock music: "Like something out of Malice in Wonderland, the hordes of shaggy rock 'n' roll singers thump across the land, whanging their electric guitars. Bizarre as they may be, they are the anointed purveyors of the big beat and, as never before, people are listening, all kinds of people."[41] While reporting on the music's dramatically rising popularity among those older than twenty, the popular national magazine told its readers, "For the past ten years, social commentators, with more hope than insight, have been predicting that rock would roll over and die the day after tomorrow," and "many cannot take rock 'n' roll, but no one can leave it." Meanwhile, *Life* magazine sneered, "Ninety percent of the 130 million single records sold last year were of this big sound [rock and roll]. Although much of the music is imitative trash."[42]

Beyond the ambivalence of the mainstream press lay the hostilities of city and town authorities to the opening of rock venues. When Ray Riepen attempted to open one such venue in Boston, he ran into this hostility. He was "told by everybody there was no way to get this done because of the police. They were not going to open anything for rock and roll—that meant dope." Town leaders and law enforcement officials often linked rock music culture with loud noise, drug use, and general debauchery. Riepen eventually prevailed, opening the Boston Tea Party ballroom in January 1967.[43] We would do well to keep in mind that for all the youth-based ferment around rock music and the counterculture of the late sixties, its adherents and participants remained a small minority of the population. Likewise, it wasn't singularly rock music, or psychedelic rock, or even folk-rock that dominated the commercial charts. Rather, *Billboard* magazine's top singles and albums charts of 1967 and 1968 had R & B/Soul, Motown, and pop artists dominating the top spots, even while the magazine's artist of the year for 1968 was Jimi Hendrix.[44]

Rock music culture remained as eclectic as ever as its influence continued to grow, especially on the college campus. Fans made little generational distinction in terms of popular and sought-after music. As mentioned above, as rock became associated with "youth," the music thus categorized retained an important diversity. Rock consisted of a wide range of artists, styles, sounds, and performances. This included the so-called oldies, such as Chuck Berry. The term "oldie," despite the prevalence of the connotation later, was not a pejorative one. Even amid the ascendancy of the "San Francisco sound" and "psychedelic rock," concerts and music festivals regularly included a broad range of musicians and styles.[45] At Monterey Pop, for instance, attendees enjoyed Jefferson Airplane, Eric Bourdon & the Animals, The Who, Jimi Hendrix, and The Grateful Dead, alongside Otis Redding, Indian musician and master of the sitar Ravi Shankar, and The Mamas & the Papas. A similar diversity prevailed at countless shows around the country during these years, including, famously, at Woodstock at the end of the decade, a music festival opened by folk artist and singer-songwriter Richie Havens.

So, when in 1969 David Hinckley, editor for Drew University's student-run newspaper *The Acorn*, wrote, "Rock now has a history," he captured this element of rock culture in a review of a recent Ricky Nelson concert at the Boston Tea Party. Writing of "nostalgia rock," Hinckley astutely pointed out the complex overlapping and intermingling of various styles that formed rock music culture. As a raft of contemporary rock bands included a few "oldies" in their performances, the trend reflected the sustained popularity of earlier rock and roll music. According to Hinckley, "Rock is now old enough to have a history, and current fans find all sorts of delights in digging Big Sister's records out of the closet. More serious types realize that Chuck

Berry, Jerry Lee Lewis, Little Richard, The Coasters, The Moonglows, and countless others of the 1950s helped shape the 1960s, from the *Beatles* on."[46] Artists and bands performing the "oldies" served to remind everyone, according to Hinckley, that "it was Chuck Berry, not Jimi Hendrix who first played his guitar all over the stage," and that it was acts such as The Coasters who'd shown the way through dancing as they played, a practice "so many local bands copy so wretchedly today." The undergraduate student and budding journalist then signed the review, tellingly, "Levon Helm."[47]

The college environment played a key role in nurturing rock music culture's persistent eclecticism. A few shrewd observers noticed the trend at least by 1966. In November of that year, *Billboard*'s Hank Fox reported, "Rock 'n' roll music is now the major form of entertainment on the nation's college campuses." Booking agencies devoted increasing energy and resources to the college scene. Ed Rubin, an agent with Ashley Famous, said the growth in rock's popularity on campus had been swift and "an amazing thing. Over the past year, it's grown 400 percent." Though the precise numbers varied by agency, performer/artist, and region, the story remained the same. Other agencies, such as William Morris, having paid little attention to rock, now devoted additional resources to campuses. A good act could make a living playing weekends on campuses, and many acts played dozens of shows there annually. One group, The New Christy Minstrels represented by Ashley Famous, played between 250 to 300 college shows each year. While the big names such as The Beatles and The Rolling Stones had priced themselves out of the college market, the vast majority of bands and artists could still do quite well there. Thus, the college campus had become the venue of choice for agents and promoters like Barsalona's Premier Talent. Because colleges welcomed rock 'n' roll, folk-rock, and R & B, they "are the biggest market today for the contemporary record artist," he said.[48]

Record company "rack jobbers," whose job it was to fill racks in campus bookstores, were among the first to see and exploit the trend. As reported in *Billboard* in early spring 1967, the store racks had been completely taken over by rock. Purchases of rock and roll albums accounted for 75 percent of all sales. Folk artists still sold well but behind such acts as Simon & Garfunkel, The Byrds, The Animals, The Monkees, and Herman's Hermits. For Simon & Garfunkel, well over 90 percent of the duo's contact with the record-buying public came with college performances. Reflecting an important shift, R & B artists saw significant growth in sales in the college market as well. According to Hank Fox writing for *Billboard*, "The upswing of record sales [for R & B] on campus has been aided substantially by a more liberal and realistic attitude of bookstore managers."[49] In other cases, the students insisted on it. In at least one case, a bookstore "told us not to stock any rock and roll," said one rack jobber. "The manager insisted that college tastes were not compatible with this type of music. But within one week the bookstore was so deluged with requests that he called us to revise its entire inventory."[50]

Over the previous year, rock music sales on campus eclipsed all others. *Billboard*'s ranking of Top Artists on Campus listed The Beatles, Jefferson Airplane, The Doors, The Rolling Stones, Aretha Franklin, The Mamas & the Papas, and The Temptations all in the top ten.[51] Hundreds of college campuses hosted music concerts of a wide variety, with rock the most prominent. And, strictly judging the commerce of popular music, it was now big business, with totals for records and tapes sold topping $2 billion, more than the revenue for all films, and more than the total revenue for all sports. Importantly, most of this revenue, nearly 80 percent by the closing of the decade, came from rock music.[52] By the latter sixties, the college campus became the site for much change as youth embraced rock music culture and led the changes of the era. The opening editorial comment in *Billboard*'s 1968 *Campus Attractions* inaugural issue placed the college student at the forefront of change in the country: "Today's collegians can no longer be considered the leaders of tomorrow. In a large sense, they are the leaders of today. Much of the social and political ferment this nation is experiencing may be traced to the campus. Campus leaders are speaking out on issues, and their elders are listening. In many cases they are following. Collegians no longer fall into molds cast by their fathers. They are creating their own molds. And collegiate tastes in music . . . are setting the pace."[53] Not coincidentally, a few enterprising college students in and around New York City had begun to organize and promote rock concerts on the campus, and thus began what is in retrospect a remarkably rich experience with and role in the evolution of rock music culture.

The Late Sixties and the Counterculture on College Campus

During the few years following 1965, area college campuses were the sites for the growth and development of sixties culture and counterculture. But the counterculture was a good deal more than protests. Students organized, discussed, wrote, studied (or not), engaged with their world, hated and feared the Vietnam War, fought against injustice, had sex, used drugs, and listened to and shaped rock music culture with remarkable individual and collective autonomy around the nation's recently expanded campuses. I want to highlight the interwoven nature of these developments.

Rather than retelling the familiar story of this or that well-known sixties place and/or personality and the commonplace trajectory of the era from inspired to weary and frustrated, I want instead to suggest something novel: the campus experience during 1967–1970 places the college campus at the very center of "the sixties" and forces a reassessment of what we think we know of 1960s political culture, rock and roll, and the counterculture. Most of the historical literature of this period treats these three as disparate and siloed. I suggest that doing so has missed a real opportunity; that the three are interrelated in fundamental ways and really cannot be viewed as separate. In this relatively brief period, an organic cultural phenomenon evolved, integrating and manifesting the realities of the day. The same processes played out at dozens of other campuses around the country in a way that points to the organic building-out of a national cultural infrastructure. While many of us are likely familiar with its more visible elements—key spokespersons, bands, events such as occupations—we know less of the interrelated nature of these phenomena. Three of these elements dominate the chapters that follow.

Campus Culture: Newspapers and Radio

It seems no college is complete without its student-run newspaper, then as now. Many of them existed well before the sixties while others had just emerged, and students at various campuses launched competing endeavors in this period when independent papers flourished. Campus papers became the single most important vehicle for the dissemination of the evolving cultural atmosphere on campuses during the sixties. Numbering well into the hundreds, these papers reflected the period far better than other, regional/national newspapers and magazines for millions of students. Their stories, images, editorials, political commentary, and letters resonated much more directly with the immediate experience of student readers. Precisely because most were entirely student run, they contained a running dialog between student writers and student readers comparable in some ways to the modern social media experience. They could be informative and provocative while also often amateurish and misguided. Content ran the gamut from silly and absurd to profane and deadly serious. Many of these campus papers became linked to and interacted with the underground press, which consisted of more than 2,600 publications of various kinds and was national in scope.[54] Following the founding of the Liberation News Service (LNS) in 1967, a kind of national syndicate of the underground press, its decidedly unconventional and radical content became a commonplace element of many college papers as young, increasingly radical college editors searched for content.[55] For all these reasons, campus newspapers today provide an invaluable resource for understanding the evolving campus culture. This is certainly true of Stony Brook's *The Statesman* and Drew's *The Acorn*.

College radio provided a similar, if less radical, function. Radio's importance varied a good deal more than the campus newspaper as some campuses did not have a radio station, and those that did often had nonstudent managers, or whose broadcast signal was weak and whose programming was frankly dull. While some college radio stations could be very provocative, others stuck to the "straight news," of sports, official campus activities, and news taken from official local and national outlets. The music programming consisted of pop vocals, country and western, jazz, and folk. Having said that, this too changed during the late sixties, and, like newspapers, more toward the provocative, with more rock music and subversive content. Additionally, as State University of Iowa's campus radio manager pointed out, the students there could not get any other signal and relied exclusively on the campus station, KWAD, for all news and entertainment. With a student population already at 6,000 in 1965, the manager told an interviewer, "by 1972, the dormitory population of Iowa will exceed 20,000." His complaint, a complaint he shared with other college radio managers, was that they "had a hard time getting service from the record companies."[56] By the late sixties, campus radio stations began converting to rock music programming, responding to student demand. In a familiar pattern, the music business belatedly and clumsily came to realize the importance of college radio. *Billboard* included a directory of hundreds of college radio stations in its annual Music on Campus issue in 1966, signaling their importance to the industry for distribution and marketing of records.[57] Within two years, college radio changed and the industry took notice.[58]

Town and Gown

The communities and towns surrounding college campuses played an important role in the developing cultural experience of the college as well. Communities not only often contributed a large number of the students for the local college, but they also became the immediate environment for students venturing off campus to interact with townspeople, to consume (food, entertainment, clothing, records, etc.), and to engage with the world beyond the campus. This was their chance to deploy the knowledge and experience acquired in classes, serving in student government, on student committees, reading, discussing, and thinking with classmates and friends.

Many towns bore the visible hallmarks of the nearby college. A variety of small shops such as restaurants, head shops, print shops, barbershops, clothing outlets, and record stores catering to local youth, both high school and college students, flourished in hundreds of towns. Their advertisements in the campus newspapers are a demonstration and acknowledgment of the mutually beneficial relationship. From a marketing standpoint, these ads were cheap and the audience, on campus, was singular, making the pitch a fairly straightforward proposition. Students also chose those local shops when advertising campus events, drawing support and a presence from the community. This was an essential element of the rock music experience at Drew University. With a small student population, student promoters figured out quickly they would need community attendance at the concerts to avoid losing lots of money. Thus, they routinely blitzed the surrounding shops with posters and even tickets to sell.

Rock Music

Finally and most importantly, there was rock music culture, the proverbial soundtrack to the sixties. By the late sixties, rock music on campuses was about as common as the subversive content of the campus newspaper; in fact, there was considerable overlap.

Beyond the sheer ubiquity of the music, rock was especially formative in the lives of millions of young people across the country. For many, rock music was a revolutionary experience, especially psychologically and culturally. As nearly all writers and commentators have noted, the meaning of this experience is impossible to quantify or otherwise nail down with precision. For instance, while one cannot know the degree to which attendees at the concerts were there for any sort of revolutionary experience, and while many may have been there simply for the entertainment, for the social or community experience, their lives were nonetheless surrounded, enveloped in the culture and politics of the time.[59]

As editor of *Commonweal*, Jonathan Eisen wrote in 1969, "Rock music must not be seen apart from the movement of young people to reshape their lives in ways reflecting their intense disenchantment with societ[y]," and, in that sense, "it is a profoundly *political* form of music."[60] Even if one did not understand or consume the music of the era as revolutionary or as an intentional element of a "movement," to have consumed it at all meant stepping onto the on-ramp of late sixties counterculture. For, as cultural studies scholar Lawrence Grossberg has argued, popular music "is so deeply and complexly interwoven into the everyday lives of fans and listeners" as to be inseparable, and has specific effects, "whether the audience is aware of them or not."[61]

By 1967–1968, incoming freshmen brought with them new styles of dress and fashion, music, and culture that sped the evolution of campus culture toward a counterculture: longer hair, drug use, anti-establishment views, opposition to (southern) bigotry, and the Vietnam War. Students witnessing these changes recalled decades later the speed with which changes came to the campus during these years. Almost from one academic term to the next, the music, fashion, and political culture changed. Stepping onto campus in 1968 was not like stepping onto campus only a couple years earlier. Several former students spoke of the sudden appearance and ubiquity of rock music. As one of them told me, "It was like a revolution coming out of the radio."[62] Contemporaneous accounts bear this out; widespread news coverage, both campus papers and those beyond, detailed the sound of rock music, drug use, long hair, growing antipathy toward the war in Vietnam, the hardening of positions regarding civil rights, and the tensions between student bodies and administrations. Campus culture, town and gown, and rock music sometimes overlapped in contradictory ways. The relationship could be mutually beneficial or it could be decidedly antagonistic, such as in various protests, drug busts, and police harassment of locals, subjects I detail in the chapters that follow. These three elements formed the counterculture tapestry of rock music culture in the late sixties.

3

"I Blundered My Way Through"

• • • • • • • • • • • • • • • • • • •

The College Impresario,
Fall 1965–Fall 1967

In 1965, *Life* magazine reported with affected puzzlement that, in spite of the disapproval of the establishment and moms and dads everywhere, "rock 'n' roll music has now jack hammered its way into becoming the most widely heard music in the world today."[1] Highlighting young people's embrace of it, the article cast a very wide net in covering what it termed "the big sound," or rock and roll (a term regularly used alongside and interchangeably with simply "rock"). This presentation, with lots of large pictures, characterized the music in very broad terms, including nearly everything also called "popular." Another contributor in this same issue attempted greater precision, identifying "seven reigning sounds," although "it takes an exceptionally sophisticated ear" to hear the differences. Those seven "sounds" consisted of four tied explicitly to cities (Detroit, Nashville, New York, Chicago), two that were regional (West Coast and "British"), and one tied to a single person, Phil Spector, the legendary producer famous for his "wall of sound" studio recording technique.[2] Both observations were attempting to grapple with an unwieldy and wide-ranging music that now dominated the popular taste. The "big beat" had gone mainstream, and while it may have seemed sudden, other mainstream reportage suggested otherwise: "The sudden public acceptance of rock 'n' roll by so many people who supposedly should know better came as no surprise to the record and radio industries. Their surveys have long shown the existence of a vast underground of adult rock 'n' roll fans, including those who were raised on Elvis Presley and, though too embarrassed to admit it, never outgrew their hound-dog tastes."[3] While it was no doubt true that the music business had already figured this out, reaction around the industry was anything but uniform. More importantly, college students took the lead, establishing the trends and conventions for music on campus in ways that kept the media and the industry struggling to stay current. Some students began to not only bring rock and roll onto campuses but also to cultivate relationships on and off campus, with local shops, booking agents, and even bands in an interdependent and organically evolving circuit. Meanwhile, campuses teemed with a counterculture energy manifest not just in music but also in the written word in campus newspapers and various other student activities both on and off campus. Having laid out the general context in the previous two chapters, this chapter will concentrate more on the two campuses that are the focus of this study: Stony Brook and Drew Universities.

"More Money Than Las Vegas"

The Industry View

First, it is important to take note of the industry's view of these changes. At exactly mid-decade, *Billboard*'s second annual Music on Campus special issue was more data-driven than *Life* or *Time* magazine, if also more hyperbolic and decidedly more celebratory. "The nation's 5,000,000 collegians, enrolled in more than 2000 institutions of higher education, form an elite that will be guiding the country's destinies for the remainder of the century."[4] The magazine's Market Research Division had been busy trying to keep up with developments on the nation's campuses. In addition to inviting a dozen or so collegians to the office for an in-depth conversation, researchers surveyed 1,800 students at thirty-seven colleges around the country. The results suggested the importance of music on campus. Students purchased 18,000,000 albums and 6,000,000 singles in the year prior. And their tastes were broad: 17 percent of them preferred pop vocalists and pop instrumentalists, 16 percent preferred folk, 14 percent rock and roll, and classical and jazz slipped to around 13 percent, with country coming in at around 7 percent. The variety of musical tastes on college campuses was, of course, not a new phenomenon. Campuses had been virtual hothouses for all sorts of musical/cultural developments for years by the mid-sixties. Now, rock and roll added to the already eclectic mix. "Few collegians are purely jazz, folk or country buffs. Most of them like many kinds of music, and the wide diversity of artists playing the college circuit reflects these tastes. It's not unusual for a college to book the Hungarian String Quartet one week, and Dave Brubeck the week after. And it's not unusual for the same group of collegians to pack the fieldhouse for all three acts."[5] The coin of the college realm seemed to be variety, and coin. The magazine proclaimed in large, bold print to the industry, "There's more money on college campuses than there is in Las Vegas." The provocative headline, however, connected to a more substantive point about colleges and live music performance. While a Vegas show cost around $15,000 to stage and, thus, the act had to perform twice daily to make money, a campus concert cost nearly nothing to stage and the profits were about the same as the Vegas show! The music promoter who made the claim spoke from years of experience booking acts. What he'd discovered is that college students liked the artists more than production, and that he could book a wide range of acts, all at similar cost and for the same audience.[6]

Seemingly always playing catch-up to these developments, the music industry, especially rock music by the late sixties, was increasingly interested in the college campus. In only a few years, the ignorance, condescension, and dismissiveness that once characterized the talent booking agencies' view had given way to enthusiasm. "Two or three years ago," said Ashley Famous agency head Ed Rubin, "college talent buyers wouldn't even have discussed the possibility of signing a rock 'n' roll artist for a concert. These concerts were devoted to jazz, symphony concerts, ballet, folk music, or a pop-standard artist." Now however, some rock artists played 80 percent of all their performances on campus. William Morris Agency head Wally Amos said that now "a good act working only weekends can earn as much as $500,000 a year" on the campus circuit. Premier Talent's Frank Barsalona was not surprised, as 25 to 40 percent of all his agency's talent played colleges every weekend, and he'd long understood rock music's appeal to college students.[7] While this interest was driven by opportunities to make money, it nonetheless had an impact on the campus music scene. More attention meant more available talent and, for better or worse, an increased presence of professionals from the agencies. An editorial in the Music on Campus special issue the following year opened by quoting the president of a long-time booking agency saying, "Schools in recent years have increased their talent budgets tremendously. . . . It is not uncommon for a college to spend three to five thousand dollars for a big pop or rock and roll act. This expanded talent budget derives from the great enlargement of student enrollment."[8] If all went well, from the industry's view, the college circuit could be properly exploited and even expanded. It seemed that with each new trend—folk, pop vocals, rock and roll, now rock music—the college hosted all. The campus was the ultimate built-in audience. This pattern required of the industry only that it pay attention and stay with the trends.

The Campus View

The trends could not have been clearer. At both Stony Brook and Drew Universities, undergraduates played host to a literal who's who of rock music. From The Animals, The Who, The Grateful Dead, Jimi Hendrix, and Jefferson Airplane to Chuck Berry, Judy Collins, Frank Zappa, Richie Havens, The Allman Brothers, and Carly Simon, plus many more, students on these campuses put on sell-out concerts in spring and fall, attended by thousands from campus and surrounding towns. Additionally, many of the most prominent intellectual/cultural/political leading lights of the era visited the campuses, all organized by students. Abbie Hoffman, Andy Warhol, Mark Rudd, Bobby Seale, Pete Seeger, Julian Bond, Ralph Nader, Allen Ginsberg, Ted Sorensen (a JFK speechwriter), Huey Newton, Dave Dellinger, Dick Gregory, Roy Innis (leader of CORE), Ralph Ellison, Nat Hentoff, William Kunstler, Jane Fonda, Tom Hayden, and many others visited for talks. There were even unannounced visits, like that from Jerry Rubin who visited Drew, spoke to students on the lawn behind Mead Hall, the main administration building, then accompanied them on an anti–Vietnam War march from Madison to the neighboring town of Morristown. Students engaged directly with the major issues of the day such as civil rights and the Vietnam War, and also manifested the cultural change of the era, with all of it broadcast via the pages of the furtive student newspapers, *The Acorn* (Drew), and *The Statesman* (Stony Brook), that, in the late sixties, read like organs of the underground press, itself emerging during these years. No other single site hosted the political/cultural variety that was routine on the college campus.

THE STUDENT ACTIVITIES BOARD AT
THE STATE U. OF N.Y. AT STONY BROOK
In association with TRIPLE "C" PROMOTIONS
presents
Direct from   First and only
England   THE   L.I. appearance

JIMI HENDRIX
EXPERIENCE
PLUS
THE SOFT MACHINE

SAT.	MARCH 9	8:00 P.M.

STONY BROOK U.
Campus Center (Gym)
Tickets: $3, $4, $5

Phone 516 246-6800   Write HENDRIX TICKETS
or 516 246 7704   Stony Brook University, Stony Brook N.Y.

BUY YOUR ADVANCE TICKETS AT:

Jimi Hendrix at Stony Brook concert poster announcement, Stony Brook University.

Stony Brook University

In 1964, Stony Brook students of the Student Polity of the Student Union created the Student Activities Board (SAB) to "improve and maintain an adequate social and cultural calendar for the student body." One of its first acts was the sponsorship of a student "sojourn" to see Peter, Paul & Mary in concert at a local venue. The committee, reflecting growing confidence in this event as students reacted positively, purchased an additional fifty tickets, on top of the initial one hundred, and committed to future "cultural offerings." From this "auspicious beginning," the SAB evolved, with considerable student input voiced in the campus paper, *The Statesman*, into a series of subcommittees with more sharply defined responsibilities. One of those was a subcommittee specifically handling music concerts. By the following academic year, Stony Brook had welcomed an eclectic range of music such as jazz artists Mose Allison, Count Basie & His Orchestra, and the Dave Brubeck Quartet, along with popular acts like The Chad Mitchell Trio, and blues man Reverend Gary Davis.[9]

Former president of Reprise Records Howie Klein recently told me, "[On] my first day at Stonybrook in 1965 . . . I was just a nerdy kid from Brooklyn, and the first thing I see is the president of the student body, Sandy Pearlman . . . and he had long hair. . . . I had never spoken to anyone with long hair." Klein approached Pearlman following the latter's presentation to the students, and, as they chatted, Pearlman asked Klein if he would run for class president, because, as Klein told me, "They needed a person on the left, which I didn't know I was at the time, to do what they needed the student government to do." This was Klein's introduction to what would be a very active college life. He went on to become class president and to chair the Student Activities Board (SAB), responsible for bringing music to campus.[10]

Rapid growth characterized so much of student life at Stony Brook in the late sixties. Amid the mud and construction, student committees and government took shape. Sandy Pearlman got himself elected moderator of the Executive Committee, positioning him to then appoint the chairperson of the SAB. The college newspaper gathered its editorial staff, honed its production, and expanded its coverage. Nearly every issue for academic year 1965 contained coverage related to civil rights and the Vietnam War, including Stony Brook's own teach-in, held at the end of the spring term. An expanded "review" section also included student opinion on changing music culture, with an especially insightful editorial on the transition from "teen culture" rock and roll to the more serious "folk-rock," with its attendant themes of social and economic justice in the October 19 issue. The Review section also began critically examining concerts held on the campus as well as reviewing new albums, such as the extensive review of The Rolling Stones's 1964 release "12 × 5."[11]

The SAB continued to feel out its opportunities. As it happened, the campus gymnasium, with a capacity of around 3,000, was frequently available for concerts. Students began organizing various shows in the facility, several series, performances called "Moods," comedic acts like Dick Gregory, alongside folk and jazz. Stony Brook quickly developed a reputation for hosting good shows—safe, no violence, not a lot of cops hanging around. Word got around. The first East Coast show for The Grateful Dead was at Stony Brook. A cocktail of factors including geography and demographics resulted in the evolution of an especially vibrant and furtive campus infrastructure and culture. This culture manifested all the elements of what is commonly understood of the sixties and of the counterculture. Campus culture also both reflected and nurtured student autonomy and power. Chair of the SAB, Klein wrote in *The Statesman* in fall 1966: "A relatively high degree of student power, primarily concerning control of funds. This is a key to understanding the essence of the Student Activities Board. The Administration is there only to advise and to provide facilities, to give us a legitimacy in the outside world and to help. At Stony Brook the Administration rarely says 'no.' That's what makes the S.A.B. significant; that's what provides the 'S.A.B. Spirit.'"[12] Meanwhile, Klein and others had been taking full advantage of opportunities both on and off campus to engage with the swiftly changing cultural world around them.

Klein, Pearlman, and other friends and students at Stony Brook like Richard Meltzer, who later became a well-known rock music writer and critic, frequently socialized together in and around Lower Manhattan, and the East Village in particular. Meltzer, a sophomore philosophy major in 1964, and Pearlman, later producer/manager for The Blue Öyster Cult, Black Sabbath, and The Clash, enrolled in a course on modern art taught by the pioneer performance artist Alan Krapow, who "aided and abetted" their meanderings from art to philosophy to rock and roll and back again in writing assignments. The professors, with their "oddball agendas," granted the students wide latitude, according to Meltzer.[13] Among their numerous off-campus adventures, Klein and Pearlman regularly went into Lower Manhattan's East Village neighborhood to see an obscure rock band a couple

Howie Klein, Sandy Pearlman, and Richard Meltzer.

times a week. Klein approached the band following one performance and got them to agree to do a show back at Stony Brook in what was the start of a rich experience as a rock music promoter. Thus did The Fugs, a provocative underground band begun by counterculture poets, play a concert at the weekend dance at Stony Brook on Long Island. What happened at Stony Brook is a good example of the degree of student autonomy and what that meant for the cultivation of rock music culture in the moment and in the future.

This group of students, happily in over their heads, took full advantage of the freedom accorded students of these years. Each recognized something in the other that seemed to push the whole group in new directions. Klein and Meltzer looked up to Sandy Pearlman, who paved the way as an outgoing, engaged, and popular upperclassman. He seemed to know everyone, and everything. Pearlman knew Patti Smith, suggested she put her poems to music, and even considered her for the lead singer of Blue Öyster Cult; ditto Jackson Browne. Pearlman was thoroughly engaged with the budding rock and counterculture. Meltzer and Pearlman had gone to Far Rockaway High School together and were longtime friends. Klein viewed Meltzer with something approaching awe: "He was known as someone who was brilliant." For many underclassmen, Meltzer "was kind of a role model" for the developing hippie culture on campus. "Hippie wasn't a thing yet," Klein said recently. The elements of that culture, rock music, the avant-garde art scene, dope, and generally thinking against the grain, were just then simmering. And, because Meltzer "was a wild and crazy guy," and brilliant, he was broadly influential around campus. Alongside these and other active and engaged students, numerous artists and musicians moved in and around the campus, a number of them, like the members of Mountain, from Long Island. The Allman Brothers were virtually "the house band for Stony Brook for about a year," according to Klein and others.[14] The tendency to take risks and push the envelope on the part of a few students highlighted the period as a key moment of change.

And, not surprisingly, not everyone was on board, especially with some of the more unconventional and adventurous events. The Fugs's performance on campus is a case in point, as it cast in sharp relief the clash between more conservative elements of the student body and those welcoming the risky and avant-garde elements of cultural change. During the concert, at least one student was outraged and screamed in Klein's face as the band clamored through their song, "Coca Cola Douche."[15] As happened with nearly every other campus dustup, this one played out in the pages of *The Statesman*. In the days following the concert, a student wrote a letter challenging the SAB's method for choosing acts, and specifically of "the monopoly—or monarchy—of its chairman." Though not mentioning names, the student challenged the "Tammany Hall" organization of "influence, patronage, persuasion and some extra-legal activities" of the SAB in choosing The Fugs. He charged a small group of students with having changed the rules only two days prior to the show in a clandestine move to allow the band to perform. He demanded, on behalf of the student body, to know the method for selection. "The in-group foisted this performance on the student body by methods which were, at least, extra-legal, and, at most, deplorably egotistical. For who were they to take it on themselves to say what student interests are? By what right do four unauthorized people decide what are the likes and dislikes of 3,000?"[16]

In the following editions of the paper, responses ranged from snarky to sincere. "We think it is disgusting that such obscenity should be allowed to be viewed by the innocent youth of America. This could only be the plot of some foreign agent." The undersigned included Leonard Shames and Barry Brown, both fans of the band.[17] The reaction suggests a relish in the back-and-forth, and a tongue-in-cheek "thank you" mocked the student's outrage.

And the SAB presented the Fugs, a singing group whose material is as controversial as its talent is debatable.

Counterculture band The Fugs perform at a dance at Stony Brook, *Specula*, 1966.

The letter focusing on the selection process scarcely concealed a more substantial reaction to the intentionally provocative performance. Besides, there is no evidence that students had ever been aware of the selection process before. Ultimately, the reaction to the concert compelled a lengthy response from Klein.

Turned out, Klein was freshman class president before becoming SAB chair. In that capacity, he had brought The Fugs to campus. Not quite a full academic year into college, he took to the pages of *The Statesman* to defend the choice, but only following the suggestion "by a hysterical friend." So, to "put an end to all the groundless rumors that have been circulating since Ed Sanders [front man of The Fugs] and the boys left the campus," Klein shared a lengthy, and insightful, backstory: "It all started way back before I was Freshman Class President, when I was wearing loafers, sweatsocks and washed every day. Lenny Shames had taped the Fugs' first album and played it for me one day. The Fugs' sound buried itself deep in my mind and didn't pop out again until I heard that Dave Buffalo Edelman had stepped on his Fugs record—the only one on campus at the time—and that Stony Brook might go Fugless."[18] Thus did Klein open his defense in colorful, storytelling style. He took the opportunity to point out his own transition, and implicitly that of other, like-minded individuals, from "straight" to the counterculture. At least, that is an obvious interpretation of one suspending daily washing and the wearing of loafers. An East Coast counterculture was at that moment in the offing, and it differed in fundamental ways from the West Coast version. Centered on a small area in southern Manhattan, this cultural flowering consisted of various avant-garde artists, writers, folkies, and speed freaks, with considerable overlap among them. Low-rent slums, garbage-strewn streets and filthy sidewalks, housing without heat, police corruption and crime characterized the neighborhood to a far greater degree than most realize today. Going into the Village was not exactly high on the list of typical tourists. Rather, conditions kept those elements out and allowed for the cultivation of a "new bohemia," as one writer has called it.[19] Klein and many other students were venturing into this developing underground culture and bringing elements of it back to campus.

In 1963, Peter Stampfel and Steve Weber began The Holy Modal Rounders, a strange combination folk-psychedelic act that performed at places like the Gaslight, traditionally a folk venue in the neighborhood. About a year later, both joined the newly formed Fugs, founded in 1964 by Tuli Kupferberg and Ed Sanders. The band came out of the city's folk and beat scene from earlier years, and its founders shared a disdain for the West Coast variety of "hippie," and a liking of The Velvet Underground, formed only months after they formed The Fugs.[20] In New York's East Village, The Fugs represented the leading edge of the counterculture. They were intentionally provocative, even abrasive, and performed songs such as "Kill for Peace" and "Strafe Them Creeps in the Rice Paddy, Daddy"; perspectives seriously at odds with the "flower power" motif of hippie culture. Their music, known only to locals, was crude, confrontational, and decidedly radio-unfriendly. Thus, Klein's exposure to it is insightful.

In my first official act as President of the Class of '69, I travelled to the Village, bought the album, with my own money, of course, and began loaning it to hundreds of eager kiddies the first week of April . . . and one day who should venture in but Bill Chappelle, chairman of the S.A.B. Bill's no turkey, and when I suggested that the S.A.B. and Freshman class sponsor a Fugs mood he ate it up. Sandy Pearlman, a Fugs devotee from way back, agreed to help out with the arrangements, and on the first night of the Easter vacation, Sam, Wendy March, Barry Brown, and I went down to the Astor Place Playhouse to hear what the Fugs were like in person. The four of us were one when it came to deciding what the boys and girls at Stony Brook would think of them so we spoke to their business manager, Nelson Barr. He told us that the Fugs get a thousand bucks a night but we hassled him a while, told him we were in no way connected with a frat and explained that the Stony Brook Viet Cong if there were a Stony Brook V.C. would sponsor the thing. We settled on $300 and told him we'd be back with some other people. That week, over twenty Stony Brook students, of all persuasions, crowded into the Astor Place for Sunday and Thursday night performances. After the Easter vacation a caravan of three cars each packed with . . . students, went to make final arrangements. The next week we went in again to sign the contract which nobody remembered to bring so we went in again and even one more time.[21]

Klein left out much of the importance of the Village to area college students. He, Pearlman, Meltzer, and others routinely went into the city to dabble in music, theater, and art. For like-minded students at Stony Brook and elsewhere (Drew students also routinely traveled to the Village for entertainment), the city offered a much broader view than the campus. And, as he quickly learned, many of the bands and their "management" were also neophytes around his own age, which made interaction and negotiation much easier. Once the industry professionals took over in later years, these relationships were no longer possible and the cost of everything soared. During these few years, as young rock music impresarios learned the ropes, they also built the basic infrastructure of rock music, nurturing it, promoting it, and spreading its influence back on campus via campus newspaper, radio, and the gymnasium or theater. The campus acted as a kind of social and cultural center of their lives and of these activities. One had regularly to reconcile the two. And the cultural traffic ran both ways:

Meanwhile, the Administration decided that the Freshmen Class couldn't sponsor it because there had been no class meeting—there was none for the Senior class concert either—and that the S.A.B. couldn't sponsor it because there was no S.A.B. [meeting] (the next week the defunct SAB had no trouble putting on the Simon & Garfunkel–Paul Butterfield Concert). Therefore the Executive Committee, in accord with Article VII, Section 4 of the Constitution . . . passed a motion (11 yes and 1 abstention) sponsoring the Fugs. Since this was a budgetary matter there was some discussion as to whether or not it had to be posted for 10 days before going into effect. When the day for the concert came, only 3 or 4 days had passed so, rather than imposing their loose interpretation of the Constitution on the Polity, the liberals agreed not to have the legislation which allocated $300 for the Fugs go into effect until the full ten days were up, in case somebody wanted to petition the E.C. to overturn the legislation.[22]

Aside from the details of the Executive Committee and its constitution, various elements of process are on full display in this defense that warrant greater attention. First and foremost, Klein's explanation involves a telling combination of understanding and adhering to the rules and taking chances to nurture and indulge in nascent countercultural experiences. Taking him at his word, the students remained committed to the process and were appropriately deliberative as they worked out how and whether to bring a provocative act to campus. The structures of governance they had earlier put in place remained intact here and, ultimately, determined the outcome. At the same time, a small number of them were determined enough to bring the band to campus that one of them, importantly, the chair of the SAB, funded the cost out of pocket: "The Fugs came, no Polity funds were paid out, no petition was submitted and that was that. (The fact of the matter is that Polity moneys have not yet been paid out for the Fugs—many weeks after their performance, and if it were not for gallant Bill Chappelle who laid out the money himself, the Fugs could have sued us for breech [sic] of contract.)"[23] Putting aside whether or not his defense really mollified anyone, The Fugs concert makes clear the conveyor-like processes involved—between student leaders and the remaining student body, between all students and the rapidly changing culture around them, and between the need to be a student within an institutional framework and the need for autonomy and control of one's direction and choices. In a recent conversation, Klein conceded that "it was not what people expected," given the band's penchant for provocation and dirty words, "but it was a *huge* success." The room was packed to overflowing and everyone had a good time. At that point, he realized music could and did actually impact people. Klein viewed the band as important, saying, "They were kind of the bridge between the beatnik music of the fifties and what was about to happen with the hippie music explosion of the mid-sixties."[24]

Area college students glimpsed the coming countercultural trends well before most by witnessing the evolutions firsthand in otherwise sequestered cultural pockets like Tompkins Square Park, the Dom, Andy Warhol's

Factory, and St. Marks Place. New York's East Village became a draw for all sorts of people intrigued by the eclectic cultural developments there. Well before they decided to form The Ramones, teenage brothers Joey Ramone and Mickey Leigh took the train south into the Village to satisfy their fascinations, while a very young Debbie Harry snuck out and boarded a bus that took her from New Jersey into the city, just to walk around: "I would just sort of sneak away. I was probably around thirteen. I would just get on a bus . . . and go into Manhattan and walk down to the village." The street life, coffeehouses, ramshackle clubs, and an assortment of hangouts littered the neighborhood and made welcoming and unconventional meeting places for all manner of curiosity seekers, misfits, renegades, and punks. These few places nurtured a wide range of artistic and intellectual trends, including rock music, as there were virtually no rock-friendly venues in the city, and certainly none outside it except college campuses.[25]

Area college students could and did sample from this panoply of experiences. Klein still recalls with fondness attending Andy Warhol's Exploding Plastic Inevitable on St. Marks Place, where The Velvet Underground regularly performed: "I never missed a show." He and countless others took full advantage of the cultural opportunities, fun, drugs, music, and entertainment freely available in the Village, without necessarily recognizing it as anything more than that. They also acted as conveyors of that cultural experience in returning to campus to organize events of various kinds. At Stony Brook, the student body had access to cultural trends just by virtue of enrollment. The remainder of the spring term at Stony Brook saw folk duo Simon & Garfunkel and The Paul Butterfield Blues Band perform in the last week of April, followed on the evening of May 7 by comedian Dick Gregory opening for Mongo Santamaria and his Orchestra, a Cuban percussionist and bandleader performing Latin jazz.[26] All were regular performers at both college campuses and various clubs in the city.

The final issue of *The Statesman* for the spring term listed the new appointees to the SAB that included Howie Klein. In the fall of 1966, Klein took over as chairman of the SAB and welcomed The Byrds, The Youngbloods, The Blues Project, Richie Havens, Dave Van Ronk, Muddy Waters, Big Joe Williams, and Sandy Bull, as well as others.[27] The spring 1967 term was similarly eclectic: The Four Tops, Jefferson Airplane, Tom Paxton, and Thelonious Monk, among others. A significant factor in this wide-ranging musical entertainment brought to the student body was, in fact, student demand.

Most students were receptive to acts they'd heard of like Motown or Brill Building, and music that enjoyed lots of mainstream radio play like The Shirelles and The Four Tops. To also bring lesser-known acts whose performance might be provocative (or laced with obscenities as with The Fugs) required some care. Student promoters had to navigate the different tastes and demands among the students, whose money, after all, paid for the entertainment. And those students were not shy about openly challenging decisions made by student leaders. Klein, well aware of this reality, explained his personal approach to booking and promoting concerts. He made sure to regularly mix in some very popular acts like Marvin Gaye, Martha & the Vandellas, The Temptations, The Four Tops, and anything else from Motown. "We had great bands and they were great concerts . . . I put on great concerts," speaking more to the acts than his own efforts. "But, that was just to pacify" the conservative elements on campus. "And they loved it, they were happy. And they were pacified." "But what I really did during my tenure which was about three years was to book all these bands that no one had ever heard of."[28] Striking the balance was often the challenge.

Because most students enjoyed more mainstream and popular performances, a few of them could be easily provoked by a single unconventional act. Klein recalled, "I would constantly be under threat of impeachment. . . . They tried it at least twice . . . for booking, once The Doors . . . and once, Jimi Hendrix." Though it seems unlikely now, audiences both loved and hated these and similar acts. The performances of just these two, now infamous, could be wild, filled with sexual energy and explicitly provocative to the audience. Though now household names and icons of the rock era, most of these bands and artists had only just emerged. "In those days, these were unknown bands. The Doors didn't have an album out when I first met them," Klein recalled. That the acts were relatively unknown played a key role in the opportunities for young, inexperienced music promoters like college students, who had money, a built-in audience, and a gymnasium, but little else.

Klein recently recalled the details of his booking The Doors for a campus concert. The band had just finished recording their first album and were in New York in March and April doing some final studio work by day and performing by night at a tiny hole-in-the-wall called Ondine.[29] They performed several times a week for a little more than a month at the club.

Because he frequently went into the city, knew something of the scene, and knew the club's manager, he was aware of the performances. He and Sandy Pearlman went to see numerous shows. The latter, in his junior year at Stony Brook, was already writing rock criticism and reviews, and was there to write about the band for *Crawdaddy!* Klein was there to enjoy the show and get high with Jim Morrison.

Or at least that's the way it turned out. After having attended most of the performances, the band invited the two students backstage, in truth a tiny space just a step from the stage. "We were getting very friendly with them [and] Jim Morrison asked me if I could get him some DMT. . . . The worst drug ever made," recalled Klein. "It's like an acid trip that takes 20 minutes. . . . It was hard to get but I got him some." Just before going on one night, Morrison said to Klein, "Let's do some of that DMT." Klein initially said no, but ultimately the two did take the drug and, when time came for Morrison to join the band onstage, "literally, the two of us are laying on the floor passed out." The band, discovering this, had to keep playing until Morrison could be brought around and join them for the performance. Klein's recollection is that they used the drug at Morrison's insistence and the band was angry about the whole affair. The band typically opened performances with extended instrumentals anyway, but on this occasion they had to play a little longer. The result, however, was that the Stony Brook students got what they came for: an invitation backstage and an agreement to play at Stony Brook. "This was in the summer and the deal was they were to come play the school in the fall for $400. They were going to be our first concert of the fall." This ad hoc arrangement might have been unusual in general, but not for a new and unknown rock band. Between the summer and fall, the single "Light My Fire" shot up the *Billboard* charts to occupy number one and, suddenly, The Doors had a hit and were obscure no more. Klein was elated, "and ["Light My Fire"] was a huge hit! So here I had this band [that] was just becoming gigantic . . . for 400 bucks!" Klein remembered. Very soon, the encroachment of an assortment of professional managers and handlers would make this impossible.[30]

The other spot in the city Klein often visited was Andy Warhol's Exploding Plastic Inevitable on St. Marks Place, where he watched The Velvet Underground perform. These scenes were great opportunities for meeting other artists. On one of these evenings, he met "three guys who had managed to just get into New York from California. Tim Buckley, Jackson Browne, and Steve Noonan." "I brought the three of them back to Stony

Brook . . . they hung out, did shows, and, little-known fact, Jackson Browne, for a week, was the lead singer of the Blue Öyster Cult." Klein went on to book each of them for concerts on campus. First up, "I hired Tim Buckley for 50 bucks" to open for The Doors. "No one was famous. These were my contemporaries. They didn't have albums out or anything like that."[31] For $450, Klein lined up a dynamic and eclectic performance with a folk/singer-songwriter opener and a psychedelic rock band headlining. This was bound to please some and infuriate others.

Knowing the student body would be divided, Klein advertised in *The Village Voice* to bring people in from the city to see these kinds of shows. While students saw the shows for free, those coming in from off campus were charged a ticket price. The gambit paid off. The show was packed, and the SAB even made money selling tickets to nonstudents. However, and predictably, The Doors stirred controversy during the concert and subsequently in the pages of *The Statesman*.[32] At one point during The Doors's performance, a fellow student and member of the student council grabbed Klein's shoulder, spun him around, and shouted, "Klein, have you paid these clowns yet!"[33] A key part of the SAB's job, as its chairman pointed out in a lengthy response to criticism of the performance in *The Statesman*, was to provide students access to "the big names," the very thing students had clamored for the previous year in a poll conducted by the SAB.[34] In retrospect, The Doors was a risky and provocative way to open the fall concert season. Still, Klein's timing could hardly have been better. Rock music exploded on the scene that year, with a few notable and high-profile happenings: The Beatles released *Sgt. Pepper's Lonely Hearts Club Band*, and the Monterey Pop Festival, which showcased Jimi Hendrix and Janis Joplin, among many others.

The remainder of the fall concert series at Stony Brook reflected these larger changes in popular music trends. A concert featuring the psychedelic soul band The Chambers Brothers went over very well with those in attendance and received praise in the paper for allowing space to dance to the music.[35] Two weeks later, the SAB organized the annual Fall Festival Weekend. The lineup, as announced in *The Statesman*, consisted of Phil Ochs and Steve Noonan with Soft White Underbelly (Blue Öyster Cult) and The Holy Modal Rounders split into two shows, one at 8 P.M. and another at 11 P.M. The James Cotton Blues Band performed at a separate dance in the campus gym. Then, on Sunday, Doc Watson, "one of the finest country-style guitarists," performed in the women's gym. Live music and dancing filled out two days of various activities that ran the gamut from speeches to con-tests, and even a sports car rally.[36] Jefferson Airplane returned for another concert on November 5, and Ravi Shankar followed on November 17. In the space of a single term, campus entertainment ran from folk-psychedelic, rock, blues-rock to singer-songwriter, jazz, folk, and Indian sitar. This is just a small sample of the entertainment provided students in that term.[37]

In the relatively brief period between fall 1964 and fall 1967, Stony Brook students organized a student government and numerous student commit-tees and began drawing top music talent to the campus. Word got around that the student promoters put on a good show, and the campus's proxim-ity to Manhattan made it an obvious choice, especially given the paucity of rock music venues.[38] These events at Stony Brook were no one-off, either. Remarkably similar developments were taking place in neighboring New Jersey at a small liberal arts college. And, importantly, many of the same art-ists and bands that had performed at Stony Brook also found their way to Drew University, often only days apart.

Drew University

When Glenn Redbord arrived at Drew to begin his freshman year in 1964, he brought with him a rich experience in booking bands. He'd been organ-izing shows on Long Island as a summer job while still in high school and had learned the ropes and established useful contacts along the way. First working for someone else and then on his own, Redbord organized shows at area beach clubs for acts such as The Platters and The Shirelles. By the time he arrived at the small, suburban New Jersey university, he saw an opportunity to bring that experience to the campus.[39] The vehicle for doing this was the Social Committee, which he chaired by spring 1966.

The Social Committee, in practice one or two students, enjoyed a rap-idly expanding budget and similarly rapidly expanding student control. As elsewhere, students took more and more of the control of funds away from administrators and faculty supervisors. In doing so, they also extended the autonomy and decision-making of various committees. The chair of the committee gathered around him a group of students loosely arranged into committees that organized entertainment for the undergraduates on campus, including weekend dances, movies, folk/pop concerts, and, after

Glenn Redbord directing concert plans. Drew University Yearbook, 1967.

1966, rock concerts. Campus entertainment varied widely during the first half of the decade. Students organized classical music performances, a variety of films, and seasonal and weekend dances. They also launched something called the Arts Festival, which brought a folk performance involving Andy Chilson & 37 Friends to campus in the spring 1966 term. Reflecting the growing popularity of rock and roll, student government president Tom McMullen voiced what was evidently a shared view of popular music options for the campus when he wrote in *The Acorn*, "One of the most difficult things to find is a good rock and roll band. High priced, no talent groups are formed all the time, with the result that mediocracy becomes the rule rather than the exception." He went on to praise a local rock and roll band lately performing at high schools and colleges in the area. The band, The Straymen, was actually made up of Drew students who had already managed considerable experience playing "proms, dances, mixers, and fraternity parties," according to McMullen. The band regularly played area college campuses including Muhlenberg, Stevens Tech, and Upsala. They had performed at Drew six times recently because, as one of the band members said, "our price is always within range of Drew's social budget."[40] Musical tastes on campus, reflecting broader, national trends, were changing as students embraced more pop music and rock and roll.

The students at Drew hosted a full calendar of popular entertainment throughout the 1966–1967 academic year, and the acts reflected the wide variety of college performances as well as the broader changes in popular music trends. In spring 1966, for instance, Colston Young, Andy Chilson & 37 Friends, The Fantastiks, The Shangri-Las, The Paul Taylor Dance Company, The Young Rascals, The Happenings, Chad & Jeremy, and Eric Burdon & the Animals by spring 1967 all made appearances.

In 1966, and amid the total reorganization of the student government at Drew, Redbord won the election to chair the Social Committee.[41] The committee and students working on its behalf enjoyed "total" autonomy. Because of his prior experience in booking entertainment, Redbord said recently, "I saw an opportunity . . . and booked two concerts for Fall 1966 and Spring 1967." Those concerts were a pop duo and an English blues-rock band, respectively.[42] Both performed in the campus gymnasium, launching what became several years of students bringing some of rock music's most iconic bands and artists to the campus. The university administration had little interest in or knowledge of what they were doing. When, for instance, the Social Committee informed the dean of students Alton Sawin that The Animals concert would cost $2,500, "he could not relate to that amount for one group for one night," according to Redbord. Nonetheless, the students proceeded, "with very little oversight." "Dean Sawin really didn't relate to what we were doing. Nor did he relate to us or to the other kids on campus . . . he didn't understand, he didn't even know who these groups might have been, what we were doing." "He was a nice guy . . . but we knocked heads often." Asked if the students felt any pressure for accountability, Redbord responded, "Absolutely none. There was no accounting."[43]

At Drew, Redbord worked with Stan Rubin, who, along with Sean LaRoche, founded College Entertainment Associates (CEA), an agency specializing in booking talent for the college campus. The CEA served as a broker, typically taking a percentage for setting up deals. A 1967 interview with Rubin cast the relationship as one in which the "callow undergraduate" needed the expertise and experience of professionals. "Few college students have either the experience or the temperament to deal with the legitimate talent booking agency, let alone the sharpshooter who promises the Supremes and delivers the Four Nosebleeds." Itself only a couple years old, CEA had worked with student promoters at Washington and Lee, Holy Cross, the University of Virginia, the University of Kentucky, Notre Dame, the U.S. Naval Academy, Princeton, Cornell, Vanderbilt, Fordham, and Georgetown. Casting his agency as "protecting" the undergraduates, Rubin told an interviewer, the "foul-ups" in the college concert business "resulted from the failure of the student impresario to grasp the elements of show business." This paternalistic view may well reflect actual experiences at one or more campuses. More importantly, though, this view as well as the founding of the CEA, the interview, and its prominence in *Billboard*'s special Music on Campus issue are a reflection of the encroachment of "professionals," and the industry at last taking the college campus seriously.[44] Likewise, the perspective fails to capture the role and acumen of the college impresario.

Exercising a surprising degree of autonomy, a group of students organized into a couple of committees booked and promoted numerous bands for concerts in the campus gymnasium. On most occasions, they managed to pack the facility, around 1,500 seats, with multiple shows per evening, turning a profit in all but one or two instances—the committee lost significant money on The Who in 1968.[45] They drove around the campus in a wide arc, blanketing local businesses and high schools in several surrounding towns with advertising and stacks of tickets to be sold. They printed large posters and displayed them in shop windows. These posters, in design and composition, were the idea of Redbord; "I invented that [format] because it was a copy of what we did out on Long Island."[46] Printed on heavy, 24 × 36 card stock with bright colors and lettering, these were hard to miss. They taped one of them, advertising Iron Butterfly for 1969, to the doors of Greg Granquist's car, a 1953 Chevy Bel Air named "Proud Mary," used to ferry tickets and the posters to area businesses. Student organizers, typically one or two of them,

Photo by Frances Edward

Greg Granquist

Greg Granquist, *The Acorn*, Drew University.

even went door to door promoting the shows. In some cases, the local papers ran ads as well. And, as always, the campus paper, *The Acorn*, ran multiple ads on the eve of the shows to generate excitement and boost attendance.

At the same time, Redbord relied on the existing network of clubs and agents, anemic though it was in 1966. He booked the English pop duo

Greg Granquist's car, fondly named "Proud Mary," was used to distribute concert tickets and posters to local businesses. Drew University Yearbook, 1969.

Chad & Jeremy in the fall and, reflecting larger shifts in popular music, turned more toward rock acts beginning in spring 1967 with The Young Rascals and opening act The Happenings.[47] "The Young Rascals and The Happenings were a very odd situation," Redbord recalled recently. He had actually booked both bands in the summer of 1966 for three concerts, "two on Long Island and one here [at Drew] . . . by the time they came here," they had hit singles, including The Young Rascals's "Groovin'," which made the band much more recognizable—and expensive. "They didn't have them when I first booked them. I paid next-to-nothing to have The Young Rascals and The Happenings. It was luck, strictly luck." Part luck, part pluck. Redbord had worked with Rubin booking summer gigs on Long Island and, thus, knew him well enough to phone him up and ask which acts were in the area. Based on availability and cost, he could then plan entertainment for the coming term on campus. He was something of a bridge between the private clubs and the college campus, understanding the process of booking entertainment for both.[48]

When Redbord booked The Who, Rubin phoned him up to let him know the band was backing out as their current tour was taking them elsewhere. He was replacing them with a band called The Animals. Redbord did not know much about The Animals, and he knew less about the current state of rock music. But Rubin did: "I knew he had his hand on the pulse" of popular rock and roll music. "I trusted his opinions." Asked if he understood his role as building something larger than the Drew experience, Redbord said, "I don't think I was consciously doing it. I think I just had the ability to do it and did it." He, like many others in college during these years, was focused on academics and what he termed his own "entrepreneurial programs." He approached these roles in a decidedly businesslike manner, as he did the numerous activities that occupied his time and energy. He took on several leadership roles while in college, including president of the Kiwanis Club, a role that frequently took him into area high schools. And, in spite of a lack of administrative or faculty oversight of the Social Committee, he always managed to balance the budget, even making money most terms.

A full-page ad in the February 17, 1967, issue of *The Acorn* announced Eric Burdon & The Animals for March 3.[49] With a string of hit singles including "House of the Rising Sun," "Don't Let Me Be Misunderstood," and "We Gotta Get Out of This Place," this latest iteration of The Animals marked a departure from previous acts or bands. The Lovin' Spoonful closed out that spring term with a concert in May. Both bands performed to enthusiastic crowds, and subsequent reviews in *The Acorn* lauded the events while also reflecting a serious engagement with rock music. For instance, a review of The Animals highlighted the strength of Eric Burdon's vocals in defining the band's sound, while also informing readers that "the New Animals have dropped the blues distinction" for which the original group gained notoriety in favor of "common electric rock." Nevertheless, the review, wrapped around various photos of the concert a week earlier, praised the quality of both bands, along with their dynamism and sound. They even wrote of Lovin' Spoonful's front man John Sebastian as standing "with Bob Dylan and Art Garfunkel among popular writers who are making a serious contribution to mass music," and, promoting the upcoming show for readers, urged, "They shouldn't be missed."[50] Within that academic year and as a result of Redbord's efforts, rock concerts became an established practice on the campus, reflecting the growing presence and importance of rock music both at the campus and across the nation.

The lack of administration or faculty involvement in various student activities no doubt helps to account for the flourishing of rock music on the campus beginning in 1967. A more substantial role for the administration would almost certainly have meant different choices of performers and

The Drew University
Social Committee

Presents

ERIC BURDON
And

THE ANIMALS

Friday, March 3

8:30 P. M. GYMNASIUM
ADMISSION $3.00 - $4.00

TICKETS ON SALE IN THE
STUDENT UNION AND AT THE DOOR

The Animals, full-page ad in *The Acorn*, 1967, Drew University.

bands, reflecting much less the youthful taste and sensibilities of the era. Perhaps more important was the rise of rock music generally during the latter half of the decade. Rock music was simply everywhere. It could be heard at numerous outdoor festivals, as that venue proliferated during these years, at diners and movie theaters, in automobiles, on television, and wafting across college campuses from speakers jammed into open windows. One former student at Drew described the rapid changes he witnessed from 1967 to 1968. In terms of the cultural life of the campus, there was "a social revolution you could see in front of you." The rules had changed seemingly overnight and rock music was everywhere: "You walked around campus there were speakers out of people's windows. We were hearing music constantly. . . . [It was] "like a revolution coming out of our radios."[51]

At Drew, rock music was just one manifestation of numerous experiences whose parts added to a larger whole. Some elements of that experience related explicitly to the sixties and the counterculture, while others did not or did so only implicitly. The final event of the spring 1967 term is a case in point. That weekend, "Spring Weekend," Drew hosted a series of diverse acts. Folk artist and activist Carolyn Hester performed in concert on Saturday afternoon. Rock band The Lovin' Spoonful performed in the gym later that evening. The rock band The Bit a Sweet from Long Island performed at an informal dance at 10 P.M. the same day. The following day, Beat poet and sixties activist Allen Ginsberg held a poetry reading on campus.[52]

Though today these names sound disparate when strung together, owing to varying degrees of fame, celebrity, and relative weight in the privileging of certain elements of the sixties at the expense of others, they coexisted seamlessly during the period. Hester, for instance, had been a regular feature of the folk revival scene in New York for years; one historian has called her "the leading lady of the folk circuit."[53] Her portrait even adorned the *Saturday Evening Post*'s cover for May 30, 1964, as the representative of sixties folk. A young, unknown, and ambitious Bob Dylan was astute enough to hitch his own wagon to her in 1961, eagerly agreeing to play harmonica on her LP, which earned him the notice of Columbia producer John Hammond. Dylan wrote of her importance in his memoir: "John [Hammond] had first seen and heard me at Carolyn Hester's apartment. Carolyn was a Texan guitar-playing singer who I knew and played with around town. She was going places and it didn't surprise me. Carolyn was eye catching, down-home and double barrel beautiful. That she had known and worked with

Buddy Holly left no small impression on me and I liked being around her. Buddy was royalty, and I felt like she was my connection to it, to the rock-and-roll music that I'd played earlier, to that spirit."[54] As Hester later said of the young Dylan, "He hadn't even written 'Blowin' in the Wind,' or much of anything yet." Together with luminaries such as Judy Collins and Joan Baez, Hester played a key role in bringing folk music into the sixties.[55]

The Bit a Sweet, a psychedelic garage rock band on its way up, signed with major record label MGM and released two singles in 1967, although long-term success did not follow and the band broke up within a few years. The Lovin' Spoonful, another rock band with local roots, formed in New York's East Village in the early sixties. Releasing hit singles "Do You Believe in Magic," "Daydream," and "Summer in the City," among numerous others, the band enjoyed major commercial success. By decade's end, however, the band split, and front man John Sebastian did a solo, walk-on set at Woodstock.[56]

And, finally, Allen Ginsberg, a key figure bridging the era's political activism and the counterculture, was by the late sixties very well known, for among others, his poem *Howl* (1956), in which he excoriated modern U.S. capitalist society and its then current insistence on a culture of conformity. He also strongly opposed the Vietnam War and spoke out forcefully in support of civil rights. An outspoken, gay, Jewish intellectual from New Jersey, Ginsberg moved remarkably fluidly between the cultural and political tides of the era, perhaps more thoroughly ensconced in both worlds than any other prominent figure. A frequent companion of Dylan, The Beatles, and many others, and a regular presence at rock concerts and festivals of the era, Ginsberg's presence, his actions, and his role were always both political and cultural to a degree that makes the distinction meaningless. And, as he told an interviewer in 1996, "I was very moderate in my use of drugs. I was more interested in the politics than the drugs."[57] So, these performances at Drew on that weekend were both disparate and part of the same thing, which was remarkably diverse or eclectic, particularly in light of subsequent categorizations such as "folk," "psychedelic rock," and "counterculture," all too often treated as separate things. The two rock bands lived a typically brief existence of only a few years of the latter part of the decade; as a folk artist, Hester coexisted, performed with, and was otherwise a very natural fit alongside rock acts, and Ginsberg, Beat poet and activist, had earlier become thoroughly enmeshed in the politics and culture of the era.

To emphasize the point, that fall the Social Committee brought folk artist Judy Collins (September) and Detroit's "Motown sound," pop/soul band The Four Tops (November) to campus, and, in between, avant-garde artist Andy Warhol made an appearance (in October) that, perhaps intentionally, disappointed and angered nearly everyone.[58] The eclecticism that prevailed at Drew during these years reflected not merely the discerning judgment of the students there, although no doubt their judgment played a part; it also reflected the larger cultural and political milieu in which the students operated.

Andy Warhol's visit to the campus is a good example. Students in attendance expected the famous artist to present his "pop art in action," a thing for which Warhol was, of course, famous. The expectation reflected student interest in contemporary artistic, intellectual, and cultural developments beyond the campus, and in New York in particular, and the pop artist was just one of numerous similar invitees to the campus.[59] By late 1967, Warhol had become, like Ginsberg, "famous for being famous," and was surrounded by the full range of artists, musicians, writers, and assorted misfits and hangers-on at his "Factory" in Lower Manhattan. The Factory served as his studio and regularly presented live music, The Velvet Underground, and the famous Exploding Plastic Inevitable multimedia events. As he dabbled in "pop art," film, and rock music, Warhol represented the cutting edge of cultural developments in and around New York City during the sixties.

Onstage at Drew that evening, Warhol sat behind very dark sunglasses. An entourage surrounded him at a table, with a single microphone placed at the center. For an hour, he said nothing beyond, "I'm really not prepared to speak tonight." The event left students puzzled and more than a little frustrated, with some confronting him as he left the stage to ask if he felt justified in the "performance." Student government president Tom McMullen also confronted Warhol and, in an image in the subsequent *Acorn* coverage, evidently grabbed the latter's shoulder as he spoke to him about the strange episode. Other coverage in the paper ran from bemused to angry. Students engaged in a running conversation about the experience (which may have been Warhol's intent), including conversation of an investigation into the details of the contract to see if there had been violations that would justify nonpayment. Someone even suggested that the whole affair had been a big hoax and that the person sitting onstage in dark glasses had not been Warhol at all but a stand-in. One student wrote, "Everyone agreed [Warhol] was worth something. Many would have been more than willing to give him bus fare (not carfare or airfare) back to whence he crawled forth." The dean, when asked, seemed to suggest the students, in getting nothing out of Warhol, had actually been given a valuable lesson. Some students writing in the paper agreed: "Maybe Warhol was getting the biggest laugh. . . . It was probably the only presentation at Drew where one didn't have to be there to know or not know everything that did or didn't go on."[60] Putting aside whatever might have been the point of Warhol's stunt, the whole episode showcased student engagement with and critical viewing of popular culture—various strands of the story remained in the pages of *The Acorn* for months afterward. That engagement ran the gamut and was on full display in the pages of the campus paper that now included columns devoted to film and music reviews, pop culture, politics, and substantial coverage of civil rights and the Vietnam War.

Like a lot of students entering college mid-decade, David Hinckley witnessed this rapid change. "When I got to Drew in the Fall of '66, there was very much a sense that the campus was run by a very traditional group [like] the Young Republicans. . . . Those were the people who . . . ran things." In his recollection, and in comparison, the campus seemed staid, conventional. "There was not a lot of 'boat rocking' going on when I got here. . . . There was great and deep suspicion of people who came onto campus who had long hair." By 1967, Hinckley had become editor of *The Acorn*, and in the intervening academic year, something had changed: "There was a visceral shift. . . . The class that came in the Fall of 1967, most of them had longer hair." Drew remained a "traditional" campus; most of those attending still had a clear focus on what they wanted to do, and they had come to Drew to get a good liberal arts education and move on to a good career. "You never had the feeling Drew was some revolutionary hotbed." "In any case, I think there was a huge shift at Drew in the time I was here." That spring, students gathered en masse in front of the Brothers College building, the same spot they had gathered as freshmen to listen to college deans and the like drone on about how to behave and what all the rules were that they'd be expected to follow. This time, however, the students were gathered in protest of the Vietnam War, shouting "stop this thing" and "stop the warmongers." There was "a big shift in the feeling on campus over that time."[61] "Faculty members and students who you'd never suspect had any political leanings . . . suddenly they were in front of the group" decrying the war.

The fall 1967 term also marked the centennial of Drew University. Various celebrations and comments noted the occasion, including the many changes that had already occurred in recent years as well as those ongoing. A commemoration in *The Acorn* noted that while the forest remained, much about the university, its faculty, and its students had changed, and for the better.[62] In only the most recent decade, an expanded and more diverse student body organized a student government, expanded the purview and staffing of the student-run newspaper, and turned the Social Committee into a highly organized entertainment booking and promotion agency for the campus. Students increasingly led the changes happening on the campus, driven by larger changes taking place around the nation and the world, all reinforced especially on college campuses by the necessary rotation of seniors out and freshmen in at the start of every fall term. As the fall term came to a close, students, like students at dozens of other of the nation's campuses, exercised an extraordinary degree of autonomy in shaping their college lives. In this sense, and especially as a whole, they both shaped and reflected broader changes in the country and the world. Thus the campus made an ideal site for a variety of social, political, and cultural developments.

Conclusion

Surveying developments in pop and rock music through 1967, Paul Williams in his "What Goes On?" news column in *Crawdaddy!* wrote, "There's still no rock scene in New York."[63] Unlike more mainstream coverage from *Time* and *Life* magazines a couple years earlier, Williams was discerning in this judgment: "Rock, which has grown out of pop music, is now something larger. More rock albums are now sold than all other types of music put together, and that's a very significant fact. It means . . . that rock fans far outnumber enthusiasts of any other 'type' of music; that, speaking either democratically or economically, rock is now the vital music of the nation."[64] Not at all surprising for a magazine devoted to rock music, Williams drew a line between that "type" and the popular music common on the radio and in dance halls—the very dance halls *Time* highlighted by announcing the recent openings of 5,000 discotheques, including twenty-one in Manhattan alone.[65]

Williams's lengthy essay took stock of pop and rock music, including perspectives from mainstream press outlets like *The New York Times*, *Life*, *Time*, *Newsweek*, and *The New Yorker* as well as the industry and charts from *Billboard*. His survey even included the important distinction between 45s and LPs, nascent rock radio on FM stations, The Beatles's *Sgt. Pepper's* album and the recent Monterey Pop Festival, all of which made rock "the most eclectic and non-specific category . . . able to absorb many different tastes and preferences."[66] So, while rock music had grown into something of its own, and Williams highlighted the Haight-Ashbury scene as the lead example of it, New York remained a few years behind. Bill Graham did not open the Fillmore East until the spring of the following year, immediately making it the premier club for rock music in New York. And the discotheques that flourished in New York in the mid-sixties more typically played host to pop music and celebrities.[67]

Williams captured an important reality in his essay, even if that reality went unmentioned; while little to no infrastructure for rock music existed in and around New York city by 1967, the music flourished on college campuses. Area college campuses provided an important site for live performance of rock music when precious few existed. And Drew and Stony Brook Universities, lying due west and east, respectively, of Manhattan, played host to nearly all rock music, in all its manifest eclecticism. Without realizing it at the time, students took full advantage of the temporary absence of an industry presence and their own relatively large budgets, freedom to act, and access to their "built-in audiences" to encourage and nurture the latest trends and developments in rock music. In the coming couple of years, both campuses teemed with rock music and its attendant cultural elements. Indeed, as will become clear in the following chapter, it is impossible to survey the two campuses without contending with the countercultural rock music and politics universally recognized as characterizing so much of American life in the late sixties.

4

"They're Rockin' in
the Ivory Tower"

• • • • • • • • • • • • • • • • • • • •

Fall 1967–Fall 1968

In 1967, *Billboard* declared, "It was a long climb that took more or less
10 years, but the aloofness of the Ivory Tower was attacked, stormed and
conquered during the past year by rock 'n' roll. . . . [R]ock 'n' roll has established not only a beachhead, but has taken over." Two years later, *Billboard*
wrote of "the rock revolution on campus," as "student power" had led to a
takeover of control of many aspects of their college lives, including purchas-
ing power.[1] Both Stony Brook and Drew brought dozens of now iconic
bands and artists to campus, from folk to psychedelic rock and everything
in between, not to mention a broad range of public intellectuals and activists. Rock music culture now dominated campus culture and entertainment.
More telling is the specific language of *Billboard*'s observations. In retrospect, the language captures some of the motifs of 1968: tumult, unrest, and
violence on college campuses across the country. The language of war
and revolution, coincident with the height of the Vietnam War, also suggests
a contest in which the university defended in vain traditional conventions
and practices of the college campus. The language of war is all too familiar

and appropriate to the period. Students repeatedly engaged in occupations and marches, both common elements of the mass movements of the period. The counterculture and rock music are likewise replete with references to war and revolution. By the late sixties, dozens of conflicts erupted in and around college campuses that cast in relief the contested terrain around civil rights, the Vietnam War, student autonomy, campus culture, drugs, and rock music—so much of what we think of as the counterculture. In this sense, the year began rather inauspiciously for the students at both Stony Brook and Drew.

Early one January morning in 1968, nearly 200 Suffolk County uniformed and plainclothes police officers launched a raid on the Stony Brook campus, fanning out on cue in search of marijuana and other drugs and thirty-eight students named in an indictment. This was the first time police had invaded the "sanctity of a major university for such a raid," according to one press account.[2] Later in the year, the start of the fall term, dozens of uniformed police and narcotics agents stormed a private home across the street from Drew in Madison, arresting 120 young people and immediately pouring gas on the fire that had been smoldering since February between the students on and off campus and the townspeople. The two highly visible and provocative episodes at the Stony Brook and Drew campuses and the surrounding communities are thoroughly intertwined with all of these, and especially rock music and counterculture.

Viewed from a law enforcement perspective, both raids failed thoroughly. Though elaborately planned and sanctioned by officials months ahead of time, neither turned up nearly the level of criminality that had been their rationale. Both also brought much more scrutiny to policing in the small towns than had been anticipated. Town residents, or "townies" as the students called them, split over the episode, and their complaints and arguments played out for weeks in local newspapers. State and even national press coverage conveyed a sense of lawlessness and unrest, with very little of it actually landing on the presumed criminals. The raids sowed distrust and suspicion that spread to other area campuses. Rumors flew at Columbia University of an impending raid when students spotted narcotics agents on the campus during registration, agents the dean referred to as "real neanderthal types."[3] In short, what unfolded in the immediate aftermath of the raids brought into the open the complicated relationship between "town and gown," or the communities and a growing campus counterculture.

Campus culture had grown more diverse, with increasing numbers embracing rapid cultural change. Those changes witnessed during the previous academic year—the growth in popularity of rock music on campus, drug use, increased political engagement and radicalization of the campus newspapers—flourished. This flowering is evident in both the range of rock music performances on the campuses during the year and the explicit turn toward the radical and countercultural in the campus papers. The campuses welcomed The Who, Richie Havens, Jefferson Airplane, Iron Butterfly, The Fugs, The Grateful Dead, The Jimi Hendrix Experience, Country Joe & the Fish, Procol Harum, Blood, Sweat & Tears, and Blue Öyster Cult, along with numerous other folk and folk-rock acts. And both campus papers began publishing radical content, some from the newly formed Liberation News Service, but much of it homegrown. While some students reacted with indifference or outright hostility to these changes, an increasing number embraced and drove them. The latter tended to set the overall tone. As president of the undergraduate student body at Penn State astutely observed in 1966, "As administrators and students came to realize, the passive majority often embraced the goals, if not the methods, of the activist minority."[4]

Politics, the Counterculture, and Rock Music on Campus

As students around the country transitioned from the fall 1967 to the spring 1968 term, protests became commonplace at hundreds of college campuses, so much so that it is now difficult to find a campus without direct student involvement in protest for change. Students certainly had no shortage of outrages: the Vietnam War was a frequent object of campus discontent. President Lyndon Johnson made an easy target with continued bromides on the success of the war in the face of mounting contradictory evidence, evidence made more convincing by his own televised resignation (announcing he would not seek re-election) at the end of March. Martin Luther King Jr.'s assassination followed a week later, resulting in massive unrest, including at dozens of college campuses. The ongoing civil rights/Black Power movement and related ferment in places like Los Angeles, Detroit, Newark, and Chicago marked the northern turn in the focus on racial discrimination and violence. Bobby Kennedy's assassination followed in June. Many students then rallied around Eugene McCarthy ("Clean for Gene") as the peace candidate for president. In this context, student rebellion is not altogether surprising.[5] But large-scale, off-campus factors have taken attention away from the scope and diversity of the organic and long-standing student engagement on campus. Those off-campus factors have become a kind of low-hanging historical fruit in that they are typically invoked as the engines of campus activism and unrest, thus obscuring the particulars of an intrinsic student counterculture that had developed years earlier. Student activism and engagement around on-campus issues were widespread and ran the gamut from dormitory crowding to matters of curriculum, but were and are less visible, especially when cast alongside broader, national events.

The fact is, by 1968, campus culture at both Stony Brook and Drew was already "counterculture," itself something decades in the making. As sixties and counterculture historians Peter Braunstein and Michael William Doyle have written, the American counterculture finds its origins in the immediate post-WWII years amid a growing antipathy with the nation's "shrill triumphalism," social regimentation, hyper-consumerism, racial segregation, militarism, and Cold War.[6] The changes on many college campuses only heightened that antipathy from the fifties and into the sixties. As historian Helen Horowitz pointed out, "Understanding the ways that contending undergraduate cultures have operated in the past clarifies that protestors in the 1960s were acting not merely out of individual conscience, but from within a collegiate culture with its own ethos and codes of behavior."[7] Similarly, one careful study of the sixties college experience pointed out the fact that students shared "an underlying cluster of values."[8] Those values, their defense and their nourishment, could manifest in a variety of ways from direct protest to drug use, from editorializing in the campus paper to the exploration of rock music culture.

The very person responsible for launching the process of bringing rock music to campus, Glenn Redbord, had nothing to do with activism, at least as commonly understood: "I and my friends were not involved in political activity. We were all too busy with our entrepreneurial programs or trying to figure out how to pay for school and then, finally, in '67, '68, figuring ways to get out of the draft. But never protesting the war . . . I was in the middle of it and had no interest whatsoever. I look back and find it hard to believe. I was not in favor of the war. But, I was not an activist." Likewise, regarding civil rights, Redbord had little interest: "I had nothing to do with it, never thought about it. It was never an interest of mine." Reflecting on this, he emphatically added, "Looking back, I'm horrified to think that it wasn't an interest."[9] Redbord echoes much of what has been written of this seeming paradox; the simultaneous existence of student protest and open rebellion alongside passivity and a reinforcement of the rules of society, both occupying the same space on the college campus. The paradoxical frame is a bit misleading though. While Redbord and no doubt many others focused on their studies, finishing their degree, and moving onto a job or career, they also participated in the cultural milieu of the day, even if not as "political activists," an often narrow understanding. Many were active, if not "activists." For his part, Redbord was engaged with the world probably more than most. He was a leader, both on and off campus. Rather than frame this as the difference between being an activist and not, I view this in terms of the larger cultural environment and its evolution and diversity, especially on the college campus. The counterculture was more expansive and more diverse than is popularly understood.

Nowhere is this diversity clearer than in the pages of campus newspapers *The Acorn* and *The Statesman*. By the late sixties, both were replete with counterculture and radical political content—or at least what would have passed for radical in the moment. Alongside concert announcements and reviews, album reviews, and artist profiles, the paper routinely featured the full range of late sixties politics, often explicitly mirroring the vibe and the feel of the underground press.[10] The papers contained coverage of the unfolding disaster in Vietnam, tips for how to avoid the draft, ads for a moratorium on the war and student walkouts, teach-ins, and marches, students campaigning against Richard Nixon, favorable commentary on the civil rights movement, critical commentary on the problem of racism at the university, and essays and editorials on the death of Martin Luther King Jr. *The Acorn* ran a full-cover tribute to both Janis Joplin and Jimi Hendrix immediately following the deaths of the young rock music stars, a similar tribute to Malcolm X, and both contained a broad range of subversive and countercultural commentary and subversive "comix" from such countercultural luminaries as R. Crumb, Jules Feiffer (who also spoke on the Drew campus), Gilbert Shelton, Ron Cobb, and Herbert Block (or "Herblock"!).[11] Especially from 1968 on, as both papers filled out their content with weekly news packets delivered from the LNS, the national syndicate for the emergent underground press in the United States, content tilted more toward the radical and the countercultural.[12]

To the students at the time, these changes appeared to come quickly. *Acorn* editor Hinckley described a transition, a "huge shift," at Drew between 1966 and 1970, much like the others I interviewed. "There was not a lot of 'boat rocking' going on when I got here," he told me. Within a couple years, the differences were palpable: long hair, bell-bottomed jeans, bearded young

drew

acorn

student newspaper
of
the college

Vol. XLIV No. 5

DREW UNIVERSITY, MADISON, NEW JERSEY

October 9, 1970

WE WOULD LIKE TO DEDICATE THIS
ISSUE TO JIM HENDRIX AND JANIS
JOPLIN 1942-1970

On the inside...

Tribute to Jimi Hendrix and Janis Joplin, *The Acorn*, October 1970.

men, marijuana, and rock music were commonplace. Bob Johnson, class of '71, history major and student government vice president, recalled, "When I arrived at Drew in 1967, there still was the rule that you were supposed to wear suits, coats and jackets to Sunday dinner. I think I wore it once. I was one of the very few [who did]." The old rules persisted, at least officially. Female and male students could be in each other's dorm rooms only with the door open and with feet on the floor. Dorm monitors reinforced these rules, as they had for years. When he returned to begin his sophomore year in 1968, "those rules were still in place; nothing was enforced." Students moved their mattresses into their significant others' rooms; "when you went into a restroom, you weren't sure whether it was a men's room or a women's room." From one year to the next, as Johnson recalled, "it was a social revolution that you just see in front of you." At the same time, rock music became the soundtrack to this set of experiences. "By my junior year, you walked around campus, there were speakers out of people's windows and you were hearing music constantly."[13] Another student, Jeff King, class of '72, sociology major, arrived in August 1968: "I had never been on campus until about two weeks before my freshman orientation. I walked in and saw a poster in the U.C. [University Center] for the Jefferson Airplane. I realized, 'hey, this is the place to be!' because if they can bring the Jefferson Airplane to my campus, thirty miles from New York City, there's gonna be a lot of music here."[14] King attended that concert he'd seen advertised in the U.C. on October 4 that year. He went on to chair the Social Committee, organizing numerous concerts of his own.

Likewise, at Stony Brook, students had arrived at a number of important realizations, having grown up during these years. In sharp contrast to Drew, the Stony Brook campus had expanded dramatically during the previous four years. A growing number of students voiced their discontent or frustration over the consequences. *The Statesman* ran an interview with a graduating senior, Pete Nack, at the end of the spring 1968 term. Nack, a very active and visible student leader during his four years, had witnessed much change, some of it negative.

> There's been a change in atmosphere over the past few years. The atmosphere a few years ago was still euphoric. . . . Now the attitude is that "this place sucks and I can't wait to get out of here." . . . I think this is the general attitude of a majority of the students. This is the change. The hatred of Stony Brook by Stony Brook students is immense. It's a strange hate—on one hand they

realize the potential and they really think it's good to graduate from Stony Brook, but they're also disgusted by the lousy conditions. And the conditions have gotten worse: four years ago there was no tripling, the classes were much smaller, you were assured of getting a tenured [professor] in half your classes, and the course offerings were fairly new (now they're the same courses and they've gotten stale over the years). Not that much attention has been given to undergrad curriculum. The general attitude is that things have gone stale, and a lot of Seniors are really disappointed about Stony Brook.[15]

Nor were Nack's observations outliers. *The Statesman* routinely contained various commentaries on all these issues, perhaps near the top of them being "tripling," the practice of placing three students in a dorm room designed for one. Another former student recently voiced precisely these issues in relating her experience at Stony Brook in the sixties. Nancy Malagold arrived at Stony Brook from Brooklyn in 1968 and was "tripled" in her freshman year, resulting in a "nightmare" of a year. She participated in antiwar protests and attended numerous rock concerts. She recalled a campus variously populated by "preppies" alongside "hippies," and remembers seeing drug use on campus. And, regarding "town and gown," Malagold emphatically insisted the "gown" was much more radical than the "town." She also recalled the mud, constant construction, and, referring to the architectural style, the "Stalinesque grotesque" buildings. Though she sympathized with antiwar protests and the civil rights movement, she believes protests and the like limited her education—administration canceled finals and made courses pass-fail following a spring '69 drug raid and later Kent State, the Cambodia bombing, and numerous bomb scares. The result, in her mind, was an easy set of courses very limited in scope. She told me recently, with much regret, that she never took a science course, only one math course, and not a single history course. "It's really a disgrace." She acknowledged her role in this, saying, "I could have taken harder courses." Still, she recalled with fondness the concerts she attended, and that of The Moody Blues in particular because during their song "Timothy Leary Is Dead," Leary actually walked out onto the stage to sing along with the band.

She and Nack both also lamented the trend of larger numbers of "vocationally oriented" student ambitions and goals. What they meant was that students, at least a growing number of them, came to college in pursuit of grades on the way toward a career, rather than a genuine intellectual curiosity without regard to grades. The fact is that with exponential growth, all of what would have remained small or relatively insignificant matters grew into something more. This crowding, along with the constant mud and construction, was a consistent theme.[16] *The Statesman* was also filled with LNS material, subversive content, and drug raids, bomb scares, and student protests/walkouts/occupations. This content ramped up toward the close of the decade, seemingly paralleling the growth of the campus and student body.

At Drew, Hinckley witnessed these changes at the *Acorn* up close and personal. Serving multiple staff roles, he went on to become editor of the paper in 1967. That summer, he attended the national conference of the United States Student Press Association (USSPA). The USSPA served as the national organization for college newspapers and held an annual conference at a member college to which were invited newspaper editors and staff. At this conference, held at the University of Minnesota in Minneapolis, growing discontent within the organization came into full view. Hinckley described "an enormous internal battle" as representatives of eighty to ninety papers from across the country fought over the leadership and the future direction of the USSPA. That body represented "traditional," "objective" journalism, according to Hinckley. In the late sixties, that meant reifying an establishment narrative and an avoidance of provocation. Jack Newfield, a writer for the *Village Voice*, described mainstream, traditional journalism at the time as "the belief in welfare capitalism, God, the West, Puritanism, the Law, the family, property, the two-party system, and perhaps most crucially . . . the notion that violence is only defensible when employed by the State."[17] For a growing number of young newspaper editors and staff, this description was both accurate and the problem.

Activists led by Ray Mungo and Marshall Bloom, editors for *Boston University News* and the *Amherst Student*, respectively, occupied key leadership roles, and Bloom was poised to become USSPA president at the 1967 conference. What they had in mind, though, was a very different student press outfit. The USSPA, then housed with the National Student Association (NSA), had been founded just after World War II and was, in many ways, just as outdated. "The USSPA was one of those bourgey [*sic*] student organizations with a budget in six figures, whose conventions are addressed by Senators and executives," according to Mungo.[18] To make matters worse, "the USSPA had always been the NSA's brainchild, ward, and mouthpiece," and many of its own members considered the NSA little more than a CIA front. They were proven correct when underground press *Ramparts* magazine published an exposé on the CIA and student group ties in its March 1967 issue.[19] Inevitably, students and their campus newspapers had been made complicit with the state, Cold War, counterintelligence, injustices of many kinds, and the war in Vietnam. The organization's conservatism, alongside heavy CIA involvement, compelled some to make a break. Ultimately, this insurgent effort was defeated in a close vote, and Mungo and Bloom broke away and formed the Liberation News Service (LNS). The LNS soon became the leading national syndicate for news for many rapidly emerging underground magazines, libraries, and papers, including hundreds of college papers, among them *The Acorn* and *The Statesman*. By the following year, nearly two hundred other papers plunked down the $15 membership fee to receive weekly news packets.[20]

Returning to campus that fall, Hinckley settled into his new role as editor of the campus paper, focusing on local rather than national news and limiting the coverage produced by other sources. In his own view and remembering himself not at all as an "activist," his approach tended more toward traditional journalism. Despite this, he acknowledged the myriad changes both on the campus and around the nation and the impact of these changes, notably what he called "advocacy journalism." In spite of what might have been his own traditional editorial approach, the content of the *Acorn* began to reflect this and other changes of the period. The paper's content contained a broad range of politics, the Vietnam War, civil rights, and rock music, this last including reviews of live shows, new albums, concert announcements, provocative comix, regular columns, and a lively editorial page. His successor, Ken Schulman, citing the free love and free speech movements and the yippies, said these changes at the school and at the paper were very much a response to larger changes happening across the country and around the world. As editor and feeling a sense of substantial engagement with those changes, he was "very interested in reporting in an activist and provocative way."[21] Under Schulman, *The Acorn* officially became a member of LNS.

Around 4 A.M. one morning in late 1965, Jann Wenner was abruptly awakened in his UC Berkeley dorm room by cops searching for drugs. After a quick search of his room, he was arrested and jailed. Luckily for him, the search did not discover the drugs hidden in his freezer, and his lawyer managed to get the possession charges dropped. Already deeply involved in both the new rock and roll and the campus Free Speech movement, his Something's Happening column for *The Daily Californian* campus paper, written under the pseudonym "Mr. Jones," became "Berkeley's window into the insular psychedelic rock scene," and Wenner "the ultimate acid insider" according to a biographer. Recognizing that activism and rock music had surpassed his interest in studying, he dropped out of college in his sophomore year and started *Rolling Stone*, a magazine dedicated to covering rock and roll. In a widely read 1969 editorial (for an issue dedicated to groupies), he wrote, "Like it or not, we have reached a point in the social, cultural, intellectual and artistic history of the United States where we are all going to be affected by politics. We can no longer ignore it. It threatens our daily lives and our daily happiness."[22] That the young rock magazine editor used the word "threatens" is clearly indicative of a particular perspective on the events of the period. Political culture did not merely demand attention; it threatened. For many young progressives such as Schulman, this sense of being threatened, of having one's values or even one's life threatened, was the galvanizing sentiment of the day.[23]

In January 1968, the month Greg Granquist became chair of the Social Committee at Drew, the Tet Offensive shook the nation's already faltering confidence in the military to bring the ever-expanding war in Vietnam to a successful end, whatever that meant. With more than 500,000 troops deployed there following several years of dramatic escalation, not only did the end of it all seem out of sight, even the terms of losing and winning had become less clear. Utterly vexed and out of options, president Lyndon Johnson, during a televised address at the end of March, essentially announced his own resignation by telling viewers he would not seek re-election. The announcement shocked many, buoyed some, and angered others.[24] Then in early April, Martin Luther King Jr.'s assassination sent shock waves cascading across the nation. Hundreds of cities, universities, and colleges erupted in anguish and violence.[25]

Two days following King's assassination, *Rolling Stone*'s other founding editor and music writer, Ralph Gleason, published an editorial in which he called out the hypocrisy of the establishment and those critical of young people, hippies, smoking grass, and rock music. He admonished cops, parents, the government, and the military for harassing and beating hippies and Blacks, for "brutalizing the Vietnamese," and warned, "It will get worse, much worse, before it gets better." And then, drawing to his close, he wrote, "Music may . . . save us yet. Certainly no hippie, no folk singer, no long-haired, guitar playing rock musician is going to fry us all with napalm or blow us up with the bomb. This would be a better country with Zally [Yablonski of The Lovin' Spoonful] as president, to say nothing of the thousands of others."[26] Gleason's preference for either a hippie, a folk singer, or a long-haired guitar player for president is instructive. His inclusive grouping is telling; on one side stood forces bent on destruction and death, and on the other, hippies, folkies, and rock musicians—all a part of the same thing—intending harm to no one. The hippies, folkies, and rock musicians brought only peace and, as Gleason concluded, "anything that offers peace in this world is attractive."[27]

Operation Stony Brook

We, as a class and as a generation, have known little peace.

—*Specula*, 1968

At the start of the year, peace was not on the agenda as nearly two hundred police officers waited in the predawn hours for the signal to begin a massive raid on the students of Stony Brook in search of drugs. As students and school officials stood around outside, police ransacked the dorms, tossing personal belongings and sending the inhabitants scrambling. Police eventually arrested and took to jail thirty-four young people from the campus, eleven of them nonstudents. In spite of the shroud of secrecy surrounding the planning for the raid, word got out quickly. In retrospect, this seems to have been the point. In a telling move, police agreed to provide a briefing for the press at 3 A.M. on the edge of the campus, just ahead of the raid. Journalists and cameras then fanned out across campus along with police. Some had been provided a tactical booklet drawn up by the police called *Operation Stony Brook* as a kind of informative guide, complete with maps of the campus and dorms and detailed descriptions of the students sought for arrest.[28]

Some alleged at the time that part of the point was visibility, as various state and county officials jockeyed for position. Suffolk County police commissioner John Barry spearheaded the raid, authorizing the planting of undercover police agents on the campus.[29] Those agents quickly became fixtures on the campus as what was termed at the time "drop-ins," or nonstudents who regularly hung around the campus. They made friends with students known to smoke marijuana and use other drugs by frequenting G Dormitory, a well-known center of activity on campus. Over the course of several months, undercover police gathered intelligence and provided

Police gather at the Stony Brook campus before launching a major raid for drugs and students suspected of involvement with drugs, *Specula*, 1968.

authorities with a richly detailed picture of student activity, including drug use and sales with impunity as school officials looked the other way. One student, well known to others as a source for pot, hung a sign on his dorm door that read, "I'm all out," to avoid the line of students coming to make a buy. The details were many and shocking, especially for the communities around the isolated, rural flagship campus. Glassy-eyed students aimlessly wandering the halls, acting "too friendly," according to one of the agents, "drop-ins" sleeping on the floor, bad LSD trips, and so on. These revelations provoked a very public debate around not only drug use but nearly every aspect of the campus experience and the youth culture dominating it, with one concerned citizen using the episode to criticize the presence of student activist Mark Rudd on the campus and the fact that the student newspaper contained coverage of "Black Power leader Eldridge Cleaver" and "his anti-white views."[30] This editorial attempted to leverage support for the state

Drug raid on Stony Brook campus, *Specula*, 1969.

university through taxes and was aimed squarely at the governor, finishing, "Governor Rockefeller, please take note."[31]

State congressional committees of jurisdiction mounted a series of hearings, requiring testimony from campus officials as well as some students. News coverage across the state was littered with various elected public figures grandstanding with bold declarations, staking out tactical ground as the public digested and made sense of the apparently out-of-control drug epidemic on college campuses. Others, of course, downplayed the incident, lest it get completely out of their control.[32] Commissioner Barry told the press a couple weeks following the raid, "It's the pusher we want, no so much the user," although the arrests evidently snared only the latter. Students and certain members of the press were not buying this argument: "It is going to create a blaze of publicity. Because of this, it is well to keep in mind that all state Senators and Assemblymen will be up for reelection in November, and there is no better way to get one's name in front of the public than through legislative hearings and investigations."[33] The Joint Committee on Crime, Its Causes, Control and Effect on Society's own final report on Stony Brook revealed serious cleavages among its members. The report ended with the dissenting "Minority Report" that blasted the whole proceeding as "already overpublicized," having no legislative purpose, "reprehensible," and unnecessarily damaging to the reputation "of a great public institution."[34] The students at Stony Brook found themselves caught in a highly visible contest between forces well beyond the campus, with clear political overtones and national implications. The result, not surprisingly, according to numerous accounts, was "the students at Stony Brook are scared. . . . They are scared of a largely hostile community that will employ any means to keep the University 'in check.'"[35]

Tensions between the campus and the community had been building over the past year. Rumors of widespread drug use combined with growing student activism drew greater attention to the campus from the community and the police. Stony Brook had "drawn fire on two fronts: drugs and draft evasion," according to one press account.[36] Suspicion and distrust between the police and the campus administration had compelled the former to plant undercover cops in the first place, at least as early as the previous September. They blended in, or at least attempted to, with the students to gather information that would be crucial in securing the grand jury indictment and in planning the subsequent raid. The police planning booklet, *Operation Stony Brook*, makes clear the level of informant assistance in describing in detail specific places students hid drugs, their particular habits and hangouts, height, weight, hair color and length, address, and whether or not they had a car. The following warning accompanied every student listed in the booklet, some thirty-eight of them: "It is not known if the subject carries a weapon, but because of his use of drugs he should be considered dangerous."[37] The police kept campus officials in the dark about their plans, out of concern that their allegiance to the students would compromise the secrecy of the operation. As part of the subsequent hearings, officials charged one administrator with tipping off the students to an impending raid of a "pot party."[38]

On the list of dozens of students police sought for search and arrest was Howie Klein, even though he no longer lived on campus. "They thought I was the biggest drug dealer in Suffolk County," and, by his own subsequent admission, they were not far from the mark. Still, he viewed the whole affair as "such a farce": "It's hilarious how lame the police were. I mean, some guy with big cop shoes and a mop-like, long-hair wig he bought for $15 from a Halloween costume shop walks up to me and asks if he can buy a nickel bag."[39] Evidently other students took a similar view, and came to refer to one of the undercover drop-ins as "John the Fed." Officials pressured a number of students to provide testimony before the grand jury. Klein was one of them, and he eventually agreed to do it. "They said they would grant me immunity if I would testify. I said I would do it, but only if I didn't testify against any person. . . . They just wanted me to talk about drug use on campus." He ended up spilling all—at least about his own activities. "My lawyer said 'tell them anything you've ever done. Get anything bad into this testimony.'" Doing so meant he could not be prosecuted for any of it in the future.[40] He managed to avoid being caught up in the campus raid largely because he had not been living on campus for a while at this point; he had been kicked off a year or so earlier due to accusations of selling drugs.[41]

In early March, amid continued fallout over the police raid, Allen Ginsberg came to Stony Brook. Some 800 students crowded the G cafeteria, lining the halls and stairways to get a glimpse of the counterculture hero. He did not disappoint, arriving amid "the odor of incense," bearded and wearing beads, old jeans, and a large, flowered tie and chanting to the gathered crowd while standing atop a cafeteria table. Moderated by Pete Nack, Ginsberg told the students, "Your professors are being asked to fink on you." Ginsberg admonished administrators for not supporting the students and also read statistics from recent research on the harmlessness of marijuana, including the Food and Drug Administration's own conclusion. He encouraged the students to appeal the case all the way to the Supreme Court, adding, "You're not powerless!" The famed Beat poet and counterculture activist spoke on college campuses routinely, tailed by the FBI (also routinely).[42]

Living off campus in a stereotypical tract-style suburban house with several others, Klein continued to explore rock music culture in New York and book bands for performances on the campus. In the last week of February, Jackson Browne, Judy Collins, The Fugs, and Country Joe & the Fish all performed. When Klein booked Jefferson Airplane for a show in spring 1967, Bill Graham, then managing the band, accompanied them. Klein hosted the band, with their large bus, at the suburban home—a hard-to-miss scene, no doubt. He, Pearlman, Marty Balin, Paul Kantner, and Bill Graham went into the city for dinner following the Jefferson Airplane show at Stony Brook. In this casual and organic way, all of them began piecing together the network of rock culture for the area around New York. Subsequently, Bill Graham began sending Klein tapes of bands that had not yet become known or hadn't yet recorded an album to play on his campus radio show. Klein then provided those bands exposure to the campus and, likewise, provided like-minded students exposure to bands each likely would not have encountered. Regarding these connections and the budding culture thereof, Klein today views all of it as part of the same thing: the Vietnam War, the drugs, the rock music, the attitude, the culture. "All of these were happening at once and rock was the easiest way that you could see this in the culture. These reactionaries hated it. They took it as a challenge to who they are. . . . They were very, very hostile to it."[43]

Student leaders were doing more than simply arranging entertainment for their classmates. They provided a critical link between campus culture and the world beyond. That link conveyed the cultural and political realities of the day in both directions—bringing the world to the campus and taking the campus to the wider world. A number of students remained very active in the burgeoning scene in and around New York's East Village. They became the key part of a local infrastructure for rock music and an important bridge linking the city to the campus. The campus hosted many concerts during the late sixties, several dozen just in the 1967–1968 academic year, the fall and spring terms. And although an official committee structure, the SAB, existed to formalize the process, the actual arrangements were dominated by only a few students, a frequent complaint on the editorial page of the campus paper. They, along with a handful of others, acted as the agents, promoters, hosts, critics, and even managers for bands and artists.

Both Meltzer and Pearlman were part of the inaugural staff of writers at *Crawdaddy!*, which billed itself as "the first magazine to take rock music seriously."[44] Pearlman, having written a series of poems titled *Imaginos*, put together a band to bring those words to music. That band, initially named Soft White Underbelly, later became Blue Öyster Cult.[45] Both he and Meltzer wrote songs for the band, and Pearlman managed. As a relatively new student at Stony Brook, Klein had looked up to and admired both Pearlman and Meltzer. Pearlman was very active in student government and provided Klein with his own entry into an active role on campus. Meltzer was a sort of heroic campus provocateur and gadfly.

Klein recently recalled, "[Meltzer] was a wild and crazy guy," and everyone saw him as brilliant. Everyone saw him as kind of a role model for "this new thing that was being born," the culture around the new rock music. Klein sees Meltzer as having been a bridge between the older, Beat culture and the emerging counterculture around rock music, the hippie aesthetic, hallucinogenic drugs, fashion, and art. Others have seconded that notion over the years, including rock music critic and historian Greil Marcus, who has both praised and puzzled over Meltzer's *The Aesthetics of Rock*, a cult-classic treatise on rock culture written while the latter was at Stony Brook. That book might be as bizarre, puzzling, and at times insightful as Meltzer himself. His role on campus was as a sort of cultural rebel—he got tossed from The Doors concert on the campus for his disruptive behavior; he later got tossed from the final Sex Pistols show in San Francisco. He also knew more about the then emerging rock music than anyone. Whenever he recommended a band, Klein then tried to book that band, without question.[46] Almost in spite of himself, Meltzer enjoyed broad influence around campus. Highly energetic, provocative, whip-smart, and a prolific writer, he was Lester Bangs before Lester Bangs, according to Klein. Meltzer was soon off to Yale for graduate school in all his enigmatic glory, which did not last very long.[47]

Pearlman (who graduated in 1966) and another Stony Brook student, Neil Louison, began hosting rock music shows at the Anderson Theater in the East Village in early February—just two blocks from where Bill Graham would open the more famous Fillmore East later that year. The first of a series of rock shows began on February 2 with Country Joe & the Fish, Jim Kweskin & the Jug Band, and (Pearlman's own creation) Soft White Underbelly (prior to their being rechristened Blue Öyster Cult).[48] At a time when very few venues hosting rock music existed at all, the Anderson filled a niche and created an easy bridge between cutting-edge rock music developments in the city and the college campus. Additionally, this arrangement created opportunities for other area campuses as well. In a now obvious and striking pattern, nearly every band and artist performing in the city and/or at Stony Brook also played other area colleges at the same time, especially Drew University.

Meanwhile, the SAB instituted its own apprenticeship program as elections brought in a new crop of students.[49] And, as the SAB continued to refine its operations, the industry itself still lagged behind in terms of rock music. This was especially true in the realm of management and promotion. There were lots of bands, especially rock bands, that could be booked ad hoc, which was preferable to waiting for a touring band to come to town and then working through an agency. "This was key!," Klein told me. "That industry was just getting started. That industry that coordinated record releases with tours wasn't really happening yet. It was possible to find artists and get them to play who weren't out promoting an album."[50] College students could and did turn this lack of precedent and infrastructure to their advantage quite easily. For instance, Klein befriended Brad Pierce, who managed a dance club called Ondine in Midtown under the 59th Street bridge and had access to The Doors. This kind of direct access to and role in the evolution of rock culture, impossible only a few years later, is precisely how many of the era's iconic rock bands came to perform at the campuses. As Klein pointed out regarding The Doors's arrangement, "I made that deal with Jim Morrison," not any management or agent.[51]

He also befriended Howard Solomon who ran the Cafe Au Go Go in the Village on Bleecker Street. The club opened in 1964 and hosted variety acts, folk, and comedy—Lenny Bruce and Solomon were both arrested there on obscenity charges in 1964—until the rock music phenomenon came along. When it did, Klein and Solomon struck a deal; Solomon would book rock bands at his club for $3,000 for the week. They would play five or six nights, with one night at Stony Brook. "I would pay $1,500 of the 3K and he would pay the other fifteen." The deal was advantageous to both; it was a steal for Klein to get a rock act on campus for essentially half-price and, likewise, Solomon got a week's worth of shows at half-price. "He booked everybody. . . . These bands became giants, but they weren't at the time," said Klein. The arrangement also provided Klein with an all-access pass to the shows at the club. "One night, John Hammond was playing there . . . and I noticed . . . his guitar player. . . . [He] was the greatest guitar player I'd ever seen in my life, a guy named Jimi James." So he approached the guitar player, later known to the world as Jimi Hendrix, after the performance, and said to him, "I book the concerts at my school, would you come and play?" Hendrix said that he would, but first he was going to England "with those guys over there," pointing to the members of The Animals, also performing at the club. That same night, he secured a commitment from John Hammond

Jimi Hendrix performing onstage at Stony Brook, *Specula*, 1968.

to play at Stony Brook. Following a stint in England, and the release of his second album, *Axis: Bold as Love*, Jimi James returned as The Jimi Hendrix Experience to start the band's first North American tour. The tour began in San Francisco and worked its way east, playing numerous college shows on the way to New York and Stony Brook on March 9.[52]

The day before, Bill Graham opened the Fillmore East in New York's East Village (then called Lower East Side), headlining Big Brother & the Holding Company. Within a few months, the Fillmore was *the* place on the East Coast for rock concerts, and Bill Graham, having honed his skills as a promoter on the West Coast (at Fillmore West), blazed the trail, offering two shows per night, three nights per week. The venue and its bizarre, fascinating, and often contentious history quickly became legendary for rock fans.[53] Among his numerous rather artful schemes navigating the East Coast scene, Graham insisted the bands and artists he booked play no other gigs during the same week within a thirty-mile radius from his club. His only exception? Colleges. Though possibly an apocryphal tale, the proximity rule for Graham's East Village club is sufficiently widespread that nearly everyone I interviewed shared it unsolicited, revealing an understanding and a relationship, if not also hard fact.

By fall of that year, this network that had been in the making for several years now flourished along with the music. A growing number of FM radio stations now programmed rock music, also called "progressive" and "underground," at least part of the time, while several, including New York's WNEW, had pioneered the format full-time the previous year.[54] The campus hosted Smokey Robinson, Sam & Dave, Tim Hardin, Joni Mitchell, Procol Harum, Blood, Sweat & Tears, Moby Grape, Blue Öyster Cult, Ten Years After, Big Brother and the Holding Company, Richie Havens, The John Hammond Trio, Janis Joplin, and Nina Simone, among others. Now nearly all of them also booked performances at the Fillmore either immediately before or after the campus show. And, reflecting the work students had done over the previous several years, they nearly always included multiple campus performances.

Rock Music Culture on Main Street, USA

In 1968, rock music and its attendant culture were facts of life for millions of Americans, but especially for young people. This was as true across the country as it was at a small liberal arts college in suburban New Jersey. Students had now set a clear precedent of active engagement with that culture. In booking and promoting bands and artists on the campus, the students at Drew were tapping into the rapidly developing East Coast rock infrastructure centered around New York City in general and the East Village in particular. This infrastructure consisted not only of talent agents but also the underground press and the counterculture. Officially part of the Social Committee but acting with a lot of independence, both Glenn Redbord and Greg Granquist discovered or chose acts based on availability—which bands or performers were then on tour or otherwise moving through the region. Booking agencies in the city handed out packets, with lists and prices for artists from which to choose.[55] The students then negotiated terms and signed a contract. The whole process required work—phone calls, negotiations, paperwork, lots of back-and-forth, promotion, and money. To do it well required a good deal of pluck and time, and several of those involved repeatedly shared examples of how the commitment to arranging and promoting the concerts, alongside commitments to the antiwar and Civil Rights causes which were also key elements of their lives, added a semester or two to their time at school.[56]

The students had taken the initiative to do this with little to no involvement from the administration and little in the way of examples to mimic. In nearly every case, acts performing in the city, most often at Fillmore East after its opening, either performed at Drew and Stony Brook just prior to or immediately following that gig, constituting something of an ad hoc circuit. When they did play at Drew, again in nearly every case, they performed at no other venue in the state.[57] One of the bands available in early 1968 was The Who, and Granquist booked the popular British group for an early spring show as his first concert.[58] Embarking on their first U.S. tour, The Who was not exactly a household name at the time, which made Granquist a little hesitant with the recommendation from Redbord. "The price was $4,500 for one show with an option of $500 for a second show. I was dubious—the price was high—but I wanted to have a concert, and I was familiar with their hit 'Happy Jack.'"[59] An ad for the show ran in *The Acorn*, and the students printed and distributed posters for it around town. Both Fenstermacher and Granquist remember the concert as very loud, complete with the famous equipment- and guitar-smashing theatrics for which the band soon became famous. Meeting the band backstage, Granquist also remembered, "My impression was they were shorter than I expected. I don't know, I guess I had an impression that all rock musicians were gonna be tall or something."[60] And though both viewed it as a good show, it did not sell out, and they ended up losing money. Granquist believed that "most Drew students were not 'hip' enough in 1968 to turn out for an English rock act with one hit. And I was not yet experienced enough in promoting off campus to tap the Morris County teen population. We only used about two-thirds of the Baldwin Gym's capacity."[61] While the band may have had a little more than one song out and had played the Monterey Pop Festival less than a year earlier, he was right to view the booking with skepticism. And, as it turned out, Drew was the only college gig during that U.S. tour. The band performed at Fillmore East the next week. Perhaps more importantly for Granquist, the budding rock impresario learned from this experience and altered his booking and promoting tactics accordingly. He put it more bluntly: "I blundered my way through as far as being a promoter."[62]

A concert with Richie Havens followed in May that turned a small profit.[63] As a folk artist and singer-songwriter, Granquist believed Havens was "more in line with Drew student tastes." In what might be an apocryphal tale, he arrived for his performance at Drew only a few weeks following a performance at an impromptu jam session billed as a wake for Martin Luther King Jr. amid the national, and even global, reaction to that tragedy.[64] Havens seemed to echo the seriousness of the times, delivering an impassioned performance at the university, which student organizers and attendees remembered fondly even decades later. Granquist recently described Havens's passion and seriousness when talking about the concert. As the concert came to an end, Havens "continued to just strum his guitar, with eyes closed, for like three minutes as he wandered off the stage, continuing to play even after the applause had died down and he was backstage. He was really into it."[65] The concert closed out the entertainment for that term, and the Social Committee had learned a good deal about the process, and costs, of organizing concerts.

As that spring term ended and the student body returned home or otherwise departed campus, Granquist hung around, and soon began thinking about booking additional concerts in the fall. "I worked at Drew during the summer as a night security guard and got a head start on planning." One of the lessons he'd taken away from his experience during the spring was simply the mathematical problem facing a small college attempting to book expensive acts. Drew's gymnasium could only hold around 1,500 people, and the bigger bands cost around $10,000, the majority of his yearly budget, for one show. At that time, no one was going to pay the $8 or $9 ticket price needed to cover the costs. So he gambled. "I took a big risk and attempted a 'first-time-ever, two-shows-in-one-evening' event . . . I was inspired by Bill Graham's Fillmore East, where the format was routine."[66] Soon after its opening in March 1968, a number of Drew students made the trek to the recently opened venue in New York's East Village to check out the latest rock acts. Everyone I interviewed for this project knew of and had taken in at least one concert at the venue.[67]

By summer 1968, Jefferson Airplane was one of the hottest acts in the country and, following an appearance at Fillmore East in July, the band left for Europe, bringing psychedelic or "acid" rock to a much wider audience. *Life* magazine added to the band's growing influence with a June issue that included the four members on the cover.[68] With that, the band "had broken through the psychedelic haze" in its rise to stardom, according to its biographer.[69] Returning to New York from a string of gigs in Europe, the band taped *The Ed Sullivan Show* in late September, held a free concert in Central Park the following day, and played the Whitney Museum in the city on October 3rd and Drew's gymnasium the next day.

The concert ad in *The Acorn* a week earlier announced two shows, with opening act Earth Opera, another psychedelic rock band.[70] The ad also highlighted the new Airplane album, *Crown of Creation*, released the previous month, under a stock photograph of the full band. Though the album did not rise in the charts like *Surrealistic Pillow* (1967), it nonetheless enjoyed much radio play via the new "album rock" on FM radio.[71] In short, this band, more than the others who had played on the campus to this point, represented the cutting edge of rock and the counterculture. Even allowing for some experience in booking bands and staging rock shows, this was "a big effort for a Drew event," Granquist remembered. He continued, "The event was a financial gamble too. The Airplane were $7,500, and $500 for the opening act, Earth Opera. That's over half the yearly Social Committee budget for a show in early October. I loved the Airplane's music though and felt confident they would sell."[72] He was right; the show sold out. The concert was a huge success, for both organizers and attendees.[73] The band put on a quintessential psychedelic rock concert, complete with light show by Glenn McKay's Headlights, a staple element of the band's visual performance. By all accounts, the show was loud and the psychedelic elements unavoidable, while the band's musicianship and vocal performance also earned plaudits in a review in *The Acorn*. Much had changed in the world of rock music since

IN CONCERT
JEFFERSON
AIRPLANE
EARTH OPERA *and* *WITH* GLENN McKAY'S HEADLIGHTS
FRI., OCT. 4, 1968
AT DREW
RT. 24 — MADISON — BALDWIN GYM
2 Shows 7:30 & 10:15   All Seats $3.50
For Information
Call 377-5552 or 377-3000
Madison Photo Shop   Millburn - Record Village
Parsippany - Mario's   Summit - Scotti's
Record & Tape Shop   Dover Record Shop
Westfield - Melody Corner Morristown - Bambergers
Drew University Center

Jefferson Airplane concert poster announcement, Drew University.

the band's formation only three years before. Rock music was now global, and the San Francisco sound, or psychedelic rock, occupied a central place in the culture. And, in a largely forgotten but important piece of that moment, the band and the music were intrinsically woven into the cultural fabric of the counterculture, hostility toward rock music and drug use, and the college campus. The interwoven nature of these developments burst into the open during the summer and fall in Madison, New Jersey, culminating in the band's performance on the campus in early October.

Hippies, Townies, Greasers, and Straights

On the evening of September 27, 1968, young people began arriving at the big house on Main Street in Madison, New Jersey, for a birthday party. The house had become a popular place to hang out and listen to music over the previous months of that year. Its residents, an interesting and varied collection of young people, welcomed everyone. On this night, the house welcomed well over one hundred people from Madison and surrounding towns. At around 10:30 P.M., an abrupt knock at the door was followed by a massive police raid as several dozen law enforcement officers quickly entered the home, aggressively searching every room and arresting everyone in attendance. Conducted by a combined force of local police and state and county authorities, they sliced open furnishings, broke windows, pulled wires from walls, dumped food on the floor, and generally ransacked the place. Besides some prescription pills in one partygoer's purse, the raid turned up nothing. Nonetheless, police arrested about 120 people, including sixty-four minors, and took them downtown for booking. A few weeks later, a local judge ordered the residents evicted.

This story remains something of a legend for the town's historical society and those old enough to have some memory of the incident. Most remember "hippie house" fondly and relish in retelling (often varied versions of) the story. No doubt the intervening decades have worn down the jagged edges of the experience.[74] The incidents during these several weeks set in motion protests, a march downtown involving several hundred, outbursts of shock and outrage from area residents in the local newspapers, episodes of violence between so-called townies or greasers and defenders of house residents, and the involvement of the ACLU. In short, the events around the old house at 47 Main Street in Madison, New Jersey, cast in relief the tensions and contradictions of sixties communal living that were a key feature of the countercultural experience of the era. These young people weren't just experimenting with alternative living arrangements, upsetting conventional social relationships and hierarchies of sex, power, and love; they were doing it in the heart of suburban, Cold War America. This was, literally and figuratively, Main Street. Their attempt at alternative living exposed the tensions within a rapidly changing postwar American society. The house's residents found themselves caught between powerful forces, and literally positioned between the hostility of townspeople and authorities on one side of the street and the progressive forces among the student body of the liberal arts college on the other. Their short-lived experiment brought into conflict powerful forces shaping and reshaping the United States during the counterculture sixties.

The communal living experiment at 47 Main Street quickly became ensnared in the era's tensions around matters of race, class, gender, and culture as the residents consisted of young men and women, Black, white, Native American, and Asian, all creating their own cultural lives. The residents endured the disapproval of some neighbors and the town's authorities because they represented the counterculture and the new rock music. In fact, as tensions mounted beginning in the summer of 1968, the derisively named "hippie house" was tied explicitly to the emergent rock music culture, the college campus, and drugs; these issues formed the rationale for the authorities to crush it. Hostile authorities and neighbors viewed this mixed living arrangement, the rock music several of the residents practiced and played, and the full-size, Day-Glo-painted prop airplane (the "Jefferson Airplane") parked on the front lawn as unambiguous signs of the era's counterculture having arrived.[75] An exclusive story in *The New York Times* that summer brought more attention to the house.

"We Were Different from Straight Society"

Tom Wetzler left home early and was living in New York's East Village in the late 1960s. While there, he learned from a friend of "this place in Madison [New Jersey] that was looking for people to live there with them." Not really satisfied with his living situation in the city, he decided to make the trek out to northern New Jersey to check it out. "I went and I looked around and they looked at me and I moved in a few days later." The whole arrangement was "pretty informal," and premised on the idea that "we were different from straight society."[76] "We were coming up with ideas for survival, just day-to-day living, and developing a life that made some sense outside of a consumer-oriented society." Very young like the others at the house (Tom was seventeen at the time), he was "still trying to figure out a lot of things." When he moved in that spring, he joined Billy Shaw and Bob Courboin, who'd been living there for a few months.[77]

By spring, a growing number of people had settled into the large old mansion on Madison's main street running through the center of town, aptly named Main Street. Only a few minutes' walk from downtown, the old house sat directly across the street from the large stone arch that formed the main entrance to the private liberal arts college Drew University. While none of the residents were students, most attended the numerous rock music concerts organized by the students and held in the campus gymnasium after 1966. Most were also aspiring musicians, and regularly practiced in the basement of the house. The residents cultivated a laid-back atmosphere and welcomed friends and an array of local young people. "We didn't do background checks" to approve of someone visiting or even living in the house, Tom told me recently with a chuckle.

One of those who hung around the house often was Doug Chapman. A former SDS leader from the University of Michigan who had spent his eighteenth birthday in jail along with his "running buddy" Bill Ayers on the heels of an anti–Vietnam War protest, Chapman returned home to Madison to figure things out and to "lick my wounds." Chapman's father was a professor at Drew, which made Madison "home," but did not mean returning as a student. "I knew the one thing I didn't want to do was to go back to college. . . . Early '68 was a difficult time in this country and I wasn't sure what the hell I wanted to do with myself." From his vantage point decades later, Chapman reminisced about the experience: "There I was in suburban New Jersey in '68. I thought, gee, I'm a cool guy. I've been to San Francisco, the Summer of Love, I was arrested in a Vietnam demonstration, I know all these heavy-duty radicals . . . I'm a cool guy, ya know, in this context of a little suburban village." There is something confessional, earnest, honestly reflective, and self-conscious without regret about this remembrance. With his Gibson SG and Triumph motorcycle, Chapman soon became a fixture at the house. The house's reputation as a cool place to hang out got around, and it became something of a beacon for those in the area seeking like-minded people. During the summer, Chapman bought a 1953 International Harvester bus, "somewhere nearby in the sticks of New Jersey for $75," that became the default transportation for various adventures.[78]

Barbara North was just seventeen when she decided to quit high school and set off to find an alternative to mainstream life. From her parents' home in Westfield, New Jersey, she'd heard about the "house," "this really cool place," and she and her friends were asking themselves, "How do we get to Madison?" She described "a freedom that was everywhere." She recalled that one day there was an event taking place in Central Park's famous "sheep meadow" that she and the others wanted to attend, so a "handful" of those at the house piled into the bus. Driving through Madison on their way out of town, "Doug just opened the door, and he said, 'We're going to New York, you wanna come?' . . . By the time we were on our way, we had a whole bus full of people." She became close with Courboin, referring to him as "Robby." "Robby would do the 'school bus run'" where he picked up kids from the area to come hang out. "The townspeople just hated them and wanted to get it shut down. . . . They waited until there was a whole lot of people there so they could make it a big hurrah, ya know?" She was one of the juveniles arrested in the late September raid.[79]

In choosing to live communally, Wetzler and the others were immediately at odds with contemporary American society, with its penchant for material accumulation and consumerism. For his part, Wetzler's realization that "people could live in style and well from the garbage" of America was a revelation. "Instinctively, we knew there was more to life than accumulating things." Not only did this mean producing less waste, but it also meant personal freedom, freedom from the dictates of society. The aim was not simply to hang out and party, free from parental or other oversight. In fact, looking back on the culture of the "hippie house," the modern observer might find it unexpectedly dull. "We only had one rule in the house and that was 'no dope on the property.'" The primary residents of the house held full-time jobs and paid the rent on time. They remained very much aware of what they were doing, especially in this small, traditional town. They spoke about this fact routinely. "We tried to have a weekly meeting at dinner so we could discuss things," although "we had no strong, central idea, other than being freaky." At the same time, he added, "we didn't want to be some sort of party house for people."[80] In spite of the effort to remain somewhat anonymous, area residents took notice. "We did become sort of a tourist attraction." The residents recognized the pitfalls of drawing too much attention. As Wetzler spelled out, "It was a double-edged sword, we liked the attention and the fun, but we didn't like the wackiness that came with it." Looking back, he conceded to "not being very good at some of the social nuances around us."[81]

Within a relatively short period, "hippie house" became a hub of activity, attracting a daily train of visitors from the area. The residential makeup was both temporary and permanent, as some came and went while a few stayed around the whole time. On a typical evening, several dozen people stopped by to hang out on the front porch, talk, and listen to music. For many, the house held an obvious appeal—the place and people were friendly, welcoming, and "cool." For Bob Courboin, the young man at the center of the house and referred to as the "den mother," the whole thing was a genuine experiment in communal living. Everyone got along reasonably well, they divided household chores, and the large house had plenty of space. The full-time residents all worked and the rent of $250 a month was shared between them. "I look forward to when the whole world will be like this," he told the *New York Times* reporter who visited. Courboin, like virtually all the others in the house, hailed from a nearby town. He had grown up in a middle-class household and briefly attended prep school. But, again like many other young people, he had become disenchanted by the "gospel of success" that seemed to envelop everyone else and determine the course of one's life. Following some early trouble with the authorities for car theft, and a stint experimenting with drug use, Courboin changed his life. Now drug-free, he insisted on that same policy for the house—the one rule in a household not overly governed by them. "Music, beauty, sex—they mean just as much without it. I can get as high on beauty now as I used to be able to with four or five joints."[82]

"Jefferson 'Airplane' Finds a Home in Madison"

Early one summer morning, a full-size, WWI-era biplane appeared on the lawn at the house.[83] The Day-Glo paint splattered front to back made the plane impossible to miss. Passing pedestrians and motorists slowed to take in the spectacle; some were bemused while others found the presence of the unusual yard ornament provocative. The plane had actually been a publicity stunt placed outside the Fillmore East for the Jefferson Airplane show.[84] Following the second of two shows there, Fillmore owner and manager Bill Graham needed the prop hauled away. A few young men attending the show quickly intervened, offering to take it. As they explained, they just needed some time to drive back home to Madison, New Jersey, to get a

The Jefferson "Airplane" parked on the lawn at 47 Main Street in Madison, New Jersey. Billy Shaw, left, Bob Courboin, right. (Photo courtesy of Bob Courboin.)

truck capable of hauling it. One of them, Courboin, knew Graham, and the latter agreed to let him have it.

The young men brought the plane back to their residence, arriving at around 5 A.M., and spent the rest of the morning reassembling it.[85] Later that morning they phoned the Madison Police Department just to make sure having it did not violate any law. The police assured them it did not. "We don't know how our neighbors are going to react yet but we hope they don't mind," another of the full-time residents, Billy Shaw, who brought the plane back with Courboin, told a local reporter. "We are on our best behavior now because we like it here and don't want to be thrown out."[86] Resplendent in shoulder-length red hair and Nehru jacket during the *Times* interview, Courboin emphasized that they were just trying to get along with the town. At the same time, he also conceded the noise complaint might be justified. The house's residents, all rock musicians, regularly rehearsed in the basement. They even soundproofed it following noise complaints from a neighbor.

The brightly painted airplane solidified in the minds of many in the small town the existence of a "hippie house" and the arrival of the counterculture. Over the next several months, the prop airplane became the centerpiece of growing tensions swirling around the occupants of the house, the townspeople, and the local college students. While many young people embraced it, the authorities and some of the townspeople did not. In fact, the presence of the plane only added to existing tensions between the residents of the house, termed in local press accounts "hippie house," and local police, the fire marshal, and various elements of the town's residents. While the residents made efforts to get along, they could not help but feel the constant pressure from the town. Some in the small town, labeled "greasers" in local coverage, continued to harass not only the residents but also Drew students involved on their behalf. Following exposure from the *Times* article that August, the antipathy only grew. As *Acorn* editor David Hinckley wrote, "The greasers, unsure as to exactly what was going on, became more violent." The situation grew increasingly tense over the summer. Largely unknown to the residents of 47 Main Street, police had begun surveilling the house in response to complaints from neighbors. Others hostile to the residents were more violent in their reaction. Late one night while everyone slept, someone doused the prop plane in gasoline and set it ablaze. The fire on the front lawn drew the local police and fire departments, and more unwanted attention to what was fast becoming a focal point in the small town.[87]

Similar tensions played out around the country among so-called hippies, counterculturalists (or simply young people with long hair), and residents in communities small and large wherein locals found these new styles, appearances, and sounds challenging to their own sensibilities and traditions. As sixties chronicler and participant Todd Gitlin wrote of this phenomenon, "Police busted dope-smokers, dealers, the keepers and occupants of crash pads, troublemakers and innocents at rock concerts, and a lot of other young people whose looks they didn't like. Restauranteurs threw young longhairs off their premises. City officials deployed housing-code violations, zoning and vagrancy laws, and all manner of obscure regulations against them."[88] Each of these reactions characterized the tensions in Madison during the year as local officials and hostile residents kept up the pressure on the residents. The fire marshal and local judge issued continued threats of further action and even eviction for such things as furniture on the front porch, excessive noise, and disturbing the peace. Courboin recently recalled, "They harassed us constantly." On the charges of having furniture on the front porch, Courboin told me, "We had no air conditioning . . . and summer was hot!" Even at the time, he recognized the house was being singled out for something larger than an old couch on the porch of an even older house. "There was a war going on," he said recently. "The country was divided and the long-hairs seemed to be the dividing line."[89] The police chief believed the "kids are alright, but they bring their troubles on themselves" and set a bad example because "now every hippie character in the county wants to join the fun."[90]

Students from the campus took a different view of the increasingly tense relationship with the town and the police in particular.[91] Unknown to the residents and the students, a local judge had already authorized a search warrant for the property in late July.[92] And although he could not have known of the impending raid, Courboin was already thinking about an alternative weeks earlier. "We've already got our eye on another place a couple miles from here." "There's 15 acres of land. We'll be isolated and nobody will be able to say we're bothering them."[93] The continued harassment and effort to run the house's residents out of town also energized the student body of the liberal arts college across the street. A number of them began to report harassment including physical altercations between so-called greasers or townies, and students identified with the "hippies."[94]

In addition to Courboin, Shaw, and Wetzler, the house's other residents included an African American male, Stan and Arkie, two male cousins who were Mongolian, Edward Running Fox Goode, a Native American known to everyone as "Cochise," as well as two young, blonde, white women. Some at the property, as well as those covering the story, believed this combination was at the heart of the town's hostility toward them. People rarely spoke candidly about race, class, and gender issues regarding the presence of hippies. Rather, one of the townspeople expressed the dissatisfaction this way: "They're always bringing their long-haired, unwashed friends around."[95] A student editorial in *The Acorn* immediately following the raid pointed out, "If an upper middle-class, white Madisonian held a similar party, there isn't a chance in the world he would have been so charged." In a small town nearly entirely made up of "white" people, the diversity of residents in the house challenged accepted conventions and assumptions, to say the least.[96]

The morning following the raid, the local *Daily Record* front-page headline read, "Police Arrest 120 at 'Hippie House.'" The coverage, mirroring what Hinckley had described as traditional journalism, presented facts, and lots of them. Those facts, however, proved divisive, even damning to the police in the eyes of many residents. More than forty officers from the towns of Madison and Florham Park, state police barracks, and the county narcotics squad "swooped down in military precision . . . on an estimated 200 people gathered for a 'birthday party,'" read the opening paragraph. "Police headquarters looked like Times Square at New Year's Eve as cops ferried carload after carload of juveniles and adults from the scene to be booked." The raid "bagged" partygoers from six New Jersey counties and New York City. Most were released to their parents after booking. A few of the charges included disturbing the peace, illegal possession of prescription drugs, and contributing to the delinquency of minors. The police chief said the raid, which had followed months of investigation, was intended to search for and seize narcotics and illegal possession of alcohol. In the course of the raid, police also confiscated dozens of other items from the house, such as "one box of green vegetation," a copy of *Avant Garde* magazine, copies of the *Berkeley Free Press*, and a pocketknife. An eighteen-year-old attendee was also charged with an automobile violation for "illegally" discharging passengers from a car—he'd opened the door of a police cruiser, allowing those inside to flee during the mayhem.[97] All told, the raid itself was something of a bust for authorities. At the police station, in the wee hours of the morning with lots of young people standing around, many with their sleepy, confused, and angry parents, the atmosphere was both tense and resigned. One of the house residents recognized the police were now just going through the motions. The arrest, said the police, "isn't our prime concern." The police had to do something. "I mean, after all, they have this huge raid, and don't find any dope. They're gonna look pretty silly if they don't charge us with something."[98]

That same morning, about one hundred "mostly sympathetic" people gathered in front of the house, several dozen Drew students among them. Joined by Courboin, Shaw, and others from the house, they marched downtown to city hall to lodge complaints against the police for property damage. Some of the students were assaulted during the march as "townies" heckled and generally harassed them along the route—several of them were later charged with and convicted of assault.[99] Students had been dealing with (and complaining about) police harassment in town for much of the year— a couple freshmen were arrested in the spring for handing out leaflets announcing a rally to support Dr. Benjamin Spock, Reverend William Sloan Coffin, Mitchell Goodman, and others, who were all arrested for opposing the draft. Students had voiced concerns over police harassment for some time, and those concerns had already reached the administration.[100] Following the raid, incidents ramped up quickly. "We have had occasional problems before between the town and the school," said Dean Alton Sawin, "but I don't think it has ever before reached the intensity it has now." Police claimed to be unaware of the incidents, while students felt increasingly nervous when leaving the campus: "We can't even step downtown any more without fear of being hassled. Many of the people at Drew University are finding it increasingly difficult to cope with the people of Madison." Students drew a direct link between increased harassment and "backlash arising from anti-hippie feeling on the part of many ultra-conservative" people.[101]

But not all "townies" sided with law enforcement, especially regarding the late September raid. One resident's letter in the local newspaper is worth quoting at length:

> The police raid on Madison's Hippie House has left me with grave doubts about this method of law enforcement. First I don't believe a search warrant should allow such extensive destruction of property. I visited the house on Saturday and was appalled at the broken drawers, scattered clothing, ripped sofas and smashed birthday cake. I believe the Borough should be required to pay for every piece of property which is damaged and does not yield illegal material. . . . Second, the incompleteness of the search casts serious doubt on its purpose. Why was one bag of dog food dumped on the floor and the other left untouched? Why were other groceries left on the shelf? Why was stuffed furniture slit open and not completely searched? Why were other items left untouched? Thirdly, I don't understand why the raid had to take place when there were so many people present. Nearly all are bound to be found innocent. Now we have some 100 more people antagonistic toward the police. Fourthly, I don't believe the ordinance against disturbing the peace is fairly enforced. What about broken mufflers, motorcycles, and especially those raucous graduation parties in June? Lastly, I believe it is absolutely outrageous that the female guests were turned over to matrons, forced to strip and submit to a search. I believe Madison would be better off if the residents of 47 Madison Avenue were allowed to live in peace subject to the same degree of law enforcement that the rest of us experience.[102]

While some residents took a dim view, one local claimed that house residents were bums who refused to work (untrue); others expressed anger and frustration with policing tactics. A couple of the letter writers recalled the violence in Chicago during the Democratic National Convention, calling what happened in Madison "the Chicago sickness," while another invoked the Soviet occupation of Czechoslovakia to condemn the heavy-handedness of the police. Reactions from area residents were swift and filled the editorial pages of surrounding newspapers for weeks afterward.[103]

As luck, or fate, would have it, the arrival of the biplane coincided with Granquist's securing Jefferson Airplane for a concert. As improbable as booking the band was the coincidence that the prop plane from the band's summer concert had come to reside on a lawn only feet away from the campus's main gate. Many of the house residents and regular visitors were musicians (several were in bands that opened for Frank Zappa when he played at Drew) and fans of rock music in particular, so the residents of the house also attended the show at the college. Barbara North remembers "standing in a huge crowd waiting for the doors to open" as she, along with Courboin, Shaw, Chapman, and Wetzler, waited to get into the concert.[104]

Moments before the concert began that evening, a few of them met with the band offstage. Their conversation brought together several seemingly disparate trends that ran parallel during much of the year—if not much of the late sixties. The house residents reminded band members that when they'd played Fillmore East back in mid-July, they had done so with a full-scale model airplane parked on the street outside the venue as a promotional stunt. As Wetzler explained their situation to lead singer Grace Slick (he now calls it "whining"), she said, "What do you want us to do about it?" It was "a little dope slap from Grace Slick."[105] Once the band took the stage, Grace Slick announced to the crowd that the residents needed help with mounting legal bills, and they "passed the basket," raising around $200 for the cause.[106] The concert that evening brought together the various elements of a months-long drama in a way that highlights the often complex interplay between the counterculture's "hippies," college students, and small-town America.

"Madison: Sorry We Didn't Mean Any Harm"

Despite the late September raid having turned up nothing, the local judge ultimately ordered the residents' eviction for October 11, "within 72 hours."[107] Amid protests and marches, the residents packed up and left. When asked of their plans for the future, Courboin said, "We'll live in the

"Hippie house" on eviction day with peace sign and note to the town prominently displayed.

bus for a while, then maybe move into another house, or a commune, or something." The whole environment surrounding their departure was subdued, a marked difference from the tension and chaos during the preceding weeks and months. According to a student reporter for *The Acorn*, while rock music continued to play amid the packing, the party atmosphere was over. Courboin, refusing to condemn the whole thing as a failure, chose instead to view it as an experiment wherein he had learned a lot. A Drew student participating in the continuing protest, put it this way: "We figure about 25% of the community was on our side at the end and that's not bad in a middle-class town like this. This was one of the major achievements of the House." Within a few weeks of the Jefferson Airplane concert, the "House" stood vacant. As the story in *The Acorn* concluded, "It's quiet now at 47 Madison. But it is not as peaceful."[108] One of the last remaining signs of the hippies was, literally, a sign. A large piece of cloth crudely painted with

The man sez...

"KEEP MOVING," protest marchers from the "Hippie House" are told by Madison Police line Saturday Group marched from the House to the Municipal Building to complain about alleged destruction of property during narcotics raid late Friday night. Included in the march were 30 to 40 sympathetic Drew students, although only one had been involved in the raid itself. Story, pictures, inside.

"Hippie house" protesters gather in downtown Madison, including Billy Shaw, Stan Laffey, and Bob Courboin, *The Acorn*, Drew University.

black lettering, the sign read, "Madison: Sorry we didn't mean any harm," painted above a large peace symbol. The sign became a regular and visible feature of the continued protests at the campus and hung prominently just in front of the large stone arch at the main entrance to campus.[109]

The Show Goes On

Meanwhile, the Social Committee closed out a busy 1968 by booking the rock band Iron Butterfly for a November 16 show.[110] The band made the stop at Drew on the way to a two-night stand at Fillmore East a week later. Granquist, again, chose the band for its provocative presence and performance. With hit singles such as the now iconic "In-A-Gadda-Da-Vida," the band represented an early example of "heavy metal," and Granquist wanted to showcase something different. As he said recently, "I recall getting some complaints from students that we were having too many psychedelic shows, and why didn't we get somebody like The Fifth Dimension instead. Whatever. I wanted to push the envelope."[111] Iron Butterfly certainly promised

IN CONCERT
THE
IRON
BUTTERFLY
SAT. NOV. 16, 1968
AT DREW
RT. 24 — MADISON — BALDWIN GYM
Show starts 8:00 p.m.   All Seats $3.50

For Information
Call 377-5552 or 377-3000

Tickets on Sale At:

Madison Photo Shop   Millburn - Record Village
Parsippany - Mario's   Summit - Scotti's
   Record & Tape Shop   Dover Record Shop
Westfield - Music Staff   Morristown -
        Drew University Center

This authentic reproduction was printed in 2016 by Brown & Bigelow - St. Paul, MN - (651) 293-7021

Iron Butterfly concert poster announcement.

that. The announcement in *The Acorn* informed readers the band "is a four-man electronic rock group. Their music is between pop and blues, and has been called 'strange and heavy.'"[112] No one could have known just how strange and heavy an experience the band would provide.

"We were feeling good about it. This was gonna be an easy show because they [the band] were already here," in a local hotel, Fentstermacher remembered.[113] About half an hour prior to showtime, someone informed him and

Granquist of a problem. One of the band members, no one can recall exactly which, lay naked in a bathtub of ice back at the hotel, as his bandmates struggled to bring him out of a drug-induced stupor. As Fentstermacher rushed over to the hotel to check things out, Granquist remained "anchored to the gym," pleading with the opening act, The International Silver String Submarine Band, to keep performing as he stalled for time. The delays piled up and the opening band continued performing, outstripping their material and improvising the rest. As Granquist said, "They were heroic. They performed three sets to hold the audience. I hunkered in the Baldwin Gym basement, trying not to think about the difficulties of refunding ticket sales, suing the Butterfly, and general disgrace. Periodically, the floor would rumble from stamping feet. In between acts I would have to announce a further delay, ask for patience, and dodge thrown objects."[114] Meanwhile at the hotel, Fentstermacher helped lift the naked, and very cold, band member out of the bath, clothe him, stuff him into a car, and race him back to campus for the show, now several hours late.[115] As they prepared to take the stage, Granquist continued to placate the increasingly raucous crowd, trying a bit of levity: "Well, we have three Butterflys here but there's one Butterfly that's just not quite here yet." Outside, Fentstermacher consoled and held back a pressing crowd, who'd already managed to break some of the plate glass at the gym entrance. "I was tryin' to be Bill Graham or something," in dealing with angry concertgoers.[116]

Ultimately, when Iron Butterfly did play, nearly four hours late, they "did a really ripping good show," according to Granquist.[117] The subsequent review in *The Acorn* echoed this sentiment, describing with high praise each musician and the individual contribution to the overall sound, which was "deafening," and "worth waiting for." The concert ended with a tour de force performance of "In-A-Gadda-Da-Vida," lasting twenty-five minutes, culminating "in several controlled fires in front of the group" and a light show, which produced "a stupefying effect on the already hopped-up audience, which cheered madly as the group walked off stage."[118] The show, and the whole "strange and heavy" evening, finally came to an end sometime well after 1 A.M.

Conclusion

By the close of that fall term, the Social Committee at Drew and the Student Activities Board at Stony Brook had grown into campus-based concert booking and promotions agencies in their own right.[119] This process centered on the students, acting as they did with much autonomy to organize, promote, and otherwise engage with the rapidly developing/emerging world of late-sixties rock culture. Their role and the degree of autonomy they enjoyed stand out. Alongside the work directly associated with arranging for the entertainment, both student groups groomed successors in an apprenticeship fashion. Granquist learned the basics of booking bands from Redbord. The former then began cultivating Dave Marsden, who followed Granquist as social chairman. Marsden then handed it off and apprenticed another student, Don Orlando, who was then followed by Jeff King, and so on. The SAB implemented its own program to insure longevity. The students put in place a process that maintained a continuity across the years from 1967 to 1971.[120]

Both student groups kept up a steady stream of rock music culture on the campus. The campus proved an ideal environment to play host to a wide array of performances amid significant cultural and social change. And this proved true across the country. In its spring 1969 special issue of *Campus Attractions*, *Billboard* now viewed the college campus as an essential site for the growth and development of popular music:

> Many of the important currents of today's [music] are not only reflected on campuses, but vital movements are begun there. Today's collegians are in the forefront in challenging society in order to improve it. Students also show a greater receptivity to all forms of art. Diversity of interests can make a string quartet or a jazz band as acceptable as the latest rock, folk or easy listening act. Music trends, especially, are being set on campus. Many of the most important artists in all areas rely heavily on collegiate bookings, while even off-campus concerts are dependent on student appeal for success.[121]

Within a couple years, popular music culture had changed a great deal, and the leading industry magazine's coverage provides a useful window for viewing that change. Where its editorials and articles once equivocated, or parsed language regarding rock and the college campus scene, the tone now made clear the dominance of both. Rock music now even acted as a leader for all types of pop music. For agents and promoters, the strategy for getting an act onto a college campus now ran through rock bands and artists. These changes elevated the college student and the social chairman impresario as well.

In the same issue of *Billboard*, writer Richard Robinson wrote of the importance of the "college scene" and of the effort by bands, artists, and agents to break into "the college circuit." Viewed as the culmination of a number of changes in and around popular music culture, the article and its tone and treatment of the college impresario is instructive. Bands now needed to be serious about the elements required to make the college circuit. Among the most important were the live performance and a hit single because, as Sean LaRoche of Premier Talent told the article's author, "album groups are competing with local groups." These local groups were seasoned, practiced, and put on a good show. LaRoche continued, "When you go into a particular market you're competing with local groups who have been on the scene for years and who are getting the same price as you're asking for your album group. College buyers don't want to take a chance on an act they haven't heard."[122] College students, audience and promoters alike, were now "much hipper" and "can't be hyped anymore." Agents had to put in the work, advertise in the expanded underground press, play gigs in and around the East Village, and take seriously the college concert promoter to get "exposure in the hipper college scene." LaRoche's variety of experiences working with college promoters included working with Granquist at Drew. Robinson wrapped up his article with a summary of the changed campus scene: "In all, college booking is becoming an art. No longer is a phone call or album and photo mailing going to elicit financial response from college social chairmen. College students are aware of 'hype' and of the fact that a group is not necessarily musically competent just because it has recorded an album. . . . Any group that wants to get into the college market has to gain a degree of professionalism that just was not necessary two to three years ago."[123] College students stood at the center of much of this forming infrastructure and culture and, although certainly not intentionally, compelled the industry to take notice.

Both campuses, along with hundreds of others, had also experienced the full range of late-sixties tumultuous change. Students took full advantage of an education beyond the curriculum in a way certainly unmatched before and likely since. In his visit to Drew in the fall, Nat Hentoff told the 360 in the audience as much. The freelance writer and public intellectual told the student audience what it likely already understood experientially: that their very legitimacy might come from someplace other than the official curriculum, which tended to be "irrelevant" and deadening.[124] More than once, the audience answered the speaker's statements with thunderous applause as his observations and declarations resonated with direct experience—experiences around coming of age, political change, the Vietnam War, Civil Rights/Black Power, and rock music.

The year also ushered in the era of the ballroom. Along with the Fillmores (both East and West), the Electric Factory (Philadelphia), the Boston Tea Party, the Kinetic Playground (Chicago), the Grande Ballroom (Detroit), the Electric Circus (New York), and Thee Image Club (Miami) all opened that year. Plenty of others also thrived, especially in relatively large cities. Often these venues opened in abandoned factories and warehouses that meant spartan accommodations and very low overhead. Ticket prices were low—actually on par with ticket prices on campuses at around $3–$5—and audience size was limited. Concert promotion on college campuses, what one industry history called "the single biggest boon to concert promotion," now combined with ballrooms of similar size to create a more or less navigable circuit for a small number of promoters and club owners who dominated, such as Frank Barsalona. From his point of view, that had been the point from the beginning: "To me, one of the most important things about Premier [Talent] is not just the acts, but that we developed the rock promoters as well. Unlike the agencies before, who went to the established promoters, we developed new promoters, young promoters—like the Bill Grahams, the Larry Magids, Don Law—people who did nothing else but rock, and who knew the music, heard about the music."[125] One result of this kind of cultivation was the dominance of local promoters during the late sixties. They, along with a few agents, also cultivated relationships with area college students.[126] Unknown to the student promotors and organizers at the time, they were living through the peak moment of rock music on campus.

5

The "Americanization of Rock"

••••••••••••••••••••

Spring 1969–Fall 1970

In retrospect, the period 1969–1970 represents the culmination for rock music and college campus culture across the United States. The student population swelled beyond 6 million, which "served to crystalize the group identity of the young," according to one well-known study. Campuses teemed with a counterculture that compelled greater attention from administrations, the national media—and, unfortunately, law enforcement. The counterculture had grown to a mainstream phenomenon by 1969. Political scientist Theodore Roszak gave the phenomenon its first serious academic treatment with the publication of *The Making of a Counterculture* that year. Among the book's many insights, Roszak wrote, "Most of what is presently happening that is new, provocative and engaging in politics, education, the arts, [and] social relations . . . is the creation of youth, who are profoundly, even fanatically, alienated from the parental generation." That fall semester, Drew University president Robert Oxnam welcomed the incoming class, also speaking to gathered parents, by saying, "We are in on the beginning of the revolution. . . . Between our generation and the young adults there is a tension—an electric guitar string that vibrates only to rock music."[1] And while some students rolled their eyes at the cynical ploy by the administrator, his statement confirmed the omnipresence of the counterculture on the campus.

Meanwhile, and to the disappointment and outrage of many of the culture's participants, both the counterculture and rock music had become decidedly mainstream commodities. Even square *Time* magazine could condescend, "The wrong people, the wrong drugs have taken over . . . English majors (ugh), fraternity boys and the down-and-outers who would have been bums anywhere are joining the culture."[2] Rock music culture grew into a mainstream phenomenon in part because the music industry finally caught on and began promoting it, resulting in soaring scale and associated costs. The hip music industry insinuated itself in the culture in all sorts of ways, with one of the most famous coming in a Columbia Records 1968 ad asserting, "The man can't bust our music!" Much has been made of this "inane" little advertisement. For many, the clumsy (yet effective?) ad attempted to position the large record company firmly in the camp of the counterculture, and against "the man," for the obvious purpose of selling records. The ad also reflected the "flux, confusion, and weirdness" of the counterculture pulsing through mainstream, capitalist America, to borrow the words of one historian.[3]

This period also witnessed the rapid expansion of large, outdoor music festivals, each attended by hundreds of thousands of fans. Like the Columbia ad, these large festivals were manifestations of far greater industry involvement and the growing scale of the counterculture, in all its musical and aesthetic features. In August 1969, several hundred thousand gathered for what is undoubtedly the most famous of them all at Woodstock—a three-day "music and arts festival" that immediately became the reference point then and now for live rock music performance. This scale of rock music, what Bill Graham called its "Americanization," all but eliminated hundreds of smaller venues that had been crucial to rock music development in the preceding few years. Within the couple of years following 1968, rock music culture on campus reached its peak. Its swift decline quickly followed. In hindsight, the college campus had been important in promoting and nurturing rock music culture, the very success of which manifested in the decline of its performance on all but the largest campuses, while even some of those declined to play host for various reasons. By the end of 1970, those now iconic bands that had become commonplace at both Stony Brook and

Drew (and at dozens of other campuses) all but disappeared, most of them opting for the bigger payday offered by arena and outdoor festival shows. The "Americanization" of rock music culture meant, among other things, that it had outgrown the limitations of the typical college venue.

Blood, Sweat & Tears and Campus Culture

These changes were not immediately obvious in spring 1969 from the campus point of view. In fact, the bookings at both Stony Brook and Drew continued with a rich and diverse selection of music entertainment. Stony Brook opened the spring term with Arlo Guthrie, Jethro Tull, Mountain, Blood, Sweat & Tears, Miles Davis, Dizzy Gillespie, Taj Mahal, Ten Years After, and Chuck Berry, while Drew kicked off the term with Frank Zappa & the Mothers of Invention, Chuck Berry, Blood, Sweat & Tears, and Blue Öyster Cult. A broad selection of public intellectuals, activists, celebrities, and political figures also made appearances on both campuses for public lectures, workshops, and activist events.

Unsurprisingly, tensions between students and administrators and law enforcement around rock music, activism, and drug use continued apace. That spring, in an effort coordinated with the administration at Drew, local police came onto the campus "in a fleet of cars" at around 11:30 P.M. carrying out a warrant to search a student dorm room. Finding a small amount of marijuana and some speed, they arrested two students, and were then met with a large, angry crowd of students who gathered to protest the arrest. The students shouted, threw cigarettes and rocks at police, and even blocked their exit so the police could not leave. They managed to exit sometime after one in the morning. Student government president Bob Smartt, an African American transfer student, attempted to calm the crowd and in a prepared statement said, "When I see an insane and unjust war taking thousands of lives every year, I cannot consider these young men criminals," a reminder that the war in Vietnam was never far from the consciousness of young men in particular. Around 150 students subsequently marched to the dean's house and demanded that he come out and explain the administration's role in the affair and how the police had obtained information to secure a warrant.[4]

In May, Suffolk County undercover agents arrested eighteen students at Stony Brook on a range of drug violations. Law enforcement began raiding various dorms on the campus at around 11 P.M., rounding up three or four at a time as they went. A crowd of around 300 students gathered in protest, shouting and throwing stones, which smashed the window of one of the security vehicles as it fled. Students spontaneously raged across the campus, overturning and setting fire to cars and throwing rocks until around 4 A.M. Student leaders were then in meetings with administration officials and emerged to urge the students to stand down and disperse. The next morning's headline in *The Statesman* read, "18 Arrested on Drug Charges; Fires, Violence Plague Campus; Polity Calls for Student Strike." Protests followed for weeks.[5] One student writing in the paper that day called the episode "a political bust," as it just happened to occur the evening before the State Senate's Hughes Committee reconvened its investigation of drug use at Stony Brook following a yearlong recess. The writer also pointed out the fact that those arrested were freshmen users rather than known dealers.[6]

While students continued to clash with law enforcement, surrounding communities, and campus administrators, these clashes served only to solidify a growing resistance among them. More and more, students came to see these establishment and authoritative voices in antagonistic terms as they adopted a countercultural perspective, something intrinsically amorphous and in flux. Around the same time of the bust at Drew, comedian Dick Gregory came to campus to encourage students, as he had at Stony Brook the previous semester, and to offer an apology for the mess left them by prior generations. "I hope you youngsters won't make the mistake of eulogizing America, but will go out and examine it," the comedian-turned-activist told the audience of more than 1,200. "We've left you kids with a hell of a mess to clean up, and then the old fools wonder why you act the way you do."[7] As he no doubt already knew, students had been actively engaged in examination and change for a while now. The campus was alive with antiwar, Civil Rights, free speech, and counterculture activity and activism to the greatest extent yet.

When Ken Schulman took over as editor of *The Acorn* that year, he set about "reporting in an activist and provocative way," immediately subscribing to the LNS press syndicate, radical content that soon dominated the pages of the paper. Schulman, among those who viewed the president's "revolution" comments with a heavy dose of skepticism—saying of Oxnam recently, "it was a co-opting move. He was very clever"—was inspired by the free speech, antiwar, and Civil Rights movements. "We wanted to report on what was happening behind the scenes." He and other like-minded students—and not all students were like-minded—wanted inclusion in the faculty meetings but were refused. The refusal only ramped up their efforts and heightened tensions between students and the administration. Following one refusal to be included in a meeting around an important campus matter one semester, Schulman along with others managed to get a tape recorder hidden in the ceiling of the meeting room. He subsequently published the faculty meeting in *The Acorn*, much to the chagrin of faculty and administration.[8]

The continuing tension and conflict at Stony Brook included walkouts, occupations, protests, teach-ins, contempt charges and subsequent jailing of professors for refusing to testify on drug abuse, physical violence and attacks on student activists by opposition groups on campus, and wall-to-wall coverage in the pages of *The Statesman*. Nearly every issue from 1968 forward is filled with these events, alongside provocative comix, ads, editorials, and guest columns, with a heavy helping of material from LNS packets.[9] The similarities between the two campuses are striking.

Both campuses invited Dixiecrat and staunch segregationist South Carolina senator Strom Thurmond to campus to speak to the student body. And, in both cases, the event went about as one would assume. Both are also particularly insightful. Howie Klein wanted to bring Julian Bond to campus because, as he said, "I thought he would make a great speaker." Given his youth, his role in the political life of the nation, his recent election to political office as an African American, and the fact that the Georgia state legislature refused to seat him all made him ideal in Klein's estimation. Klein welcomed Bond to town by making a reservation at a "prohibitively expensive" restaurant in Suffolk County. He decided unilaterally to give Bond the unusually large honorarium of $7,000 for speaking, and generally catered to his guest's every want, and he and Bond had "a fabulous dinner that evening." In an effort to blunt criticism from conservative elements on campus and to achieve "balance" in campus speakers, he then invited the South Carolina senator. Klein instructed an assistant to treat the Senator to a $10 meal at a nearby pizzeria. He was later roundly heckled and mocked by the audience during his talk on the campus.[10]

Likewise, Drew student government president Bob Smartt, who also controlled the speakers committee, sought to mollify campus Republican leader Harold Gordon who had complained about the "liberal leanings" of the campus speaker program to that point—Smartt had earlier welcomed

Students heckle at Thurmond lecture

A different type of Academic Forum series, which this year brought three major speakers, instead of a series of minor speakers, culminated this spring in the appearance of Senator Strom Thurmond of South Carolina, who was greeted by students in sheets and African clothing.

The Senator was heckled during his speech in Baldwin gymnasium, and marshmallows were thrown at him. At the conclusion of his speech, Harry Litwack told the senator, "I had to see you to believe it. Now I've seen it and I know it's true. All I can say is, fuck you!"

To the scattered cheers which greeted this remark, the Senator said, "I'm shocked that you people at a University like this would cheer a man who uses such language."

Earlier the Senator had invited anyone who wished to disagree with him to come on stage and speak. No one came forward. A group of about 100 students in the side bleachers were the major hecklers in a crowd of about 1200.

In introducing Thurmond, SG President Robert Smartt, who arranged for his appearance, expressed the hope that "you will listen to what he has to say and show yourselves tolerant of a man who has been invited here by the students of the University."

Tom Quirk, who dressed in a Ku Klux Klan uniform at the lecture and at an earlier reception, charged that Thurmond's "campaign and policies" were being aided by the $1500 fee he received from that the University, and that that was the cause of his protest.

Quirk was rebuked for his costume by University President Robert Oxnam, who reportedly told Quirk, "I hate this man's ideas as much as you do. But he has a right to his beliefs."

In his speech, which was on political affairs in general, Thurmond called for the development of sufficient U.S. armaments "to keep us at least even with the Soviet Union." He stated that he favors state decisions on such matters as school desegregation and that he favors the U.S. Vietnamization policy, although "We could have won the war in 60 to 90 days using proper warfare techniques."

The anti-Thurmond protests brought a sharply worded response from University Services Director Mark Jordan, who wrote that the University must be prepared to deal firmly with those "who would deny others their right to speak."

He echoed the comment of Dean of Students Alton Suwin, who expressed shock that "Drew students would ever be so disrespectful to an invited guest."

In a letter to Dr. Oxnam, Smartt apologized for "the unfortunate and unpardonable conduct of a small minority of our students ... the responsible and mature majority of students will reject these playpen radicals at the polls."

Recall proceedings were begun against Quirk, in part for his actions. He was overwhelmingly kept in office, however, in the recall voting.

Quirk insisted that "We did not disrupt his speech while he was delivering it nor did we attempt to prevent him from giving it. We merely expressed our views on what he was saying."

Other speakers in the Forum series were Ted Sorenson, former Kennedy aide who is now a U.S. Senate candidate from New York, and Roy Innis, national director of CORE, who spoke in November to a small crowd. Innis devoted part of his visit to a private discussion with Hyera, the black student Union.

Thurmond speech.

Drew University students carry out a planned protest of Dixiecrat senator Strom Thurmond, an avowed segregationist, on his visit to the campus, *The Acorn*, year-end supplement, May 1, 1970.

Roy Innis, leader of the Congress of Racial Equality (CORE) to campus. Much like Klein, Smartt often had to balance satisfying sharply contrasting constituencies on campus. "The whole thing had become a pain in the ass. . . . Harold pushed and pushed and pushed. I said, 'Ok Harold. . . . you want a Republican, I'll give you a Republican,'" and promptly invited Thurmond. The South Carolina senator was not on the list of appropriate conservative figures Gordon gave to Smartt, quite intentionally. At the talk that evening, students reacted to the speaker in ways sure to make the pages of *The Acorn*. One of them, Harry Litwack, walked down front following the talk and said to Thurmond, "I had to see you to believe it. Now I've seen it and I know it's true. All I can say is, f-ck you!" Meanwhile, a group of students stood prominently in the audience holding large signs that spelled out "BIGOT." One student wore Ku Klux Klan garb during his talk while others threw marshmallows. Smartt viewed the whole thing as a bit of theater. Smartt had dinner with Thurmond afterward at a local steakhouse and got the impression he, too, saw the affair as theatrical to a degree. "I think [Thurmond] was laughing his ass off," Smartt told me recently. Thurmond, seemingly relishing the hostility from the student audience, made no effort to tailor his remarks that evening to his audience, offering caustic bits of hawkish foreign policy and domestic political commentary unapologetically. Gordon, on the other hand, was furious.[11]

Alongside the obvious and remarkable degree of student autonomy to organize and plan campus life, it is striking the degree to which politics on the campuses played out through the panoply of invited guests.[12] Not only were students free to shape campus life, they were also free to reach beyond the campus and fully integrate political, social, and cultural elements from the national scene. In both cases, students selected an obnoxiously provocative political figure precisely to mock and push back against pressure from conservative or reactionary elements on campus. Knowing students in general would revile the senator and all he represented was precisely the point in both cases.

The cover of the January 24, 1969, issue of *The Acorn* showed the intimidating visage of a glowering Frank Zappa, cigarette in one hand, with long, dark hair, heavy mustache, eyes too dark to see, and shirt unbuttoned exposing his full chest above the caption, "This man is evil." Zappa was in many ways the perfect counterculture provocateur in that he combined performance art with rock music in a decidedly eclectic and idiosyncratic fashion. Aside from his intentionally alarming image, he and his Mothers of Invention band traded in highly provocative, sardonic wordplay with audiences.[13] At Drew, the band's antics did not go down so well. The band treated the students like a bunch of hillbillies—"They totally misjudged where they were," read a subsequent *Acorn* review. "Zappa 'began with a stream of invectives about New Jersey, and how terribly provincial we are here. This kind of thing may go over big in Idaho or Kansas (two places with which Zappa compared us) where kids love to be shocked and to think their parents would be scandalized. But New Jersey teenie boppers, whatever their hangups, simply do not have virginal ears. In this context, Zappa's very average obscenities would have been merely boring, were not they so dripping with contempt about 'teens' and 'boys and girls.'" While the music was very good, at least according to multiple subsequent reviews, "the Mothers interrupt[ed] themselves with a heavy-handed dose of buffoonery, revealing, I suppose, the depth of their inner cynicism about everything, including their own efforts." Students weren't about to let Zappa, or Andy Warhol or Strom Thurmond, simply phone it in by gliding into town, spoon-feeding them whatever was their particular gimmick, then collect the check and split town. In this instance, students used Zappa's provocative image seemingly uncritically and to good effect (on *The Acorn* cover), but subsequently roundly criticized his condescension and refusal to take them seriously and on their terms.[14]

Likewise, students confronted changes beyond the campus in the music industry. Both campuses booked Blood, Sweat & Tears for spring concerts, March 8 at Stony Brook and March 22 at Drew. These events, too, are insightful as they highlight broader changes in rock music's "Americanization" as well as the importance and role of the college campus. The band represented something new in rock music, what music writers called "jazz rock." An eclectic ensemble cast fronted by the already famous Al Kooper who had recorded with such music counterculture luminaries as Bob Dylan, The Blues Project, and Jimi Hendrix, the band included a brass section and combined elements of rock, pop, jazz, folk-rock, and even big band sounds. Mike Jahn, writing in 1968 for *The New York Times* as its first full-time rock journalist, called them "one of the best rock bands in the country," in a review of a November 1968 concert at Hunter College in New York.[15]

The band played at Stony Brook back in October 1968. A subsequent review of that performance praised the band's "amazing musical versatility." The campus welcomed the band back for a second performance the following March. Students had enthusiastically embraced the band the first time around with "thundering applause" and standing ovations. "It will be no easy task to duplicate their first triumphant concert," read the announcement in *The Statesman* in the first week of March. But duplicate it the band did, and at a cost of less than $2,000. The band was among a number of up-and-coming acts managed by Frank Barsalona. Several, including this one, quickly achieved commercial success around 1969.[16]

Granquist booked the band for a concert at Drew for a real bargain, paying a single fee for a double show. The concert, centered around "Winter Weekend," featured two performances of three acts, rock band Rhinoceros, "oldie" Chuck Berry, and Blood, Sweat & Tears.[17] Though relatively unknown, those who knew the rock scene believed the band was headed for commercial success. Granquist had managed to book the band just as their "You Make Me So Very Happy" hit the airwaves and shot up the charts. The band was suddenly "really riding high," according to Granquist. "But they weren't riding high when we got the contract signed." Indicative of changes in the business of rock, Barsalona visited the campus to preside over a problem with what was just emerging as one of his own hot commodities in Blood, Sweat & Tears. While the show was underway, word got to Granquist that the lead singer, David Clayton Thomas, had just been examined by a doctor who had told him to rest his voice, and they were, for this reason, not going to do the second set. Turned out Barsalona showed up to

Blood, Sweat & Tears performing at Stony Brook, *Specula*, 1969.

make sure the band didn't perform the second show. Neither Granquist nor Fenstermacher actually believed the story of the throat ailment. Rather, both believe the story was a cover to get out of the gig now that the band was taking off.[18] In any case, the two suddenly found themselves without a second performance from the headliner, with a second audience rapidly arriving. They quickly improvised; Fenstermacher chased after Chuck Berry, already packed up and out in the parking lot. After pleading with him and offering to pay him more, Fenstermacher convinced him to play a second show. Memories vary as to how much money it took to get him (and his band) to return, but Fenstermacher is confident it was $50.[19] Not for the first time, student promoters had to scramble and piece together a show to accommodate changes swirling around their campus.

Barsalona carved out a very particular role for himself in rock music promotion in the area around New York, a role that included on-site management and control and mentoring young college promoters at both campuses. Mary Beth Olbrych recalls with fondness the role he played for her at Stony Brook: "He was a mentor." After taking over as concert chair from Klein sometime in 1968—"he gave me a few phone numbers," she told me—she began booking acts for campus on her own. In that capacity, she frequently called on Barsalona, visited his office, and even stayed at his home from time to time and got to know his wife well. One morning, she went into his office and sat down as Barsalona was on a phone call. Suddenly, Bill Graham burst into the office and screamed at her, "Who the f-ck are you!," evidently angry that she had booked a band then also performing at his Fillmore East. Barsalona quieted him temporarily with a wave of his hand, hung up the phone, then clearly explained the situation to Graham. The latter was furious that Olbrych was booking rock bands at Stony Brook and taking money away from his club—even though he had only opened the venue in the spring of 1968. Graham argued the campus was within his unofficial fifty-mile rule (the rule that bands could not play within a fifty-mile radius of his club at the same time). In any case, as Barsalona explained that morning, Olbrych booking bands for Stony Brook was actually good for Graham's business as those concerts sustained rock music's presence in the area and made for more robust performances at his club on the weekends. The argument seemed to satisfy him, if only temporarily.[20]

By 1969, both campuses found themselves in the middle of larger and more powerful economic interests tied to rock music and reflecting its growth. The resulting tension was routinely manifested as various brokers—agents, promoters, artists, administrators, and law enforcement—moved in to take greater interest in the various goings-on. Drew closed out spring term hosting Soft White Underbelly (Blue Öyster Cult) in May, while the fall term welcomed John Mayall, Canned Heat, and Jethro Tull. At the same time, The Who, The Moody Blues, and Joe Cocker—as well as lots of other minor artists—performed at Stony Brook. In short, even amid the changes then reshaping the popular music landscape generally in the United States, rock music on campus thrived.

The "Americanization of Rock"

Looking back on 1969, rock music's boosters had plenty of reason for optimism. *Billboard* was especially bullish on the college campus as the site for a broad range of entertainment. The 1970 Campus Attractions special issue described the campus this way: "From pure entertainers to lecturers and artists in the cultural area . . . the campus is rapidly becoming a medium in its own right."[21] The unique nature of the college provided, as it had for years now, a key site for eclectic cultural developments. Frank Barsalona told *Billboard* that British rock groups in particular continued to flourish on college campuses, highlighting the fact that around 40 percent of Ten Years After's bookings were there. Viewing the colleges as "a captive audience," and especially "responsive" to rock music, he continued, "It could have been more, but the problem with British groups is that usually their tour coincides with an LP release that has to be promoted. So they have to play the Fillmores or the Tea Party . . . because they are good promotion dates." Other limitations such as immigration regulations meant these bands had to cover the country in a quick seven weeks. "We don't have the flexibility of an American group which could always play the date a week or so later. . . . But the college market is certainly healthy—the market exceeds supply," he added. Barsalona described in this interview a changed environment for rock music live performance.[22] Rock was now big business and tours intentionally organized around LP releases were one piece of that rapidly developing infrastructure.

The lack of an industry infrastructure and presence that had created opportunities for enterprising college impresarios like Howie Klein, Greg Granquist, and others had at last given way to greater music business management and control. To be sure, the college campus remained a key element of this system brought on by increased industry involvement. Rock music was the most popular form on campuses, and sales there had increased by more than 20 percent over the previous year. Students and administrators charged with providing entertainment had also grown more experienced and savvier, and often knew more of the lay of the land than other, nonlocal brokers such as record labels, regional promoters, and managers. Over the years following 1969, campuses continued playing host to rock music, while the industry became a greater presence. The latter both reflected and caused the exponential growth of rock music into a billion-dollar business. The signs of a changing rock music landscape were increasingly clear.

Although Barsalona's point was to highlight the continued health of the campus market, these larger changes inevitably adversely impacted that market. He went on to mention some of the troubling trends. For instance, Led Zeppelin, another British rock band whose debut self-titled album was released early that year, cost $25,000 to book, pricing them well beyond the college budget. "I know we agents consider it an inexhaustible funnel to be tapped, but I have noticed some colleges using films or a speaker where last year a group would have been booked," he conceded. He estimated that the average college auditorium held between 7,000 and 8,000 and an entertainment budget limit of $15,000 for the given academic year. "This applies, I think, to between 70 or 80 percent of the college market," he said. Presumably recognizing the obvious math problem and reflecting a promoter's optimism, he added, "But I think the price structure will correct itself. As a buying force collectively, colleges are bigger than most. It's too important a market to lose."[23]

The trend, however, was moving the other way. The sheer scale of rock music continued its exponential growth—when The Doors played the massive Madison Square Garden in 1969, they were paid a whopping $52,000 for a single night's work.[24] For both private clubs and colleges, that meant fewer booking opportunities. Clubs like the Fillmore East, with a capacity of around 2,700, quickly reached a point where the money involved in rock music made hosting it impossible. Or, as rock writer Robert Cristgau wrote of all venues of that size, "the music had outgrown them."[25] So too with college campuses. Both Drew and Stony Brook hosted the vast majority of the music entertainment in the campus gymnasium, with limited seating capacity—around 1,200 for Drew and around double that for Stony Brook. The primary reason both Fillmore East and Drew began offering two shows per evening was precisely to get around limited seating capacity and not lose money. Private clubs needed to make money to stay open. And while colleges did not necessarily need to make money, the students worked within very real budget limitations; they needed to at least break even. After 1968, nearly all costs associated with rock music soared. The rock music business was quickly outgrowing both these important rock music venues.

Looking back, this trend was actually evident almost from the start. Record company executives began noticing rising costs of studio time in 1967. One well-known producer complained, "The Beatles really spoiled it for everyone by spending so much time in the studio." Of course, other bands quickly followed suit by returning to the studio to spend many hours rehearsing, overdubbing, layering, rerecording, and just tinkering. The cost of producing an album soared—the Beatles spent some 900 hours in the studio endlessly polishing the Magical Mystery Tour album released in November in the United States. The production costs of some rock albums ran to more than $80,000. Such extravagance then got passed along to the consumer, an early sign of things to come.[26]

A year after Drew's concert impresarios began the two-show format (copying the Fillmore East), Stony Brook began charging students for some concerts in fall 1969. As it turned out, The Who was the inaugural concert for which students were charged, at $3 per ticket. SAB concert chairperson May Beth Olbrych explained in *The Statesman* several days following the concert, costs for rock music were steadily rising. "The increase in the market for rock entertainment has caused vast increases in prices," she explained. "Because of inflation and a cut in the SAB budget, we have been forced to establish a series of pay concerts." Going forward, students would be charged for groups costing more than $6,000. The Who concert had cost $10,000 and the band "refused to do a second show." When The Who played Drew in spring 1968, the fee was $7,500. The SAB also made available useful comparative costs for bands and artists who had already performed on campus: Janis Joplin in 1968, $4,000 for two shows, in 1969, $9–15,000 for one show; The Band in 1969, $6,000 for two shows, in the fall, $12,000 for one show; Blood, Sweat & Tears in 1968, $1,750 for one show, in 1969, $10,000 for one show; Jimi Hendrix in 1968, $3,000 for one show, in 1969, $100,000 for one show.[27] Though at times wildly uneven, the costs associated with hosting rock music in general soared.

In part responding to student criticism and general budget cuts, *The Statesman* ran an in-depth series of three articles in October 1969 detailing matters for the student body. Olbrych, who became SAB concert chairperson that academic year, pushed back on student complaints that the SAB received such a large share of the total student budget. The reason the board received $93,000, over a quarter of the entire budget allotment, was that it provided entertainment for all students from concerts, "moods," and speakers to dances and various theater programs. Olbrych explained, "The SAB . . . is practically unique in America": "We are one of the few schools in the U.S. where students are solely in charge of hiring talent. At the University of South Carolina, for example, the students pay a $125 activities fee and an administrator alone determines who will speak or perform. Two years ago the kids wanted to have Martin Luther King speak on campus and the activities director replied that King had nothing to say to the students."[28] This series of articles is just one of numerous examples of the ongoing conversation among the students through the pages of their newspaper as they reacted to and dealt with broader changes impacting their campus lives. In short order, they had made the transition from virtually unlimited possibilities to facing very real limitations of the kinds of experiences they could afford to accommodate on the campus. The most severe economic limitations hit rock music, a music and music culture that had become a staple of campus life within one four-year cycle. In that same four years, rock had also become mainstream as the late-sixties soundtrack for the country, for better or worse.

American Talent Associates ran a full-page ad in *Billboard* in 1970 that screamed, "Stop the Rape of the Rock Industry" in large, bold letters over an urgent plea to consumers to do their part to save it. The ad explained, "Drastic measures must be taken to halt the gross over-pricing of rock groups to the extent that they're running out of promoters and places to appear. Don't buy a show just because the price is high. This can be stopped only by you."[29] The advertisement is in some ways reminiscent of the more famous Columbia Records declaration, "But the man can't bust our music," if also more plaintive. The San Francisco–based talent agency urged others to join it in an effort to control the rising costs of everything out of concern for its own survival, as well as that of other promoters and talent groups. Appropriately enough, the ad ran in *Billboard*'s "Rock Now" issue, an issue devoted to an assessment of the state of affairs for rock music—and much of that assessment was bleak.

The opening editorial introducing the topic for the issue, penned by editor Ed Ochs, blasted the rock industry for having "over-advertised rock product to the point of diminishing returns, shaking down the consumer then boring him, while wishing to attract as little attention as possible to what they would call a straight business deal." *Billboard*'s relationship to the music industry had for years ebbed and flowed. In the sixties, many of the influential trade magazine's writers and editors viewed the industry with unalloyed hostility. Ochs continues, "The industry is sailing down the same river it sold rock, the same Lethe-like river of forgetfulness into which drugs flow; already polluted with the vinyl flotsam and jetsam of planned obsolescence and escape: all into the goldfish bowl of pop music. Of the product that slides through *Billboard*'s review department each week—200 singles and 150 albums—almost all of it is 'chewing gum for the mind,' while much of the good merchandise grows more and more misunderstood and mismanaged by an industry with self-serving myth about self-censorship. How unmusical!"[30] This critique reads as something of a departure for a trade publication squarely positioned as a "service" magazine, that is, providing a link between music culture and the music business. In some ways, the magazine had shifted. *Billboard* hired Ochs in 1967, just out of college and twenty-two years old, precisely to cover the emerging rock music scene, and his first assignment was the Jefferson Airplane concert at Hunter College. As a student at Syracuse University in upstate New York in 1964 and 1965, he had been exposed to some of the trends in popular music such as Bob Dylan, Donovan, Otis Redding, and the early West Coast bands. "Someone lent me their albums. It was all new to me," he told me recently. Coming directly from the college scene in 1967, Ochs well understood the importance of the campus as a breeding ground for the latest music trends. "*Billboard* . . . acknowledged this trend by making an effort to report on concert activity on college campuses, even naming a Campus Editor at one point.," Ochs said.[31] This and other changes at the magazine reflected the growing importance of rock music, and now, at least in the eyes of some of its editors, the industry was making a mess of things.

The industry model for popular music's growth and development (or commercialization?) resulted in a glut of music, much of which could scarcely be called rock, organized around LP release tours while prices soared. Ochs, responding to a question about his own 1970 editorial decrying the trends and the industry model for music production, told me this:

> It's safe to say that the major record companies put out a lot of bad records with the hope that one might click and pay for the other fifteen mediocre albums in that group of releases. Sure, I wondered out loud in the public square if some of these groups were signed by record company heads who didn't have a clue about the music they were putting out, or they were signing groups because they played at their pool party or wedding, or as a favor for a friend of a friend, etc. Even worse, when a really talented new artist with a great record went unpromoted in favor of a "push" album, I would lose my mind and write about the record that everyone missed. One music executive called my reviews of lost gems "the department of lost causes," and so it was. Bill Graham and I had our own history, and while we agreed a lot, we also had our disagreements. This is something we agreed on. But this was the formula of record companies back then—put out fifteen or twenty records, promote the hell out of one or two of them while the others languish in the shadows and soon disappear, never to be heard. One hit paid for all the failures of their throw-a-bunch-of-records-out-there-and-see-what-sticks approach, but it didn't work out well for some excellent records condemned to anonymity by poor management.[32]

Other writers and critics like Paul Williams, Ralph Gleason, Robert Cristgau, and Michael Lydon had begun to sound like a chorus about these developments by 1969 and 1970.

For his part, Bill Graham had grown increasingly frustrated at the industry's colonization of rock music. Several months before Ochs's biting editorial, Graham took to the pages of *Billboard* to offer his "Open Letter to Managers and Agents," which opened in typically blunt fashion: "I don't think I need inform you of the grave problems that exist presently in the rock industry. The cost of talent, along with the existing political strife, has crippled the concert and ballroom business to such an extent that a great number of locations have either filed for bankruptcy or closed for the summer months. Those staying open are fighting for their very existence. The Fillmores, East and West, fall into that category."[33] The problem, as he outlined it here, was at least twofold. On one hand, the economics had taken artists away from the clubs, ballrooms, and concert halls and placed them in large arenas and at outdoor festivals. As such, those big-draw artists no longer performed in the smaller venues that had given them so much initial support. On the other, there were simply no new acts coming along to fill the gap, and, without the support of the big-name artists and bands, these circumstances would lead to "the death of the visible and audible rock scene." Graham pleaded with managers and agents to do what was no longer in their economic interests to do: continue to privilege the rock circuit of small venues.

At the same time, competition between those small venues also eroded their role. One of Graham's partners, Paul Baratta, broke from him and began promoting concerts at the Winterland, near Fillmore West. Other ballrooms, such as Pepperland, began operating in suburban San Rafael, and its operators gambled that it was just far enough from San Francisco to survive. The entire ballroom system or circuit was in a "state of flux," according to some of those close to the business.[34] The rise of large-scale concerts in arenas and at outdoor festivals added another element of conflict and instability to a business in flux. Larger crowds and rising prices meant greater chaos from audiences either too large to control or, in cases where a promoter booked a very famous artist in a club or ballroom, angry fans outside the venue who could not get tickets. At a Sly & the Family Stone concert in Dallas, Texas, those angry fans outside hurled bricks through the venue windows. One concert complained, "It's getting to be a far cry from the peace and harmony of the Woodstock Festival," referring to the iconic three-day music and art festival in upstate New York in late summer 1969. It is worth remembering that even Woodstock involved its share of overwhelming crowd size—the festival was intended to be by ticket-only. After overflow crowds began simply trampling the makeshift fencing, one of the coordinators announced from the stage, "It's a free concert from now on," much to the disappointment of the promoters who'd planned for a profit. Now, cities and towns began denying permits to host large-scale shows simply to avoid violence and property damage that had become increasingly associated with rock shows. Many continued chasing the "glories of Woodstock" for years in spite of these mounting obstacles.[35]

If 1968 was the year of the ballrooms, as so many of the most famous of them began then, 1969 can be thought of as the year of the outdoor festival. From the first of the large outdoor "pop" festivals at Monterey in 1967 until 1970, some 2.5 million people attended around thirty such festivals. In 1969, rock music fans attended more than fifteen of them, including the most recognized of them all, Woodstock. An estimated 50,000 attended the Monterey Pop Festival, while some 400,000 attended Woodstock, and a jaw-dropping 600,000 attended the Summer Jam in Watkins Glen, New York, in 1973—for only three bands, each paid more than $115,000.[36] These massive outdoor music festivals are indicative of the growth of rock music and its takeover of mainstream tastes. Both also mark rock music culture's evolution beyond the college campus. With growing popularity and a music industry now paying very close attention and pouring unprecedented resources into it, the once "underground" music now commanded big money.

Barsalona himself declared in 1970, "rock now is big business," a fact about which he was notably ambivalent. "Sure, prices have risen drastically, but so has the cost of performing. Let's be fair about this." As an agent, he also found it difficult to make the whole thing work as artists demanded more, club owners often could not meet those demands, and, of course, there were always very real limits of what fans would pay. Most in the business viewed the ceiling for ticket prices at around $6. While some larger shows and festivals charged as much as $10, most clubs could not get away with it. Barsalona said of this increasingly untenable reality, "I really have no solution for the problem. If audiences feel they are paying too much, then they should not go. If enough people stay away from the concerts, perhaps the agents and managers will get the message. But disrupting a concert or crashing the gates is not the answer."[37] Consistent with his reputation for nurturing artists and bands, he did not blame them, but fought to get them what he thought they deserved, and, when pushed, even getting them more. Although he did not explicitly say it, others did point to the growing power of the rock star ego as one of the factors in the growing costs as acts like Led Zeppelin and The Doors demanded unheard-of prices for performing.[38] Rock as big business meant big problems for promoters and fans.

Bill Graham described the process with some frustration in a 1970 article for *Cue* magazine:

> Five years ago, when the current phase of rock began, the majority of promoters were young kids who dug rock. Young, good kids who said, "Hey, you're into p.a. and *you* get a truck and pick up the group. We'll get a couple of benches together . . ." That was the beginning. . . . It was a hundred-dollar business. Then it became a thousand-dollar business, and some young people had to get knowledgeable about what they had to do to run dances. But then rock became a million-dollar business and a multi-billion-dollar business. When that happened, America took over. America came in.[39]

The increased scale simply priced out most small operators. A weary Graham went on, "A few years ago, the giants were making three, four thousand. Five thousand was big money. That goes for the Byrds at the top of their career in '65–'66 and the Lovin' Spoonful. Now, $5,000 is made by a group that has number 120 on the charts."[40] To be sure, rock culture, its aficionados, and the industry which sustained and promoted it had coexisted in a complicated tension for years. Jefferson Airplane's Paul Kantner explained this tension from his point of view: "The record companies sell rock and roll like they sell refrigerators. . . . They don't care about the people who make rock." Everyone from artists and rock journalists to agents and promoters groused about the complicated relationship at one point or other. As rock became a billion-dollar business, and the expense or pay involved grew beyond everyone's wildest dreams toward the end of the decade, some concluded that rock's best days had passed. For his part, Bill Graham shuttered both his East and West Coast venues in 1971, following his lament of the "Americanization of rock," by which he meant the triumph of business over the music or the art.[41] Whatever the particular complaint, grievance, and perspective, the business of rock music had changed, and this altered rock music culture in significant ways.

Conclusion: "The Campus Has Been Invaded"

All of these broader changes brought significant challenges to the campus rock performance scene after 1969. Rock remained far and away the most popular music on campus. However, that popularity came at a cost. "Now that college concerts represent a business grossing hundreds of millions of dollars," read *Billboard*'s 1970 Campus Attractions issue, "the campus has been invaded by agents, sub-agents, promoters and others." Having announced the storming and conquest of the campus by rock music back in 1967, the magazine now followed with a second, and very different, invasion. While the first had been a cultural phenomenon driven by students, this one was launched by an industry bent on profits. The big record companies moved in and established a presence on campuses across the country, buying ads in the campus paper and on the radio station, and setting up campus representatives within the organization—Warner Brothers had twenty-five of them. *Billboard* couched this invasion in terms of the numerous problems it was causing. Corruption in the form of kickbacks, payoffs, and various under-the-table offers placed student promoters in a bind and steadily drove up prices. "As the same time," the editorial continued, "turmoil has developed within the colleges themselves between administrations, appalled at the lack of knowledge and sophistication of student bookers, and students rightfully desiring more freedom in choosing their own kind of performer."[42] Agents and promoters from beyond the campus exploited a complicated situation they often misunderstood.

Georgia Tech's concert chairman told *Billboard* costs associated with hosting rock music had risen 50 percent in three years. Some college promoters came to view the agents with whom they had to work in booking artists as willfully ignoring their reality. The agents seemingly made little distinction between colleges and private clubs, making the same demands of each. The college, however, sought neither to make or lose money and the budgets were fixed, which meant limited off-campus promotion, a more limited, if also built-in, audience, and fewer shows during a given week and during the summer. One of them expressed the growing frustration this way: "We have been in this same location for 200 years. It's a sure bet we will be here for the concert. Perhaps the agency should pay *us* a guarantee that the artist will be here also." *Billboard* added to this by highlighting the artists' role in perpetuating the problem: "The agent, who in fact only deals in money, should not be expected to solve these problems. The artist, on the other hand, should be as concerned for the future of this business as the colleges themselves. For many artists, due to the peculiar nature of nightclubs and television, it remains the only place to make an honest living."[43] Students had already begun organizing to deal with some of these mounting problems. They double-booked shows, cast wider nets to gather an audience from beyond the campus, formed consortia to lock in prices in large groups, and launched record stores owned and operated by students to control prices.[44] Students from George Washington, Georgetown, Catholic, Maryland Universities, and George Mason College formed the Student Union Board Association (SUBA) to organize their own, low-cost "peaceful concerts." The aim was, according to one report, "to thaw the deep freeze on live concerts that has settled over theaters, parks, stadiums, and indeed whole cities, because of concert trouble. With $2 ticket price and careful planning," the report continued, "the collegiates hope to forestall the past year's concert troubles over high prices, gate-crashing, tension-causing waits or no-shows, poor accommodations and poor relations with the police, the local residents and storekeepers."[45] Pooling limited resources meant not only affording top talent, an explicit goal of the project, but also charging less per ticket and providing an increasingly professionalized management of big shows. Of course, this response lent legitimacy to the changes as well, especially the growth in scale of rock music performance, simply by attempting to accommodate it. The SUBA also relied on a remarkable degree of student cooperation and administration buy-in, a reality in need of constant maintenance and nurturing. In other words, the arrangement did not last long.[46]

Here was the inevitable clash: rock remained in the highest demand on college campuses and, for that reason, quickly grew more and more expensive, larger in scale, and more problematic for a host of reasons. Both Drew and Stony Brook experienced that full range of related issues in continuing to host rock music through the late sixties. The two campuses likely hosted more than most others, which makes them outliers in terms of volume, but especially insightful in terms of the broader national trends.[47] Those trends included mounting ever larger individual shows tied to LP releases and U.S. and world tours, all of which cost millions to pull off. In this sense, the two campuses presented here served as incubators for and barometers of the changes impacting rock music. As numerous iconic rock bands encountered commercial exposure and success, often playing campuses, demand for the music only grew.

At the same time, college radio had blossomed, with dozens of stations going FM and adopting the "progressive rock" format pioneered in New York a couple years earlier.[48] Although many college campuses had radio stations, limited technology, transmitter power, and range meant very few people heard it beyond the dorms up the hill—exactly the case at Drew where Granquist hosted his late-night show. He jokes now he was pretty sure not a soul was listening. Howie Klein, too, in hosting his own show at Stony Brook, believed very few students were listening; the benefit had been Bill Graham feeding him the latest underground music to play. College radio was wildly uneven; often very few students listened and almost no one outside of campus, and many college radio stations had faculty and/or administrative supervision determining programming. By decade's end, the situation had changed significantly. Following the expansion of FM broadcasting and several New York–area stations adopting a "progressive rock" format, area colleges also expanded their capability. More popular and powerful FM stations coupled with a progressive rock format now pushed rock music back onto campuses like Drew and Stony Brook. Bob Johnson shared precisely this experience from his days as a student at Drew. Already a fan of that pioneering New York FM station, WNEW, he heard the same "revolution" on the campus: "a revolution coming out of our radios."[49] It is likely impossible to exaggerate the importance of rock music to the late-sixties experience, especially on college campuses.

Within a few years, however, the level of rock performance on the campus dropped significantly. This pattern is not as counterintuitive as it might at first appear. While music on the campus remained, concerts involving high-profile, chart-topping rock bands completely disappeared.[50] The sheer scale of the rock music business—the money for the bands and the huge audiences—grew to such proportions that smaller operators, places like Stony Brook and Drew with venues seating fewer than 3,000, simply could not compete for shows. Smaller venues along the East Coast in general folded one by one. In 1970–1971, most of the ballrooms shuttered for good, including Fillmore East and the Boston Tea Party, begun only a few years earlier.[51] At the end of that brief period, huge festivals and concerts and growing consolidation among a few of the companies had fundamentally altered the music industry. By the early 1970s, according to one history of the music business, "only some twenty-odd promoters or promotion companies control more than 90 percent of the money made in rock appearances." The moment in the history of rock music when a few "dropouts from other parts of the industry," with little more than a few thousand dollars backing, could launch a successful concert promotion business were gone. Following his dramatic exit from New York, San Francisco, and the Fillmores, Bill Graham moved into promotion of large-scale shows. Even the "good guy" and genuine fan of rock music Frank Barsalona became one of a small number of rock industry titans into the seventies.[52]

Of course, live performances of rock music did not simply disappear one day from colleges. Rather, the bands and available artists shrank as the industry colonized and popularized them. The trend varied from place to place but is nonetheless clear following 1968: fewer and fewer of the iconic bands performed at either Stony Brook or Drew. The seemingly subtle differences in the ebbing of rock music performance on these two campuses are indicative of the shrinking margins the student impresarios had to consider. Stony Brook, with its larger budget and greater seating capacity, held on longer, while rock music at Drew virtually disappeared after 1970. The artists booked after 1969 in both cases consisted mainly of folk and singer-songwriter and pop vocal acts, or lesser-known bands not currently on tour. Further, record companies now scheduled tours to promote album releases in a cycle across several years that wrested control of the bands and artists away from local promoters like those on college campuses and at private clubs. The artists booked in the fall reflect the changes. In 1970, Tim Buckley, Mountain, Van Morrison, Livingston Taylor, The Byrds, and The Flying Burrito Brothers played Drew; in 1971, Gordon Lightfoot, Cat Stevens, The Allman Brothers, Carly Simon, and Sha Na Na. At Stony Brook, and considering its significantly larger budget, the volume of rock concerts continued beyond 1971, but fell off sharply after that. Thus did Stony Brook mix in some much more affordable acts like the cast of Hair, The Flock, The Spencer Davis Group, Sha Na Na, Larry Coryell, and Pacific Gas & Electric.

By fall 1971, a lengthy article on the state of campus concerts in *The Statesman* lamented the passing of "Stony Brook's incredible golden age of concerts." This was now the historic point of reference when dealing with the difficulties and limitations faced by the current SAB chairman. Among the challenges explicitly acknowledged were the scheduled tours. Tours necessarily limited an artist's availability, especially given that college campuses were no longer a priority. The concert chairman, Dennis Wagner, who had also booked concerts at Suffolk County College prior to transferring to Stony Brook, had seen the changes firsthand. The task of booking concerts was now more difficult, and his strategy reveals limited options. The SAB now employed around 120 people, all tasked with organizing security, light-ing, and crew, various technicians, "an enormous amount of extra paper work including checks, accounting records, personnel and equipment con-tracts, etc." Consequently, the SAB announced it would now avoid large-scale concerts—"a lot of people go to concerts just crashing, having no interest at all in the music"—in favor of several, smaller shows, and that meant folk and singer-songwriter artists. Students reacted negatively and clearly preferred the "big-name" artists, even if that meant gate-crashing and other security problems. The article concluded that "Stony Brook has lost much of its prestige," and even floated the idea to "decrease the impor-tance of concerts in general," while acknowledging "something would be needed to fill the void at a perennial 'big concert school' like Stony Brook." A year later, major budget cuts made the decision for the SAB—a proposed 10 percent cut that meant the budget was decreased to $8,000.[53]

At Drew, Don Orlando began booking concerts for the Social Commit-tee following Granquist and Dave Marsden, having worked with both of them. In the course of planning concerts in 1970, he released the list of avail-able bands and the costs in *The Acorn*. The list, provided to him by George Brown at College Entertainment Associates, included a couple dozen acts ranging in cost from $5,000 to more than $16,000. With a budget in the $30,000 range for the whole Social Committee, Orlando faced different options than had existed only a few years earlier. During his tenure as con-cert chair, he booked Tim Buckley, Mountain, Van Morrison with Livings-ton Taylor, The Byrds with The Flying Burrito Brothers, Gordon Lightfoot, and Cat Stevens in the spring 1971. For his final concert in 1971, Orlando booked The Allman Brothers. The band was "on the way up"—having recorded the now famous "Live at Fillmore East" album two weeks earlier—and still cost $5,000. This figure now represented the low end for rock bands. Jeff King, taking over from Orlando as concert chair, managed some decidedly eclectic and popular bookings, such as Sha Na Na, Carly Simon, Jerry Jeff Walker, Rita Coolidge, and Crazy Horse. But, at least for Drew, the days of booking iconic rock bands were gone. One of the inexpensive events King organized was the screening of the Monterey Pop Festival in the gym. The film was projected against one large wall of the gym, and students lay around on the floor as though at the actual festival.[54]

In some ways a last gasp, these latest bookings at both campuses still reflected an impressive eclecticism and range of performers. That element of music performance on the campuses actually remained intact over the

Dave Marsden, then chair of the Social Committee, seated in front of concert posters, *The Acorn*, Drew University.

next several years, even as the presence of well-known rock bands disappeared. The same pattern prevailed elsewhere. Even at larger schools able to afford big rock bands, some administrators began banning them altogether. As *The Chronicle of Higher Education* pointed out in 1970, administrators, along with students in some cases, at Georgetown University, the University of Maryland, and Boston University started limiting on-campus shows to students and banning the most popular rock groups following a number of incidents involving property damage and violence brought on by overflow crowds.[55] And the financial risk involved—rock bands' agents and promoters now routinely squeezed six-figure guarantees into the contracts, plus a percentage of the gate—meant courting potential disaster. Some of the larger schools began hiring professional promoters for campus concerts, such as Ted Gehrke at San Jose State University. Coming from a background in concert promotion, Gehrke championed the trend of hiring professionals and called the college promoters "amateurish," recalling how, as an independent promoter, he used to "chew up the student agents. I got twice what my groups were worth."[56] Whether accurate or not, the tone captures the predatory and opportunistic nature of the transition taking place in the world of rock music on campus. That transition was more abrupt for some than for others, and, not surprising given the money involved, scale mattered.

The role of the college campus, while acknowledging much variation across the nation's many campuses, had changed. The change meant different things to different campuses. For institutions of limited size, such as Stony Brook and Drew, the changes meant no longer playing the role of incubator for the latest developments in music and other cultural phenomena. In a sense, both campuses had become victims of their own success in cultivating these latest cultural trends. What had begun as an organic process of cultural experience quintessentially embedded in changes in midsixties America grew into a mainstream cultural reality within the broader context of American liberal capitalism. And although both campuses continued hosting a wide range of music well into the seventies and beyond, neither would again play the role they had created for themselves during 1965–1970, at least not in music culture.

Conclusion

• •

> Revolution is more than listening to
> rock music, getting stoned, and putting
> posters on the wall.
> —Abbie Hoffman

On the afternoon of October 3, 1971, yippie provocateur Abbie Hoffman walked onto the stage in the gymnasium at Drew University, leaned into the microphone, and made a shocking announcement: "I don't have any answers anymore. That's why I'm giving up speaking at schools, cutting my hair and going away." After spending several tumultuous years playing the highly visible role of troublemaker, and revolutionary, Hoffman was now done, the product, no doubt, of frustration, harassment, burnout, and his own inimitable, highly energetic approach to political activism. He assured the largely student audience in attendance that day that Drew would "go down in history for hosting his last appearance." Quickly snapping back to his more-typical self, Hoffman then asked his audience, "Did any of you see me at Fairleigh Dickinson [a small college just down the street from Drew] earlier in the year? That was my last appearance too!"

As had been his practice for years now, the colorful, manic, "youth movement superstar," as the state's leading newspaper characterized him, provoked, cajoled, soothed, and admonished his listeners that day. The difference now, in 1971, seemed to be that he had genuinely lost some of his former zeal for achieving revolution. The sixties were gone, long hair had become a mere affectation, "the rock music has gotten bad and the dope is lousy," Hoffman complained. The possibility of a genuine revolution had turned into commodity and fashion. "Revolution is more than listening to rock music, getting stoned, and putting posters on the wall. . . . All of that is meaningless unless it is tied to the struggle," he said. Hoffman now called on young people to get involved in the democratic process, especially at the local level, to engage as citizens in bringing about change. "Perhaps it is possible," he speculated, "to have a socialist revolution that supports the needs and interests of the people and to do it peacefully through electoral change." Calling on the young people to cut their hair and get out and vote, Hoffman then dramatically cut some of his own hair and tossed the lock onto the stage for affect.[1]

Hoffman's visit captured quite a lot of attention. First, his image covered the front page of *The Acorn*, the student newspaper, while inside, the story, "Abbie Hoffman: Good PR for Drew," opened, "This is the most publicity Drew has received since Dr. Martin Luther King, Jr. spoke here," quoting Hoffman. *The Star Ledger*, the state's leading daily, reported the campus visit as "a second 'final' Jersey goodbye." The story got the attention of *The San Francisco Chronicle*, *The Detroit Free Press*, *The Gary Indiana Post-Tribune*, *The Baltimore Evening Sun*, *Time*, and *Life*. In total, about fifty national dailies picked up the story of the talk at Drew, most highlighting Hoffman's advice to go out and vote, and, of course, the cutting of his hair. The unique activism of Hoffman and Jerry Rubin, the two leading yippies, had long relied on a gullible media eager for provocative headlines. It seemed to have worked here as well, even if much of the coverage lacked any substance and was snarky in tone. What none of these stories reported on, and what Hoffman likely did not know, was that an FBI informant sat in the audience that day, dutifully taking down all that he said. As part of that agency's infamous COINTELPRO operations, agents and informants surveilled hundreds of activists and public figures on the political left. Nor was this the FBI's first visit to the small campus in Madison; they had also followed comedian Dick Gregory there for his talk, and likely others. In an era filled with tensions between young people and authority of various kinds, it is altogether fitting that those authorities continued to focus on the college campus as both source of and springboard for cultural/political rebellion and dissent.

My point here is not to tell the story of Hoffman's trajectory through the 1960s. Rather, it is to place him, and his message that day, within a

Abbie Hoffman at Drew, *The Acorn*, Drew University.

particular physical and temporal context. What that day's speaker likely did not know was that the small, private liberal arts college, tucked out of the way in the sleepy little town of Madison, New Jersey, had for several years been a sixties hotspot; that is, students were not simply recipients of a culture born elsewhere and conveyed there. Rather, much of what we know as "the sixties" originated in these places and spaces, relatively removed from the historical spotlight. In fact, Hoffman's visit to the campus marked the apogee of an unusual cultural and political period for colleges around New York, as it had for the nation—Stony Brook's *The Statesman* had just run an article by Hoffman borrowed from an LNS packet earlier in the year. Hoffman wasn't just signing off for himself at the end of his own arc through the counterculture sixties. Whether or not he was aware of it, he did so on a campus that had been a key site for the rock and counterculture and that was also arriving at the end of an historical arc. Hoffman's admonishment specifically invoking drugs, rock music, and a haircut thus held a special resonance for the student audience. They had, in every way, lived that very historical arc; in a sense, they had been present at the creation of late-sixties culture and had nourished it as an organic experience.

At the end of Abbie Hoffman's talk that day at Drew, Jeff King furtively snatched up that lock of hair and has kept it all these years. That, along with the original concert posters and dozens of other pieces of memorabilia from the period at Drew, make up a fascinating presentation Jeff provides each summer at the annual reunions held on the campus. For him, these were indeed formative years. Nor is he alone. His presence each summer is the highlight of the day as hundreds of former students linger around his table, chat with him about the old days, take away complete sets of replica concert posters that he provides, and generally wax nostalgic about the years when the campus hosted rock music. Likewise, the university has held various exhibitions and commemorations of this rich music history, and those replica concert posters adorn the halls of various campus buildings. Still, however, one has to explain all those rock concerts to students, to place them in the proper historical context, so far removed are they now from the conventional narrative.[2] They are not, in my experience, automatically connected to the historical experience that is the sixties for most people, for they haven't been woven into that narrative over the decades. They instead come off as something disparate, odd, and curious.

The same is true of Stony Brook. Stony Brook continued hosting rock music well into the seventies, albeit mixed with folk, blues, pop vocals, and singer-songwriter acts. In 1971–1972, Procul Harum, Jethro Tull, The Beach Boys, Pink Floyd, the Kinks, Yes, and Steve Miller Band, among literally dozens of other artists, all played there. Given the much greater volume, it comes as little surprise that lots of people of a certain age are familiar with this storied past. A former student and professor there has even founded the Long Island Music Hall of Fame that features the campus experience in the sixties. Nonetheless, many if not nearly all are shocked to learn of the rock music concerts and related counterculture on the campus in the late sixties. While former students recall the experience with fondness, it remains a curiosity for others.[3]

While the vast literature on the sixties overflows with stories of yippies and Hoffman's and Rubin's activities, the Civil Rights movement, the antiwar movements, and the overt political activism from very select college campuses like Berkeley, rock music culture as an essential element of all these experiences on the college campus is notably absent. A few of those elite campuses dominate this part of nearly all historical accounts of the period, academic and otherwise. The emergence and development of rock music, its role in both campus culture and the counterculture, are at best tacked on as something different, or, just as often, simply ignored altogether. The result is a simplistic history of the changes and developments of the era that omits much, imposes awkward barriers between events intrinsically and inextricably interwoven, and lends itself to caricature.[4]

This book is offered to counter that tendency. In highlighting the experiences on two campuses, my point has been to draw attention to the numerous possibilities for further exploration of other campuses. It is clear that hundreds of them developed similar student cultures, that those students enjoyed much freedom in their decisions and control of their campus lives, and that they enlivened their campuses with entertainment of their own choosing and making. Hundreds took advantage of campus radio stations, set up their own committees for organizing campus life, spent and accounted for considerable money, established relationships between the campus and surrounding communities, and challenged administrations for control of most aspects of the college experience. Much of this rich fabric has been overlooked in service of a narrative born in the immediate aftermath of the sixties and perpetuated with broad effort as part of our national discord around the fundamental issues involved and fought over, then and now.[5]

Even seemingly obscure or out-of-the-way college campuses should not be viewed simply as sites for showcasing something developed elsewhere. Rather, they should be viewed as hothouses for these developments alongside hundreds of campuses making up a kind of national cultural mosaic. That is, seemingly disparate pieces—individual campuses, varying student populations, geographical diversity, and a range of educational missions—functioned, under particular circumstances, as a single thing. As higher education grew rapidly in the fifties and sixties, one of the standout developments was an emergent campus culture characterized by a remarkable degree of student autonomy. Planners and leaders in higher education imagined what historian John Thelin has called "an academic metropolis," whose purpose was to provide for a modern society and its economic needs. Those leaders had not, Thelin argues, taken account of "student impact on campus, community, and culture." That impact was broad and pregnant with implications for society. "The new collegiate subcultures merged into the counterculture of alternative organizations, markets, music, publishing and other ventures whose appeal took administrators, city officials, parents, and legislators by surprise," writes Thelin.[6] Likely a significant understatement, the resulting campus culture grew into something with broad national implications for change in the late sixties.

At Stony Brook and Drew, students not only hosted an eclectic range of culture, politics, and entertainment, they simultaneously shaped it; they were actors in the shaping of a late-sixties counterculture. They cultivated and curated the music across dozens of campuses, nurturing its development in the absence of a network of other sites or a pre-existing circuit. As the new rock music emerged around mid-decade, venues were few and far between, let alone anything approaching a national or even regional circuit. Given the near-total absence of a support system, the new music made its way haphazardly from a few clubs around San Francisco and New York onto campuses as college students and other cultural sophisticates became adoptees. Already sites for a broad range of music culture from classical to pop vocals to folk, campuses became key sites for rock music's live performance almost immediately. *Billboard* called out the music industry in 1966 for failing to do more than go "through the perfunctory motions" to take advantage of what had become the most dynamic market for live music performance. In this third annual "Music on Campus" special issue, the industry magazine highlighted the remarkable growth and diversity of music on campuses in only a couple years. A college student population grown to nearly 6 million had money, were regularly in one place, were all about the same age, and increasingly preferred rock and roll. One historian has called this unique cocktail "the single biggest boon to concert promotion, along with the ballrooms, in the late sixties." Still well outside the mainstream, the new rock music lacked exposure and promotion. Thus, campus newspapers and underground press organs filled the gap, constituting the most significant means of spreading the word on the latest bands and performances.

Students themselves took the lead in seeking out the latest happenings and opportunities. As it turned out, the absence of any formal structure for doing so meant lots of opportunity.[7]

The further we get from "the sixties," the more the participants (especially in the counterculture) become caricatures and/or dangerous elements in terms of popular culture representations. The 1994 blockbuster (and winner of the Academy Award for Best Picture) *Forrest Gump* springs to mind, although there are many others. The simpleton Forrest stumbles through an era of profound change, noticing just enough of it for the film to convey a hostility to many of the most important of those agents of change: the Black Panthers, hippies/countercultural types, women, etc. The lead character navigates the era with a dumb triumphalism. His unintentional personal triumphs, in the end, reinforce a refusal to think critically, to scrutinize, even to learn. What's the point, after all, since "life is like a box of chocolates," the film's enduring tagline. *Forrest Gump* is, ultimately, an American love story, dripping with the kind of nostalgic historical and cultural visuals, sounds, and dialog that make up so much of the American film-scape of the era. Meanwhile, the film's soundtrack is a smorgasbord of the era's most recognizable offerings, from Elvis Presley and Duane Eddy to Jefferson Airplane, Joan Baez, The Doors, and, of course, Bob Dylan. Thus a dizzying range of music is yoked to a reactionary reading of sixties social, cultural, and political change. Think of the movie as a younger generation's *The Big Chill*, another post-sixties film that imposed an interpretation onto the decade more appropriate for its release date of 1983 and "Reagan's America" than to the historical context at the center of the drama.[8]

My research, I hope, makes clear the problems in burying the lives of ordinary people in myths and simplistic narratives that diminish the complexity of their actual experience. That complexity reveals a good deal about changes during that era and how those changes came about and impacted both individuals and communities.

Appendix A: Bands/ Artists at Drew University, 1967–1971

● ●

Year	Band/artist	Public figure
1964–1967	The Young Rascals (Feb. 1967) Lotti & the Giraffes (Feb. 1967) The Animals (Mar. 1967)	Martin Luther King Jr. (Feb. 1964) Roy Wilkins (Apr. 1964) Seymour Melman (part of a "think-in" on campus) (May 1965)
	The Lords (1967) The Sorts (1967) The Shaggy Boys (Mar. 1967) The Lovin' Spoonful (May 1967) Carolyn Hester (folk singer) (May 1967) Bit a Sweet (Long Island rock band) (May 1967) Judy Collins (Sept. 30, 1967) The Four Tops (Nov. 1867)	Floyd McKissick (Nov. 1966) Andy Warhol (Oct. 1967) Ralph Nader (Oct. 1967) Allen Ginsberg (May 7, 1967)
1968	Clockwork Orange (Feb.) The Who (Mar.) Richie Havens (May) Earth Opera (Oct.) Jefferson Airplane (Oct.) Iron Butterfly (Nov.)	Ted Sorensen (JFK speechwriter) The "hippie house incident" Nat Hentoff (Sept.)

(continued)

Year	Band/artist	Public figure
1969	Frank Zappa & the Mothers of Invention (Feb.)	Dick Gregory (Mar.)
	Rhinoceros (Mar.)	Roy Innis (Nov.)
	Chuck Berry (Mar.)	The Black Panthers (Newark chapter)
	Blood, Sweat & Tears (Mar.)	
	Soft White Underbelly (aka Blue Öyster Cult) (May)	
	John Mayall (Oct.)	
	Canned Heat (Oct. 11)	
	Jethro Tull (Nov. 14)	
1970	Tim Buckley (Feb. 14)	Strom Thurmond (Feb.)
	Mountain (Apr. 25)	Jerry Rubin (Apr.)
	Van Morrison (Oct.)	Pete Seeger (Sept.)
	Livingston Taylor (Oct.)	William Kunstler (Nov.)
	The Byrds (Nov. 14)	Sydney Hook (Dec.)
	The Flying Burrito Brothers (Nov. 14)	
1971–1974	Gordon Lightfoot (Feb. 26, 1971)	Abbie Hoffman (Oct. 1971)
	Cat Stevens (Apr. 22, 1971)	Jane Fonda and Tom Hayden (Oct. 1972)
	The Allman Brothers (Apr. 2, 1971)	Bobby Seale (Nov. 1973)
	Carly Simon (Nov. 13, 1971)	William F. Buckley (Jan. 1974)
	Sha Na Na (Dec. 10, 1971)	

Appendix B: Bands/ Artists at Stony Brook University, 1967–1971

●●●●●●●●●●●●●●●●●●●●●

Year	Band/artist
1967	The Four Tops
	Daily Flash
	Jefferson Airplane
	Tom Rush
	Ian and Sylvia
	Tom Paxton
	The Bagatelle
	Jaki Byard Trio
	Thad Jones
	Mel Lewis Band
	Thelonious Monk
	The Grateful Dead
	Tim Buckley
	The Doors
	The Chambers Brothers
	Soft White Underbelly/The Blue Öyster Cult
	The Holy Modal Rounders
	The James Cotton Blues Band
	Steve Noonan
	Phil Ochs

(continued)

Doc Watson
Kaleidoscope
Ravi Shankar
Charles Lloyd
Babatunde Olatunji

1968

Jackson Browne
Judy Collins
Country Joe & the Fish
The Fugs
Jimi Hendrix (The Jimi Hendrix Experience)
The Soft Machine
The Spencer Davis Group
Beacon Street Union
The Vagrants
Vanilla Fudge
Janis Ian
The Grateful Dead
The Incredible String Band
Children of God
Orpheus
Smokey Robinson
Sam and Dave
Tim Hardin
Joni Mitchell
"Spider" John Koerner
The Churls
Procol Harum
Blood, Sweat & Tears
Moby Grape
Rhinoceros
Blue Öyster Cult/Soft White Underbelly/Stalk-Forrest Group
Ten Years After
Big Brother and the Holding Company
Reverend Gary Davis
Richie Havens
The John Hammond Trio
Janis Joplin
Nina Simone
The Youngbloods

1969

Earth Opera
Flatt and Scruggs
Arlo Guthrie
Jethro Tull
Mountain

Beau Brummels
Blood, Sweat & Tears
Miles Davis
Dizzy Gillespie
Taj Mahal
Ten Years After
Chuck Berry
Slim Harpo
James Cotton Blues Band
The Band
Soft White Underbelly/Blue Öyster Cult/Stalk-Forrest Group
The Byrds
Gordon Lightfoot
Turley Richards
The Flock
The Spencer Davis Group
The Who
Sha Na Na
Larry Coryell
Pacific Gas and Electric
The cast of Hair
Bludwyn Pig
The Moody Blues
The Band
Mother Earth

1970

Laura Nyro
Turley Richards
Melanie
Jerry Jeff Walker
Renaissance
Van Morrison
John Mayall
Van Morrison
Tube Groove
Pig Iron
James Taylor
Quicksilver Messenger Service
Roland Kirk
Cannonball Adderley
The Allman Brothers Band
Chicago Transit Authority
Jefferson Airplane
Blue Öyster Cult/Soft White Underbelly/Stalk-Forrest Group
Mad Dogs & Englishmen
Joe Cocker

(continued)

Canned Heat
Traffic
MC5
Ten Years After
Mott the Hoople
The Allman Brothers
Mountain
Bloodrock
Grand Funk Railroad
Swallow
The Allman Brothers
Miles Davis
Santana
James Cotton Blues Band
B. B. King
Raphael Grinage
The Allman Brothers
Bonnie Delaney and Friends
The Grateful Dead
New Riders of the Purple Sage
The Grateful Dead
Small Faces
Rod Stewart
Poco
The Allman Brothers
Hot Tuna
Cat Stevens
Traffic
Leonard Cohen
Miles Davis
Leon Thomas (Dec. 12)

1971   Bill Monroe and His Bluegrass Boys Cowboy
Tom Rush
Freddie King
Leon Russell
Soft White Underbelly/Blue Öyster Cult/Stalk-Forrest Group
The Soft Decline
Procol Harum
Seatrain
John McLaughlin and the Mahavishnu Orchestra
The J. Geils Blues Band
Jethro Tull
Roberta Flack
Les McCann
The Allman Brothers
The Wet Willie Band

Year	Band/artist
	Boz Scaggs
	The Beach Boys
	Charlie Chin
	Shawn Phillips
	Corbitt and Daniels
	The Youngbloods
	Frank Zappa and the Mothers of Invention
	The Holy Modal Rounders
	The J. Geils Band
	Johnathan Edwards
	The Flying Burrito Brothers
	Pink Floyd
	Donny Hathaway
	The Kinks
	Yes
	Pentangle
	Soft White Underbelly/Blue Öyster Cult/Stalk-Forrest Group
	The Byrds
	John McLaughlin
	"Spider" John Koerner

Notes

Introduction

1   Michele Regenold, "Rock and Roll and Beyond: Georgia Dentel, the Woman Who Put Grinnell College on the Musical Map," Grinnell College, News, September 20, 2015, accessed October 4, 2021, https://www.grinnell.edu/news/rock-and-roll-and-beyond; "1966: Jefferson Airplane Lands in Grinnell," uncredited, *The Scarlet & Black*, October 27, 2011, accessed October 4, 2021, http://www.thesandb.com/arts/1966-jefferson-airplane-lands-in-grinnell.html; Bill Graham and Robert Greenfield, *Bill Graham Presents: My Life Inside Rock and Out* (New York: Doubleday Press, 1992), 166.

2   Claude Hall, "They're Rockin' in the Ivory Tower," *Billboard*, Music on Campus, April 8, 1967, 26.

3   John R. Thelin, *Going to College in the Sixties* (Baltimore, MD: Johns Hopkins University Press, 2018). Lizabeth Cohen expertly deals with the inexorable complexities and contradictions of these postwar changes. See Cohen, *A Consumer's Republic: The Politics of Mass Consumption in Postwar America* (New York: Vintage Books, 2003), especially chapters 3 and 4. See also Thomas D. Snyder, ed., "120 Years of American Education: A Statistical Portrait," National Center for Education Statistics, U.S. Department of Education. (Washington, D.C.: 1993).

4   See the March 28, 1964, issue of *Billboard*, Music on Campus.

5   See, for instance, the March 27, 1665, issue of *Billboard*, Music on Campus, and the March 19, 1966, issue of *Billboard*, Music on Campus.

6   Keir Keightley, "Reconsidering Rock," in *The Cambridge Companion to Pop and Rock*, ed. Simon Frith, Will Straw, and John Street (New York: Cambridge University Press, 2001), 123; Michael Kramer, *The Republic of Rock: Music and Citizenship in the Sixties Counterculture* (New York: Oxford University Press, 2013), 22.

7   David Farber, "Building the Counterculture, Creating Right Livelihoods: The Counterculture at Work," *The Sixties* 6, no. 1 (2013): 3–4. Joshua Clark Davis,

From Head Shops to Whole Foods: The Rise and Fall of Activist Entrepreneurs (New York: Columbia University Press, 2017).

8   Farber, "Building the Counterculture," 3. For a similar argument and critique of sixties historiography, see Andrew Hunt, "When Did the Sixties Happen? Searching for New Directions," *Journal of Social History* 3, no. 1 (Autumn 1999): 147–161. Davis, *From Headshops to Whole Foods.*

9   Alice Echols, *Shaky Ground: The Sixties and Its Aftershocks* (New York: Columbia University Press, 2002); John McMillian, *Smoking Typewriters: The Sixties Underground Press and the Rise of Alternative Media in America* (Oxford: Oxford University Press, 2011); Kimbrew McLeod, *The Downtown Pop Underground: New York City and the Literary Punks, Renegade Artists, DIY Filmmakers, Mad Playwrights, and Rock n Roll Glitter Queens Who Revolutionized Culture* (New York: Abrams Press, 2018).

10 Students on both campuses had established rich and furtive cultures well before the advent of rock music culture, routinely hosting prominent activists and intellectuals. In 1964, for instance, Martin Luther King Jr. visited the Drew campus and gave a talk. Shortly following his visit, the infamous "barbershop incident," as it has come to be called, exposed deep division within the community of Madison. A local barber refused to cut the hair of a Black man provoking the students at Drew to launch a serious movement in opposition to segregation and racism in the town. The NAACP came to town, including Roy Wilkins, to join in marching and picketing local businesses that supported the offending barbershop. Ultimately, a court ruled against the barber. On the barbershop incident, see "4 Held in Protest of Jersey Barber," uncredited, *The New York Times*, May 14, 1964.

11 See Julian Foster and Durward Long, eds., *Protest! Student Activism in America* (New York: William Morrow & Co., 1970) and Thelin, *Going to College in the Sixties.*

12 Thelin, *Going to College in the Sixties*, 110; emphasis added.

13 Keightley, "Reconsidering Rock." Elijah Wald, *How the Beatles Destroyed Rock 'n' Roll* (New York: Oxford University Press, 2009), 237–238. David Hajdu, *Love for Sale: Pop Music in America* (New York: Farrar, Straus & Giroux: 2016), 162–169.

Chapter 1   Postwar America, the Revolution in Higher Education, and Popular Music

1   Albert A. Logan Jr., "Campuses Weigh Banning Rock's 'Super Groups,'" *The Chronicle of Higher Education*, vol. 5, no. 10, November 30, 1970, 4. Larry A. Van Dyne, "Rock Music Drowning Out the Classics in Campus Concert Halls," *The Chronicle of Higher Education*, vol. 6, no. 13, January 3, 1972, 3. William A. Sievert, "Rock Superstars on the Campuses," *The Chronicle of Higher Education*, vol. 9, no. 5, 1974, 11.

2   James Miller, *Flowers in the Dustbin: The Rise of Rock and Roll, 1947–1977* (New York: Simon & Schuster, 1999), chapter 5. Peter Biskind, *Easy Riders, Raging Bulls: How the Sex-Drugs-and-Rock 'n' Roll Generation Saved Hollywood* (New York: Touchstone, 1998). Peter Braunstein and Michael William Doyle, eds., *Imagine Nation: The American Counterculture of the 1960s & 1970s* (New York: Routledge, 2004).

3 Sievert, "Rock Superstars on the Campuses," 11. See also Bob Glassenberg, "Campus: A Circular World," *Billboard*, 8th annual Campus Attractions, section 2, March 27, 1971, 4. Bob Glassenberg, "Group Price Inflation Must Stop Say Concert Managers," *Billboard*, Campus Attractions, section 2, March 28, 1970, 26.

4 Ed Ochs, "Rock Now!," *Billboard*, November 14, 1970, R-3.

5 Claude Hall, "They're Rockin' in the Ivory Tower," *Billboard: Music on Campus*, April 8, 1967.

6 James T. Patterson, *Grand Expectations: The United States, 1945–1974* (New York: Oxford University Press, 1996), 68.

7 Thomas D. Snyder, ed., "120 Years of American Education: A Statistical Portrait," National Center for Education Statistics, U.S. Department of Education (Washington, D.C.: 1993). In 1900, only about 4 percent of high school graduates in the United States went on to college. By 1968, nearly half of them were on college campuses. See Julian Foster and Durward Long, eds., *Protest! Student Activism in America* (New York: William & Morrow Co., 1970), 555.

8 Patterson, *Grand Expectations*, 312–313. On postwar economic growth, see also William H. Chafe, *The Unfinished Journey: America Since World War II*, 7th ed. (New York: Oxford University Press, 2011), 106–107.

9 Helen Lefkowitz Horowitz, "The 1960s and the Transformation of Campus Cultures," *History of Education Quarterly* 26, no. 1 (Spring 1986): 10.

10 "A New, $10 Billion Power: The U.S. Teenage Consumer," uncredited, *Life*, August 31, 1959, 78.

11 Both Jacob and Kerr quoted in *Protest!*, 13. See also Terry Anderson, *The Movement and the Sixties: Protest in America from Greensboro to Wounded Knee* (New York: Oxford University Press, 1995), 18–19.

12 "The Careful Young Men: Tomorrow's Leaders Analyzed by Today's Teachers," *The Nation*, March 9, 1957, quotes are from 201 and 210, respectively. See also Louis E. Reik, "War of the Generations," *The Nation*, March 16, 1957, 451.

13 Todd Gitlin, *The Sixties: Years of Hope, Days of Rage* (New York: Bantam Books, 1987), 21; Foster and Long, *Protest!*, 555. Kenneth J. Heineman, *Campus Wars: The Peace Movement at American State Universities in the Vietnam Era* (New York: New York University Press, 1993), 77. Chafe, *The Unfinished Journey*, 307–310. The entire higher education "ecosystem" expanded as well: staff, facilities, even high schools experienced dramatic growth. College faulty doubled in ten years from 281,506 to 551,000. See John R. Thelin, *Going to College in the Sixties* (Baltimore, MD: Johns Hopkins University Press, 2018), 12–13.

14 Foster and Long, *Protest!*, 556–557. Thelin, *Going to College in the Sixties*, 12.

15 Paul Goodman, *Growing Up Absurd: Problems of Youth in the Organized Society* (New York: New York Review Books, 2012), 194.

16 Among the enormous historical literature on the topic are Maurice Isserman and Michael Kazin, *America Divided: The Civil War of the 1960s* (New York: Oxford University Press, 2000); David Farber, ed., *The Sixties: From Memory to History* (Chapel Hill: University of North Carolina Press, 1994); Gitlin, *The Sixties*; Anderson, *The Movement and the Sixties*; and Kenneth J. Heineman, *Campus Wars: The Peace Movement at American State Universities in the Vietnam Era* (New York: New York University Press, 1994).

17 Horowitz, "The 1960s and the Transformation of Campus Cultures," 2–11. See also Foster and Long, *Protest!*, chapter 2.

18 Foster and Long, *Protest!*, 123–132. The study's author summed up this way: "In summary, the student activists in this sample were distinguished by their talent rather than their alienation, by their intellectuality rather than their academic performance, and by their leadership rather than by their anomie"; this quote is on p. 132.

19 Thelin, *Going to College in the Sixties*, 96 and 109. Interestingly, Kenneth Heineman points out that "liberal arts and social science majors predominated in the ranks of protestors" because of what they were taught in college. "This may be explained by the nature of the social sciences and the humanities, which encourage critical approaches toward analyzing authority (and attract critical students), offer no specific avenues to jobs, and require sensitivity to, and reflection on, social problems." See Heineman, *Campus Wars*, 78.

20 Thelin, *Going to College in the Sixties*, 96.

21 See "Mapping Rock Music in the U.S., 1967–1971," sixtiesrockgeo.com.

22 "Meeting the Increasing Demand for Higher Education in New York State: A Report to the Governor and the Board of Regents," Heald Report, November 1, 1960, 1.

23 "Meeting the Increasing Demand," 4. Another commission, also appointed by the governor, came to very similar conclusions regarding the medical professions. See "Education for the Health Professions: A Comprehensive Plan for Comprehensive Care to Meet New York's Needs in an Age of Change," June 1963, also known as the "Muir Report" after its chairman Malcolm Muir.

24 "Meeting the Increasing Demand," 9 and 15, respectively. On the CUNY system, see "A Long Range Plan for the City University of New York, 1961–1975," CUNY Digital History Archive, https://cdha.cuny.edu/items/show/3162. See also Thelin, *Going to College in the Sixties*, 57–58.

25 The Heald Report, President Shirley Strum Kenny, "Celebrating Our First 50 Years, 1957–2007," 2007. For more on the expansion of New York higher education and New York University in particular, see Themis Chronopoulos, "Urban Decline and the Withdrawal of New York University from University Heights, the Bronx," *The Bronx Historical Society Journal* 46, no. 1 and 2 (Spring/Fall 2009): 4–24.

26 *Specula*, 1967, 11. Interview with Nancy Malagold, June 18, 2021.

27 Neil Lawer, "Rockefeller Cites Growth in Education," *The Statesmen*, November 1, 1966, 2.

28 I interviewed the following participants who were either students at Stony Brook or resided in the area: Howie Klein, November 8, 2020; Norm Prusslin, November 9, 2020; Charles Backfish, April 21, 2021; Nancy Malagold, June 18, 2021; Moyssi, December 7, 2021; Mary Beth Olbrych, December 15, 2021.

29 Established in 1957 as *The Sucolian*, for "State University Campus on Long Island," when the campus was located on Oyster Bay, the name was changed to *The Statesman* in 1958. See https://www.sbstatesman.com/about/.

30 "S.A.B. Organized, Activities Planned," uncredited, *The Statesman*, October 14, 1964, 1. David Fersh, "Peter, Paul and Mary—A Triumphant Trio," *The Statesman*, October 14, 1964, 10. Bob Levine, "Moan Along with Mary," *The Statesman*, October 14, 1964, 10. Student responses in *The Statesman* capture the seriousness and scrutiny, the support and criticism that was commonplace on the campus. See,

in particular, the comments of a young Richard ("Richie") Meltzer, "SAB, What and Why?," *The Statesman*, October 28, 1964, 3. Joel Kleinberg, SAB chairman, "—Activities Board Organizes," *The Statesman*, October 28, 1964, 8–9.

31 John T. Cunningham, *University in the Forest: The Story of Drew University* (Florham Park, NJ: Afton Publishing, 2002), 221–235. See also Dave Caldwell, "A Town Right Out of Central Casting," *New York Times*, June 15, 2008, accessed June 16, 2018, https://www.nytimes.com/2008/06/15/realestate/15livi.html ?pagewanted=all&_r=0.

32 I interviewed the following participants who were either students at Drew University or resided in the area: Bob Johnson, July 11, 2018; Barry Fenstermacher, May 8, 2018; David Hinckley, June 18, 2018; Don Orlando, June 25, 2018; Jeff King, June 2, 2018; Barbara North, October 21, 2019; Glenn Rebord, August 6, 2018; Greg Granquist, June 27, 2018; Ken Schulman, July 3, 2018; Harry Litwack, June 1, 2019; Dave Marsden, May 5, 2021; Bob Courboin, July 4, 2018; Bob Smartt, August 17, 2018; Tom McMullen, June 11, 2018; Tom Wexler, September 28, 2018. At Drew, concert promotion as well the entertainment committee generally was a heavily male-oriented affair.

33 This list excludes numerous concerts held at high schools. See sixtiesrockgeo.com.

34 James Miller, *Flowers in the Dustbin: The Rise of Rock and Roll, 1947–1977* (New York: Simon & Schuster, 1999), 25–27. Wexler quote in David P. Szmatmary, *Rockin' in Time: A Social History of Rock-and-Roll*, 6th ed. (New Jersey: Pearson/ Prentice Hall, 2007), 17. See also Jerry Wexler, "Rhythm & Blues Influence Worldwide," *Record World*, March 12, 1966, 50.

35 Ed Ward, *The History of Rock & Roll, Vol. I: 1920–1963* (New York: Flatiron Book, 2016), 45–49.

36 Steve Chapple and Reebee Garofalo, *Rock 'n' Roll Is Here to Pay: The History and Politics of the Music Industry* (Chicago: Nelson Hall, 1977), 54.

37 In 1959, 8,000 jukebox operators controlled nearly 500,000 boxes and bought nearly 50 million records. Thomas Lee Davidson, "1960 Music Machine Survey," *Billboard*, Music Machine Survey, May 9, 1960, 66–80. "The Operator's Stake in the Record Industry," uncredited, *Billboard*, Music Machine Survey, May 9, 1960, 63. On the importance of the dj to the record industry, see *Billboard*, Special Disk Jockey Supplement, October 7, 1950, 36. See also Chapple and Garofalo, *Rock 'n' Roll Is Here to Pay*, 54.

38 Audio Feedback, *Billboard*, November 30, 1959, 14. "U.S. Won't Set Limit to Nip Radio Import," uncredited, *Billboard*, June 16, 1962, 39. Cari Romm, "How the Transistor Radio with Music in Your Pocket Fueled a Teenage Social Revolution," *Smithsonian Magazine*, November 19, 2014. For a deep dive on the development of transistor technology, see Robert J. Simcoe, "The Revolution in Your Pocket," *Invention & Technology Magazine* 20, no. 2 (2004).

39 Reebee Garofalo, *Rockin' Out: Popular Music in the U.S.A.*, 4th ed. (Upper Saddle River, NJ: Pearson/Prentice Hall, 2008), 82.

40 Melissa Rugieri, "Sister Rosetta Tharpe: Singer Influenced Key Rock 'n' Roll Figures," *The Atlanta Journal-Constitution*, March 12, 2018, accessed May 11, 2022, https://www.ajc.com/entertainment/music/sister-rosetta-tharpe-singer-influenced -key-rock-roll-figures/UTzkpIsRNvvenWoaTGamtM/.

41 Ed Ward, *The History of Rock & Roll, volume I 1920–1963* (New York: Flatiron Books, 2016), 45.

42 Robert D. Cohen, "The Delinquents: Censorship and Youth Culture in Recent U.S. History," *History of Education Quarterly* 37, no. 3 (Autumn 1997): 254.

43 Cohen, "The Delinquents," 256; Reebee Garofalo, "Setting the Record Straight: Censorship and Social Responsibility in Popular Music," *The Journal of Popular Music Studies* 6, no. 1 (August 1994): 1–37; Trent Hill, "The Enemy Within: Censorship in Rock Music in the 1950s," in Anthony DeCurties, ed., *Present Tense: Rock & Roll and Culture* (Durham, NC: Duke University Press, 1992), 43; Lawrence Grossberg, "The Framing of Rock: Rock and the New Conservatism," in *Rock and Popular Music: Politics, Policies, Institutions*, ed. Tony Bennet et al. (New York: Routledge Press, 1993), chapter 12. See also Marty Jezer, *The Dark Ages: Life in the United States, 1945–1960* (Boston: South End Press, 1982), especially chapters 11 and 13.

44 David Hajdu, *Love for Sale: Pop Music in America* (New York: Farrar, Straus and Giroux, 2016), 116. Chapple and Garofalo, *Rock 'n' Roll Is Here to Pay*, 56–62. Hill, "The Enemy Within," 62–69. Ward, *The History of Rock & Roll*, 235–236. See also Jude Sheerin, "How the World's First Rock Concert Ended in Chaos," *BBC News*, March 21, 2012, accessed June 14, 2021, https://www.bbc.com/news/magazine -17440514, and Bernard Weinraub, "The Man Who Knew It Wasn't Only Rock and Roll," *New York Times*, October 14, 1999, accessed June 14, 2021, https://www .nytimes.com/1999/10/14/arts/the-man-who-knew-it-wasn-t-only-rock-n-roll .html. *Billboard*, January 18, 1960, also contained a variety of useful coverage of the ongoing payola hearings.

45 "R&R Still Beams Plenty of Life, Beat Currently Dominates 60 % of 'Hot 100' Chart for Slowest Fade Yet," uncredited, *Billboard*, January 18, 1960, 6.

46 Bob Rolontz, "Today's Music Picture; Still Dirt under the Rug," *Billboard*, January 8, 1960, 2.

47 Paul Ackerman, "Where Do We Go from Here?," *Billboard*, Who's Who in the World of Music, December 28, 1963, sections 2, 21, and 30. The numbers measuring a particular genre's popularity can be complicated. For instance, *Billboard* maintained separate charts for R & B and country.

48 Thomas E. Noonan, "Economic Analysis and Outlook," *Billboard*, December 28, 1963, 24–25.

49 "The Built-In Audience," *Cashbox*, uncredited, The International Music-Record Weekly, November 9, 1968, 3.

Chapter 2 "The Sound of the Sixties"

1 Nancy Nickerson, "Spontaneity Marks Afternoon Concert," *The Swarthmore College Phoenix*, April 14, 1964. Union College also hosted jazz musician Dizzy Gillespie and R & B musician Bo Diddley. Early in the year, officials also voted to change the campus radio station to rock and roll format to "satisfy student demand." See *The Concordiensis*, February 21, 1964, March 13, 1964, and, on the shift to rock-and-roll format, see the January 10, 1964, issue.

2 Michael Schumacher, *There but for Fortune: The Life of Phil Ochs* (New York: Hyperion, 1996), 77.

3 Robert Cantwell, *When We Were Good: The Folk Revival* (Cambridge, MA: Harvard University Press, 1996), 174–187, 273–274.

4 Schumacher, *There but for Fortune*, 54. On the folk revival, see also Greil Marcus, *The Old, Weird America: The World of Bob Dylan's Basement Tapes* (New York: Henry Holt & Co., 1997), 20–28.

5 "Folk Singing: Sybil with Guitar," uncredited, *Time*, November 23, 1962.

6 "The College Campus: Incubator for Recording Talent," uncredited, *Billboard*, Music on Campus, March 28, 1964, 31.

7 "The College Campus," 32.

8 Aaron Sternfield, "Collegians Shape the Nation's Musical Tastes," *Billboard*, Music on Campus, March 28, 1964, 11.

9 Sternfield, "Collegians Shape the Nation's Musical Tastes," 11. The directory of colleges begins on page 91. Drew University made the list of colleges in this inaugural issue. See page 94.

10 "College Concert Stage, Major Pop Showcase," uncredited, *Billboard*, Music on Campus, March 28, 1964, 13–14.

11 George H. Craig, "They're Supposed to Lose Money," *Billboard*, Music on Campus, March 27, 1965, 86. The college, not the social committee, also sponsored classical music concerts, although by the early 1960s they were not nearly as popular with the students as popular music acts.

12 Thomas Lewis, "New Colleges Are Sleepers," *Billboard*, Music on Campus, March 27, 1965, 78. The following are all in the same special issue of *Billboard*. Jim Albright, "Encore at Oregon State," *Billboard*, 84. Eliot Tiegel, "California's Cultural Diamond," *Billboard*, 62. In a similar feature on UCLA in *Billboard*, the article text wrapped around a large image of serious students looking on as Delta Blues legend Mance Lipscomb strummed his six-string guitar. See also Jeffrey Davidson, "Cowboys Dig Basie," *Billboard*, 87. Jack Miller, "Talent Packages Answer for Small Schools," *Billboard*, 86. G. Jerry Merges, "Cadets Get Varied Musical Menu," *Billboard*, 82. Winston F. Jones, "Eastern Kentucky Blossoms as Talent Showcase," *Billboard*, 80. Jerry Chaskelson, "Missouri Backs Up Concerts with Advertising Barrage," *Billboard*, 76. Gary A. Kraut, "Boston U. Bows as Pop Talent Showcase," *Billboard*, 76. Robert C. Welling, "W. Virginia Students Have a Voice in Concert Acts," *Billboard*, 74. Steve Smirnoff, "UND Formula: Fit Concerts into Social Calendar," *Billboard*, 70. Harold B. Bob, "Buffalo Market Shows Promise," *Billboard*, 72. David L. Bieber, "Anatomy of College Concert: Blood, Sweat, Tears—and Time," *Billboard*, Music on Campus, March 19, 1966, 72.

13 John Cocks, "A Day with Bob Dylan," *The Kenyon Collegian*, November 20, 1964. The student presence in the campus newspaper content and editorials is also pronounced and typical.

14 Aaron Sternfield, "Nation's Colleges Offer Music Industry Lush Market of 5,900,000," *Billboard*, Music on Campus, March 19, 1966, 16. See also Gary A. Kraut, "Boston Dealers Ignore B.U. Concerts," *Billboard*, Music on Campus, March 19, 1966, 78.

15 "Campus Showcases," *Billboard*, Music on Campus, March 19, 1966, 26.

16 Sternfield, "Nation's Colleges," *Billboard*,16 and 18. Paul Ackerman, "Alexander Observes the College Scene," *Billboard*, Music on Campus, March 19, 1966, 76. *Billboard* had established its own college bureau of student reporters in 1964. By 1966, it had grown from six to ninety-five college reporters covering dozens of

campuses and 1 million students. "On the College Campuses of North America," uncredited, *Billboard*, Music on Campus, March 19, 1966, 131.

17 Jack Maher and Tom Noonan, "Chart Crawls with Beatles," *Billboard*, April 4, 1964, 1.

18 Keir Keightley, "Reconsidering Rock," in *The Cambridge Companion to Pop and Rock*, ed. Simon Frith, Will Straw, and John Street (New York: Cambridge University Press, 2001), 118–119. Jack Hamilton also appropriately complicates the "British invasion" narrative. See Jack Hamilton, *Just Around Midnight: Rock and Roll and the Racial Imagination* (Cambridge, MA: Harvard University Press, 2016), esp. 91–95.

19 "The Sound of the Sixties," uncredited, *Time*, vol. 85, issue 21, May 5, 1965, 94.

20 Paul Williams, "Get Off of My Cloud," *Crawdaddy!*, February 7, 1966.

21 Jon Landau, Letters to the Editor, *The Justice*, November 8, 1966, 2. Landau also wrote the review of the Cream concert at Brandeis in 1968. See Jon Landau, "Cream on Its Way," *The Justice*, March 26, 1968, 4. He also began writing for *Rolling Stone* while still a junior at Brandeis.

22 Steve Jones and Kevin Featherly, "Re-viewing Rock Writing: Narratives of Pop Music Criticism," in *Pop Music and the Press*, ed. Steve Jones (Philadelphia, PA: Temple University Press, 2002), 27–37. Jon Landau, "Growing Young with Rock and Roll," *The Real Paper*, May 22, 1974. While at Oberlin, Jonathan Eisen launched the underground paper *The Activist* and served as its editor from 1960 onward. He later became editor of *Commonweal* and published two edited volumes of rock music writing in 1969 and 1970. See Jonathan Eisen, *The Age of Rock: Sounds of the American Cultural Revolution*, Vol. 1 (New York: Vintage Books, 1969). Contributors to these volumes included everyone named above and numerous others.

23 Kristin White, "Where Have All the Folkies Gone?," *Billboard*, Music on Campus, April 8, 1967, 24–25.

24 Fred Goodman, *The Mansion on the Hill: Dylan, Young, Geffen, Springsteen, and the Head-On Collision of Rock and Commerce* (New York: Times Books, 1997), 24–25. See also Frank Barsalona's obituary in *The Telegraph*, December 23, 2012.

25 Dave Marsh, "How One Man's Dream Changed the Industry: Premier Talent: 20 Years of Rock and Roll," *Billboard*, August 18, 1984, 36–42. Chapple and Garofalo, *Rock 'n' Roll Is Here to Pay*, 124–131, 138–139.

26 Those few venues included the Boston Tea Party ballroom, the Electric Factory in Philadelphia, the Winterland Ballroom in San Francisco, Thee Image Club in Miami, and the Fillmores (East and West). None of these served as exclusive rock music venues prior to 1967–1968. Claude Hall, "Hip Rockers Facing 2 Obstacles," *Billboard*, July 13, 1968, 12. For FM radio and the new rock, see "Progressive Rock Play; An Analysis of Its Use," *Billboard*, July 13, 1968, 16. Even around northern California, the situation was catch-as-catch-can into the late sixties. See Geoffrey Link, "Rock Acts in Search of Nitery as Club Shortage Hits Bay Area," *Billboard*, April 5, 1969, 5.

27 Marsh, "How One Man's Dream," 5 and 42.

28 "Frank Barsalona: The Lisa Robinson Interview," *Billboard*, August 18, 1984.

29 "Music Store Sales Up 7% Reports NAMM President," *Billboard*, December 16, 1967, 12. "Music (Played and Listened to) Strikes Happiest Sales Notes Ever in 1967," *Cashbox*, December 16, 1967, 7.

30 "Music Store Sales Up 7%," 12.

31 Simon Frith, Will Straw, and John Street, eds., *The Cambridge Companion to Pop and Rock* (New York: Cambridge University Press, 2001), 118, 122–130. For an industry perspective on the advent of "rock" as art, see "Art-Form Called Rock," *Cashbox*, December 9, 1967, 3.

32 For a discussion of the complex relationship between technology (the LP) and the aesthetics and art of rock music, see Alan Durant, "Rock Revolution or Time-No-Changes: Visions of Change and Continuity in Rock Music," *Popular Music* 5 (1985): 97–121, especially 102–104.

33 George Lipsitz, "Who'll Stop the Rain? Youth Culture, Rock and Roll, and Social Crisis," in *The Sixties from Memory to History*, ed. David Farber (Chapel Hill: University of North Carolina Press, 1994), 161. As perhaps the most obvious example, progressive rock band *Pink Floyd*'s album, *The Dark Side of the Moon* (1973), spent fourteen years on *Billboard*'s Top LP charts and sold over 25 million copies worldwide, more than any other rock album. And yet, the band had little success in the singles charts.

34 Keightley, "Reconsidering Rock," in *The Cambridge Companion to Pop and Rock*, chapter 5; quote is from p. 123. Among many other useful insights, Keightley points out the numerous contradictions in rock culture: "Rock may wear subcultural clothes, identify with marginalized minorities, promote countercultural political positions, and upset genteel notions of propriety, but from its inception it has been a large-scale, industrially organized, mass-mediated, mainstream phenomenon operating at the very centre of society," p. 127. Eisen, *The Age of Rock*, 1:xi. Meltzer's *The Aesthetics of Rock* is excerpted on pp. 244–253.

35 Among the many detailed narratives of the album's production is James Miller, *Flowers in the Dustbins: The Rise of Rock and Roll, 1947–1977* (New York: Simon & Schuster, 1999), 250–260. For a more recent account, see "The Beatles," *MOJO, The Music Magazine*, The Collector's Series, The Blue Issue, 1967–1970, 2018.

36 "The Beatles: *Sgt. Pepper's Lonely Hearts Club Band*," uncredited writer, *International Times*, June 2, 1967. To be sure, reception for the album was not entirely positive. *New York Times* critic Richard Goldstein hated the album and wrote in his review, "The obsession with production, coupled with a surprising shoddiness in composition, permeates the entire album. There is nothing beautiful on 'Sergeant Pepper.' Nothing is real and there is nothing to get hung about." Richard Goldstein, "We Still Need the Beatles But," *The New York Times*, June 18, 1967. For additional insight into contemporary reactions to the album, see Robert Christgau, "Sgt. Pepper, the Monkees, the Candymen, Frank Zappa, Miscellaneous," *Esquire*, December 1967. Also reprinted in Robert Christgau, *Any Old Way You Choose It: Rock and Other Pop Music* (New York: Cooper Square Press, 2000), 41–50. Other useful contemporary reactions include Joan Peyser, "The Music of Sound, or *The Beatles* and the Beatless," and Richard Poirier, "Learning from *The Beatles*," both Eisen, *The Age of Rock*, 126–137 and 160–179, respectively.

37 Steven D. Stark, *Meet the Beatles: A Cultural History of the Band that Shook Youth, Gender, and the World* (New York: Harper Collins, 2005), chapter 11; Abbie Hoffman quote is on p. 199. Elijah Wald, *How the Beatles Destroyed Rock and Roll: An Alternative History of American Popular Music* (New York: Oxford University Press, 2009), 232–237.

38 Richard Goldstein, "Monterey Pop Festival: The Hip Homunculus," *The Village Voice*, June 29, 1967. Peter Doggett, *There's a Riot Goin' On: Revolutionaries, Rock*

Stars, and the Rise and Fall of the 60s (New York: Canongate, 2007), 105–106. "The Hippie Movement," uncredited, *KRLA Beat*, July 1, 1967.

39 Goldstein, "Monterey Pop Festival." For a more critical, contemporary analysis of the advent of the "hippie" and "The Hip Community," see Richard Goldstein, "The Flower Children and How They Grow," *Los Angeles Times*, May 28, 1967.

40 Michael J. Kramer, *The Republic of Rock: Music and Citizenship in the Sixties Counterculture* (New York: Oxford University Press, 2013), 18–19. For a contemporary, critical yet insightful analysis of the burgeoning hippie/counterculture phenomenon, see Goldstein, "The Flower Children and How They Grow." For other, contemporary accounts, see Jacoba Atlas, "Hippies: How? Why? What Does It Mean?," *KRLA Beat*, August 26, 1967, and Jim Delehant. "Birth of the San Francisco Scene," *Hit Parader*, August 1967.

41 "The Sound of the Sixties," 94.

42 "The Sound of the Sixties." "Hear That Big Sound," *Life*, May 21, 1965.

43 Goodman, *The Mansion on the Hill*, 23. Also, phone conversation with the book's author, Fred Goodman, October 12, 2018.

44 *Billboard*, 1968 Record Talent Edition, Who's Who in the World of Music, section 2, December 30, 1967. *Billboard*, 1969 Record Talent Edition, Who's Who in the World of Music, section 2, December 28, 1968.

45 For an early exploration of the "San Francisco Sound" from one of the earliest, serious magazines of rock music criticism, see Gene Sculatti, "San Francisco Bay Rock," *Crawdaddy!*, October 1966.

46 Levon Helm, "Rock Now Has a History," *The Acorn*, September 19, 1969. Of course, this article wasn't actually written by Levon Helm, singer-songwriter-drummer for The Band. Rather, it was written by David Hinckley, a writer for and editor of the student-run newspaper at Drew University. He signed the artist's name as a lark—and, as he told me recently, for lack of faculty supervision: "I look back and cringe at some of the things we were doing." Interview with the author.

47 Helm, "Rock Now Has a History." See also "Oldies-but-Evergreens," *Cashbox*, April 27, 1968, 3.

48 Claude Hall, "Rock Big Thing on Campus," *Billboard*, November 26, 1966, 1, 30.

49 Hank Fox, "Rock Takes Over as Colleges' Mod Look," *Billboard*, March 11, 1967, 16. Aaron Sternfield, "College Concert Dates Sell Records," *Billboard*, April 8, 1967, 58.

50 Sternfield, "College Concert Dates, 58. See also "College Bookstore, Golden Opportunity for Rack Jobbers," *Billboard*, April 8, 1967, 37–39.

51 "Top Artists on Campus," *Billboard*, Campus Attractions, April 13, 1968, 8.

52 Lipsitz, "Who'll Stop the Rain?," 161.

53 Aaron Sternfield, "Collegians Set the Pace," *Billboard*, Campus Attractions, April 13, 1968, 4. Campus Attractions replaced Music on Campus with this inaugural issue.

54 Katie Anastas, "Underground Newspapers: The Social Media Networks of the 1960s and 1970s," *Mapping American Social Movements Project*, University of Washington, accessed July 10, 2021, http://depts.washington.edu/moves/altnews _geography.shtml. Katie Anastas and James Lewes, "Mapping the Underground/ Alternative Press, 1965–1975," accessed July 10, 2021, http://depts.washington.edu /moves/altnews_map.shtml.

55 Interview with Ken Schulman, July 3, 2018. Jack Newfield, Nat Hentoff, I. F. Stone, and William Kunstler, "LNS," *The New York Review of Books*, Letters to the Editor, September 21, 1968.

56 Paul Zakaras, "Big Ten Broadcasters Air Gripes on Record Service," *Billboard*, Music on Campus, Campus Radio Report, March 19, 1966, 34. Ray Brack, "Servicing College Stations, Problem-Fraught, but Profitable Task," *Billboard*, Music on Campus, Campus Radio Report, March 19, 1966, 35. David C. Schattenstein, "College Broadcasters Know Local Commercial Market," *Billboard*, Music on Campus, March 19, 1966, 38.

57 "Radio Stations on Campus," *Billboard*, Music on Campus, March 19, 1966, 31. Hank Fox, "It's NOT All Jazz and Folk," *Billboard*, Music on Campus, March 19, 1966, 42.

58 Paul Brown, "The Record Company and College Radio," *Billboard*, Campus Attractions, March 22, 1969, 32.

59 The rhetoric of revolution was ubiquitous during the era and subsequent attempts to deal with and explain its use have, so far as I can tell, failed to achieve a consensus. One historian explains it this way: "Revolution was experienced as a collective dream; it did not have policies or programmes. It owed more to aesthetics than ideologies and its politics were acted out within the industries that produced it." See John Street, "Rock, Pop, and Politics," in *The Cambridge Companion to Pop and Rock*, 244. See also Nick Bromell, *Tomorrow Never Knows: Rock and Psychedelics in the 1960s* (Chicago: University of Chicago Press, 2000). Doggett, *There's a Riot Goin' On*.

60 Eisen, *The Age of Rock*, xiv. Eisen, as a student at Antioch College, launched the underground paper *The Activist*. He ended up finishing his undergraduate education at Oberlin and took *The Activist* with him, evidently. Eisen made clear the paper was a publication of the Students for a Democratic Society (SDS) and had no affiliation with Oberlin.

61 Grossberg, "Reflections," 34. Part of that complexity involves an ever-present tension between the authenticity of rock music and its commercial basis. As historian Keir Keightley has argued, "Rock may wear subcultural clothes, identify with marginalized minorities, promote countercultural political positions, and upset genteel notions of propriety, but from its inception it has been a large-scale, industrially organized, mass-mediated, mainstream phenomenon operating at the center of society." Keightley, *The Cambridge Companion to Pop and Rock*, 126–127.

62 Interview with Bob Johnson, July 11, 2018. Other interviews with former students at Drew include Ken Schulman, David Hinckley, Greg Granquist, Tom McMullen, Barry Fenstermacher, Doug Chapman, Bob Smartt, Dave Marsden, Harry Litwack, Don Orlando, Glenn Redbord, and Jeff King. See also Thelin, *Going to College in the Sixties*, 107–108.

Chapter 3 "I Blundered My Way Through"

1 "Hear That Big Sound," uncredited, *Life*, May 21, 1965, 82–91.

2 Thomas Thompson, "Music Streams," *Life*, May 21, 1965, 93–94.

3 "The Sound of the Sixties," uncredited, *Time*, May 21, 1965.

4 Aaron Sternfield, "The College Campus, Record Marketplace, Talent Proving Ground," *Billboard*, Music on Campus, March 27, 1965, 7.

5 Sternfield, "The College Campus."

6 Aaron Sternfield, "There's More Money on College Campus Than There Is in Las Vegas," *Billboard*, Music on Campus, March 27, 1965, 14.

7 Claude Hall, "They're Rockin' in the Ivory Tower," *Billboard*, Music on Campus, April 8, 1967, 26.

8 Paul Ackerman, "Alexander Observes the College Scene," *Billboard*, Music on Campus, March 19, 1966, 76.

9 "S.A.B. Organized, Activities Planned," uncredited, *The Statesman*, October 14, 1964, 1. Marilyn Vilagi, "Allison Jazz: Mood Music," *The Statesman*, September 30, 1964, 9. David Fersh, "Peter, Paul and Mary—A Triumphant Trio," *The Statesman*, October 14, 1964, 10. Bob Levine, "Moan Along with Mary," *The Statesman*, October 14, 1964, 10. Student responses in *The Statesman* capture the seriousness and scrutiny, the support and criticism that was commonplace on the campus. See, in particular, the comments of a young Richard ("Richie") Meltzer, "SAB, What and Why?," *The Statesman*, October 28, 1964, 3. Joel Kleinberg, SAB chairman, "—Activities Board Organizes," *The Statesman*, October 28, 1964, 8–9. *Specula*, 1965, 101.

10 Interview with Howie Klein, November 8, 2020. Howie Klein, "S.A.B.: An Exercise in 'Student Power,'" *The Statesmen*, October 4, 1966, 5.

11 "Moderator Still Unknown," uncredited, *The Statesman*, May 4, 1965, 1. "Behind the Shades with S. Pearlman," uncredited, *The Statesman*, May 11, 1965, 4. "S.A.B. Selections Released," uncredited, *The Statesman*, May 25, 1965, 1. Karl Boughan, "A Meaningless Election," *The Statesman*, May 18, 1965, 5. "Vietnam Dilemma: Forum and Teach-In," uncredited, *The Statesman*, May 25, 1965, 2. Karl Boughan, "The Sociology of Music, *The Statesman*, The Music Box, October 19, 1965, 6. Jean Schnall, "Across the Nation," *The Statesman*, May 25, 1965, 2. Steve Sidorsky, "12 × 5," *The Statesman*, November 9, 1965, 5. See also Elaine Cross, "'The Spectrum of Folk,' Three Primary Colors," *The Statesman*, November 9, 1965, 5. *Specula*, 1966, 64–65.

12 Klein, "S.A.B., an Exercise in 'Student Power.'" Also, interviews with Norm Prusslin, November 9, 2020, and Charles Backfish, April 21, 2020, both former students.

13 Richard Meltzer, *A Whore Just Like the Rest* (Boston: Da Capo Press, 2000).

14 Interview with Howie Klein, May 23, 2021. Interview with Norm Prusslin.

15 Interview with Howie Klein.

16 Peter A. Perrone, "The Facts about The Fugs," *The Statesman*, Letters to the Editor, May 10, 1966, 5. *Specula*, 1966, 75. Neil Akins, "EC Acts Unconstitutionally in Fug Concert Procedure," *The Statesman*, April 26, 1966, 24.

17 Leonard Shames, Barry Brown, Harold Feinberg, Stephen Capsos, "The Fugs and Thanks," *The Statesman*, Letters to the Editor, May 24, 1966, 4.

18 Howie Klein, "Howie Klein's Fact about the Fugs," *The Statesman*, May 24, 1966, 5.

19 Patrick Burke, "The Fugs, the Lower East Side, and the Slum Aesthetic in 1960s Rock," *The Journal of the Society for American Music* 8, no. 14 (2014): 541.

20 Kimbrew McLeod, *The Downtown Pop Underground: New York City and Literary Punks, Renegade Artists, DIY Filmmakers, Mad Playwrights, and Rock 'n' Roll Glitter Queens Who Revolutionized Culture* (New York: Abrams Press, 2018), 137–141. Ginsberg's *Howl* is quoted on p. 138. See also Jon Kalish, "The Fugs: At the Forefront of the Counterculture," *All Things Considered*, NPR, April 6, 2010, accessed July 20, 2021, https://www.npr.org/templates/story/story.php?storyId=125628216; and Jon Kalish, "'Fug You': The Wild Side of Ed Sanders," *Weekend Edition Saturday*, NPR, May 4, 2012, accessed July 20, 2021, https://www.npr.org/2012/05/05/152029486/fug-you-the-wild-life-of-ed-sanders.

21 Howie Klein, "Klein's Facts about the Fugs," *The Statesman*, May 24, 1966, 5.

22 Klein.

23 Klein.

24 Interview with Howie Klein. Meltzer, *A Whore Just Like the Rest*, 12. Jon Pareles, "Sandy Pearlman, Producer, Manager, and Lyricist for Blue Öyster Cult, Dies at 72," *The New York Times*, July 26, 2016.

25 McLeod, *The Downtown Pop Underground*, chapter 4 and pp. 181–182.

26 Advertisement for comedian Dick Gregory, *The Statesman*, April 19, 1966, 9.

27 Steve Sidorsky, "Blues Bag, Proverbial History of the Blues," *The Statesman*, November 22, 1966, 7.

28 Interview with Howie Klein. Klein email to the author, July 25, 2021. Klein actually explained this to the student body in a separate letter to the editor; see Howie Klein, "Concert Poll Results," *The Statesman*, Letters to the Editor, November 15, 1966, 4.

29 That debut album, universally considered a landmark rock album, is littered with R & B, jazz, pop, and blues influences. For a contemporary review, see Paul Williams, "Rock Is Rock: A Discussion of a Doors Song," *Crawdaddy!*, May 1967, 42. The review is also in Paul Williams, ed., *The* Crawdaddy! *Book* (Milwaukee, WI: Hal Leonard Corporation, 2002), 166–167.

30 Interview with Howie Klein.

31 Interview with Howie Klein. Blue Öyster Cult has an interesting history explicitly tied to Stony Brook. The creation of Sandy Pearlman, he and Meltzer conceived of and wrote the material for the band, initially naming it Soft White Underbelly.

32 Ilene Zatal, "Doors Almost 'Light Fire'; Large Crowd," *The Statesman*, September 27, 1967, 1. "Concert Problems," uncredited, *The Statesman*, September 27, 1967, 6. "SAB Concert Roasted," uncredited, *The Statesman*, September 27, 1967, 6. For a review of the concert, see John Eskow, "Doors 'Orchestrate Latent Psychoses' of Audience," *The Statesman*, September 27, 1967, 9.

33 Interview with Howie Klein.

34 Madeline Tropp, "SAB Chrmn Defends Concert," *The Statesman*, October 4, 1967, 7. This letter also laid out in detail how the SAB was organized and how it worked. The SAB now consisted of fifteen members and eleven subcommittees, chaired by eleven of the members of the SAB. One of those subcommittees was the concert committee, chaired by Howie Klein. See also "The S.A.B.—From Those Who Know," uncredited, *The Statesman*, December 6, 1967, 11.

35 Jane and Mitch, "Soul Brothers," *The Statesman*, October 11, 1967, 9. Next to the review of this concert was a thoughtful tribute to Woody Guthrie, who had passed away the previous week. See "The Passing of the Man," uncredited, *The Statesman*, October 11, 1967, 9.

36 "S.A.B. Sponsors Fall Weekend," uncredited, *The Statesman*, October 18, 1967, 1.

37 This brief listing leaves out the atypical summer concert by The Grateful Dead.

38 Interview with Norm Prusslin.

39 See Aaron Sternfield, "Protecting the Callow Undergrad," *Billboard*, Music on Campus, April 8, 1967, 42.

40 John Osbourne, "Chilson's 37 Friends Give Big Folk Sing," *The Acorn*, February 28, 1966, 2. Tom McMullen, "Drew's 'Straymen' Form a Most Exceptional Band," *The Acorn*, March 7, 1966.

41 "Student Association Elections," uncredited, *The Acorn*, April 18, 1966, 1.

42 Interview with Glenn Redbord, August 6, 2018.

43 Interview with Glenn Redbord. Lack of administration involvement did not mean lack of accountability to the students who ran these programs. Despite little to no administration oversight, the Social Committee made money, and even left a surplus in the budget for the following year, a pattern repeated in the following several years. Additionally, students published the numbers in *The Acorn*, the student-run newspaper.

44 Sternfield, "Protecting the Callow Undergrad," 42.

45 Interview with Greg Granquist, April 2, 2018.

46 Interview with Glenn Redbord.

47 "Chad and Jeremy This Saturday," *The Acorn*, September 22, 1966. "Rascals in Concert with Happenings," *The Acorn*, January 27, 1967.

48 Interview with Glenn Redbord.

49 Full-page ad for The Animals, *The Acorn*, February 17, 1967, 8.

50 Full-page ad for The Lovin' Spoonful, *The Acorn*, April 21, 1967, 8. Stuart Horn, "Burdon Betters Band," *The Acorn*, March 10, 1967. Frances Edwards, "New Style Not Enough to Ruin Eric Burdon and New Animals," *The Acorn*, March 10, 1967.

51 Interview with Bob Johnson, July 11, 2018. On the prevalence of rock festivals, see *Billboard*, Music on Campus, March 19, 1966, 30, and *Billboard*, Music on Campus, April 8, 1967, 106. See also Terry Anderson, *The Movement and the Sixties: Protest in America from Greensboro to Wounded Knee* (New York: Oxford University Press, 1995), 176–177.

52 "Spoonful to Come in the Spring," uncredited, *The Acorn*, April 7, 1967. "Poet Ginsberg Reads on Reading Week Eve," uncredited, *The Acorn*, April 21, 1967.

53 C. R. Burns, "Carolyn Hester: Texas Songbird," *East Texas Historical Journal* 51, no. 2 (2013): 67.

54 Bob Dylan, *Chronicles* (New York: Simon & Schuster, 2004), 277.

55 Margaret Moser, "Double-Barrel Beauty: How Carolyn Hester of Waco Rose to the Height of the Folk Revival, Gave Bob Dylan His Break, and Lived to Tell the Tale," *The Austin Chronicle*, December 19, 2008. Bob Thompson, "The Ballad of Carolyn Hester," *The Washington Post*, January 12, 2005. Don Heckman, "Folk Singer Carolyn Hester Is Back—Still Feisty, Full of Concerns," *The Los Angeles Times*, February 11, 1989. Interestingly, a brief biography of Hester is included in an encyclopedic volume on the counterculture. See Gina Misiroglu, ed., *American Countercultures: An Encyclopedia of Nonconformists, Alternative Lifestyles, and Radical Ideas in U.S. History* (New York: Routledge Press, 2009), 376.

56 Keith Altham, "The Lovin' Spoonful: Nice, Abnormal Spoonful!," *New Musical Express*, April 22, 1966. Chris Welch, "The Lovin' Spoonful: Spoonful—The Most on the Coast," *Melody Maker*, April 23, 1966. Julie Besonen, "An Anthem for Every Urban Summer," *The New York Times*, August 12, 2018.

57 Ginsberg's biographer writes, "By 1967, he was a national figure . . . famous for being famous," and that he had become "guru to the burgeoning youth movement." Barry Miles, *Ginsberg: A Biography* (New York: Harper Perennial, 1989), 372–373. Gary Pacernick, "Allen Ginsberg: An Interview by Gary Pacernick," February 10, 1996, accessed Augusts 19, 2018, https://www.thefreelibrary.com/All an+Ginsberg%3A+an+interview+by+Gary+Pacernick.-a019918392. Some, like historian Terry Anderson, use descriptive language such as "cultural activist" and

"political activist" to describe people like comedian Dick Gregory (who also spoke at Drew), folk singer Phil Ochs, and Ginsberg, while also explaining how both types were thoroughly intertwined in all sorts of ways. See Anderson, *The Movement and the Sixties*, 142.

58　The ads announcing Judy Collins are in *The Acorn*, September 29, 1967. For a review of the show, see Penny Peterson, "I Like Judy Collins' Voice," *The Acorn*, October 6, 1967. The ad announcing The Four Tops is in *The Acorn*, November 3, 1967. Robert Manson, "Tops Turn Audience on 'Full,'" *The Acorn*, November 14, 1967. For the ad promoting Warhol's visit, see "Warhol to Explain His Creations in Action," *The Acorn*, October 6, 1967.

59　Other well-known artists, thinkers, and public figures making a stop at Drew during these years included: Seymour Melman (as part of a "think-in" on campus), Floyd McKissick (leader of CORE, 1966), Ralph Nader, Ted Sorensen (a JFK speechwriter), Dick Gregory (legendary comedian and activist), Roy Innis (leader of CORE), Strom Thurmond, Sydney Hook, Ralph Ellison (African American author of *Invisible Man*), Abbie Hoffman, Nat Hentoff, Jerry Rubin, William Kunstler (famed civil rights attorney), and Pete Seeger.

60　For coverage of the show and subsequent controversy surrounding Warhol, see Sharon Manitta, "People React to 'Nothing,'" *The Acorn*, October 13, 1967; Shepard Bliss, "Warhol Another Christ?," Letters to the Editor, *The Acorn*, October 13, 1967, 5; "Warhol Show Controversial," uncredited, *The Acorn*, Year End Review, 1967, 3; "To Be or Not to Be," uncredited, *The Acorn*, October 13, 1967; "Warhol Evokes Disapproval," uncredited, *The Acorn*, October 13, 1967; and Tom Doremus, "Shaddup and Pass the Coin," *The Acorn*, October 20, 1967.

61　Interview with David Hinckley, June 18, 2018. Interview with Bob Johnson.

62　"University Celebrates Hundredth Birthday," uncredited, *The Acorn*, November 3, 1967, 6–7.

63　Paul Williams, "What Goes On?," *Crawdaddy!*, July/August 1967, 27.

64　Williams, "What Goes On?"

65　"The Sound of the Sixties."

66　Williams, "What Goes On?"

67　Mike Gross, "'Rocksteria' Grips New York as Clubs Sprout Up with Teen Acts," *Billboard*, April 16, 1966.

Chapter 4　"They're Rockin' in the Ivory Tower"

1　Claude Hall, "They're Rockin' in the Ivory Tower," *Billboard*, Music on Campus, April 8, 1967, 26. Eliot Tiegel, "Student Power Leads to Campus Rock Revolution," *Billboard*, Campus Attractions, March 28, 1970, 16.

2　Michael Dorman, "A Drug Raid on Campus," *Newsday*, November 15, 1998.

3　Francis X. Clines, "Stony Brook Fears Distrust Left by Raid May Do More Harm Than Narcotic Problem," *The New York Times*, March 11, 1968, 44. The Columbia dean's quote is from "University Doubts Truths of Rumors on Narcotics Raid," uncredited, *The Daily Spectator*, February 8, 1968.

4　Quoted in Thelin, *Going to College in the Sixties*, 95–96.

5　Foster and Long, *Protest!*, 62 and 578. Thelin, *Going to College in the Sixties*, 94–96.

6　Peter Braunstein and Michael William Doyle, eds., *Imagine Nation: The American Counterculture of the 1960s & 1970s* (New York: Routledge Press, 2002), 8.

7   Helen Lefkowitz Horowitz, "The 1960s and the Transformation of Campus Cultures," *History of Education Quarterly* 26, no. 1 (Spring 1986): 26.

8   Foster and Long, *Protest!*, 140.

9   Interview with Glenn Redbord, August 6, 2018.

10 See especially John McMillian, *Smoking Typewriters: The Sixties Underground Press and the Rise of Alternative Media in America* (New York: Oxford University Press, 2011), 36, 71–74. And, of course, Abe Peck's *Uncovering the Sixties: The Life and Times of the Underground Press* (New York: Citadel Press, 1991).

11 The content referenced here is spread out over many articles, letters, editorials, and ads. *The Acorn* Year End Review, 1967–1968 and *The Acorn* Year End Review, 1969–1970 provide a useful catalog and summaries. See specifically "Campus Politics During Year Mostly Anti-War, Anti-Johnson," *The Acorn*, Year End Supplement, 1967–1968, and "Blackness—Our Essence," *The Acorn* special supplement, February 26, 1971. In 1967, a group of Drew students boarded a bus and attended the antiwar demonstration at the Pentagon. See Sueann Chase, "Busload from Drew Numbered Among Pentagon Protestors," *The Acorn*, October 30, 1968.

12 Interview with David Hinckley, June 18, 2018. See also Ray Mungo, *Famous Long Ago: My Life and Hard Times with the Liberation News Service* (New York: Citadel Press, 1970); Peck, *Uncovering the Sixties*, 71–72; McMillian, *Smoking Typewriters*, chapter 4.

13 Interview with Bob Johnson, July 11, 2018.

14 Interview with Jeff King, June 2, 2018. Former students I interviewed from classes earlier than 1968 recalled a more staid and traditional campus culture, while those from the classes of 1968 and later recall a campus culture in rapid and significant change.

15 Richard Puz, "The Nack, and How We Lost Him," *The Statesman*, May 14, 1968, 4.

16 Interview with Nancy Malagold, June 18, 2021. Thelin also finds crowding to have been among the most significant problems.

17 Newfield quoted in McMillian, *Smoking Typewriters*, 84.

18 Mungo, *Famous Long Ago*, 7.

19 Mungo, *Famous Long Ago*, 8. Sol Stern, "A Short Account of International Student Politics and the Cold War, with Particular Reference to the NSA, CIA, Etc.," *Ramparts*, March 1967, 29–39. The CIA's role in the NSA represented the cutting edge of Cold War liberalism, the perfect combination of "hard-line anti-communism in foreign affairs and dynamic liberalism on domestic issues," according to one history. See Hugh Wilford, *The Mighty Wurlitzer: How the CIA Played America* (Cambridge, MA: Harvard University Press, 2008), 133. Karen M. Paget, *Patriotic Betrayal: The Inside Story of the CIA's Secret Campaign to Enroll American Students in the Crusade Against Communism* (New Haven, CT: Yale University Press, 2015).

20 LNS membership grew to nearly 800 subscribers a few years later. Jack Newfeld, Nat Hentoff, I. F. Stone, and William Kunstler, "LNS," *The New York Review of Books*, Letter to the Editors, September 21, 1972. Harvey Wasserman, "The Joy of Liberation News Service," in *Insider Histories of the Vietnam Era Underground Press*, vol. 1, ed. Ken Wachsberger (East Lansing: Michigan State University Press, 2011): 139–156. McMillian, *Smoking Typewriters*, 103. Peck, *Uncovering the Sixties*, 71–72.

21 Interview with David Hinckley. Interview with Ken Schulman, July 30, 2018.

22 Joe Hagan, *Sticky Fingers: The Life and Times of Jann Wenner and Rolling Stone Magazine* (New York: Alfred A. Knopf, 2017), 56–58. Quoted in Abe Peck, *Uncovering the Sixties*, 174.

23 Interview with Ken Schulman. All the men I interviewed were young at the time and commented on the threat they felt from the Vietnam War, the threat of being drafted.

24 A useful, detailed summary of the events of spring 1968 is John Prados, *Vietnam: The History of an Unwinnable War, 1945–1975* (Lawrence: University of Kansas Press, 2009), 241–249. Anderson, *The Movement and the Sixties*, 190–192.

25 Doggett, *There's a Riot Goin' On*, 149–160. Maurice Isserman and Michael Kazin, *America Divided: The Civil War of the 1960s* (New York: Oxford University Press, 2000), 227–228. For some reactions in *The Acorn*, see "'Some Will Have to Sacrifice,'" *The Acorn*, April 19, 1968, and Shepard Bliss, "Epistle from Chicago," *The Acorn*, April 19, 1968.

26 Ralph Gleason, "The Final Paroxysm of Fear," *Rolling Stone*, April 6, 1968.

27 Gleason, "The Final Paroxysm of Fear."

28 *Operation Stony Brook*, Police Department, County of Suffolk, NY, January 17, 1968. I obtained a copy of the booklet after an FOIA request. It arrived substantially redacted.

29 "Grand Jury's Term Extended for Drug Probe," uncredited, *The Long Island Advance*, February 15, 1968.

30 "Trouble at Stony Brook," *The Suffolk County News*, uncredited editorial, December 26, 1968. See also Bernie Gould, "Rural Long Island Campus Goes to 'Pot,'" *Ogdensburg Journal*, February 6, 1968.

31 "Trouble at Stony Brook."

32 Report of the New York State Joint Legislative Committee on Crime, Its Causes, Control and Effect on Society on the Drug Abuse Problem at the State University of New York at Stony Brook, May 20, 1968, 11. See also Charles Dumas, "Legislature Fires on State University," *Adirondack Daily Enterprise*, January 25, 1968, 2. Daniel Lasser, "Charges Fly in State Drug Hearings," *The Spectrum*, February 6, 1968. "34 at Unit of SU Taken in Drug Raid," uncredited, *Press-Republican*, January 18, 1968. Bernie Gould, "The Stony Brook University Drug Story," *Adirondack Daily Enterprise*, February 7, 1968, 10. Sharon Cooke, "NY Crime Hearings Continue; Prof John Herr Is Grilled," *The Statesman*, February 9, 1968. Sharon Cooke, "Stony Brook Students Receive Praise from O'Brien, Diamond," *The Statesman*, April 26, 1968. "DeFrancesco Faces Grand Jury," uncredited, *The Statesman*, May 14, 1968. Sharon Cooke, "Hughes Hearings End; Gutman Has Last Word, *The Statesman*, February 16, 1968. Sharon Cooke, "N.Y. Crime Hearings Drag On; DeFrancesco, Fox Are Heard," *The Statesman*, February 13, 1968.

33 Lance Phillips, "Police Want SUSB Drug Pushers—Barry," *The Long Island Advance*, February 8, 1968. Alex Rankin, "Albany Open Line," *The Williamson (N.Y.) Sun and the Williamson Sentinel*, February 8, 1968, 7. "A.B.," uncredited, *The Statesman*, February 6, 1968, 4. Sandy Petrey, "Legalize Marijuana," *The Statesman*, February 6, 1968, 3. Ron Atlas, "A Pound of Flesh," *The Statesman*, February 9, 1968, 1. The campus paper also reprinted national coverage highlighting the national drug interdiction by officials as a sham. See "The Indecent

Society," reprinted from *The New Republic*, *The Statesman*, February 6, 1968, 4. Michael and Robert F. Cohen, "Guifredda Denounces SUSB, Lewis Attacks Resolution," *The Statesman*, February 23, 1968.

34 Report of the New York State Joint Legislative Committee on Crime, Its Causes, Control and Effect on Society on the Drug Abuse Problem at the State University of New York at Stony Brook, May 20, 1968, 60–61.

35 Quote is from "After the Bust," *The Statesman*, uncredited Guest Editorial, April 30, 1968, 6, excerpted from *The Spectrum*. See also Marcia Milstein, "Boomerang Barry's Bust," *The Statesman*, October 8, 1968, 8.

36 Charles Dumas, "State University Draws Fire on Two Fronts: Drugs and Draft Evasion," *Ogdensburg Journal*, January 25, 1968. See also Donald M. Bybee, acting associate dean of students, "Drugs on Campus: Statement and View," *The Statesman*, February 8, 1967, 5.

37 *Operation Stony Brook*.

38 "Stony Brook Dean Gave Pot-Party Raid Tip," uncredited, *Press-Republican*, February 1, 1968, 2. "Stony Brook President Denies Charges of Non-cooperation in Drug Inquiry," uncredited, *The Spectrum*, February 2, 1968, 3. In a subsequent agreement between the university and the police commissioner, the latter agreed that "there is no evidence to support" the claim that a professor had tipped off the students at a pot party. See "Toll, Barry Make Deal," uncredited, *The Statesman*, March 8, 1968. Report of the New York State Joint Legislative Committee on Crime, Its Causes, Control and Effect on Society on the Drug Abuse Problem at the State University of New York at Stony Brook, May 20, 1968, 24.

39 Howie Klein, "Turns Out, My Prosecutor, Harry O'Brien, Was a Democrat," *Down with Tyranny* (blog), July 13, 2021, https://www.downwithtyranny.com/post/turns-out-my-persecutor-harry-o-brien-was-a-democrat. See also Howie Klein, "Narcs Tried Busting Me in 1968—One, Now a Chauffeur, Picked Me Up at the Airport This Week," *Down with Tyranny*, July 19, 2014, https://downwithtyranny.blogspot.com/2014/07/narcs-tried-busting-me-in-1968-one-now.html?m=0. Klein said he had been "kicked off campus" much earlier for dealing drugs.

40 Interview with Howie Klein, November 8, 2020. Check out p. 80 and 23 of *The Specula*, 1968, for a quote on the construction workers attacking student activists on campus; p. 88, 92–93 on the drug raid; p. 162 on Ali visit; p. 240 on Jackson Browne performing; p. 272 on subpoena.

41 Klein and several other Stony Brook students were arrested later that summer in an apartment in New York for various drug charges. See "9 Nabbed in Drug Raid," uncredited, *Press-Republican*, June 19, 1968, 2.

42 Freda Forman, "Allan [*sic*] Ginsberg Meets University Community," *The Statesman*, March 8, 1968. Clines, "Stony Brook Fears Distrust," 44. Federal Bureau of Investigation (FBI), The Vault, Irwin Allen Ginsberg, accessed August 23, 2021, https://vault.fbi.gov/irwin-allen-ginsberg/Irwin%20Allen%20Ginsberg%20Part%201%20of%201/view.

43 Interview with Howie Klein.

44 John Rockwell, "*Crawdaddy!* Party Mirrors Magazine," *The New York Times*, June 9, 1976.

45 Pearlman initially named the band Soft White Underbelly after a Winston Churchill remark during World War II.

46   Interview with Howie Klein, May 23, 2021.

47   Richard Meltzer, The Aesthetics of Rock. (New York: Da Capo Press, 1987) and A Whore Just Like the Rest. (New York: Da Capo Press, 2000). Interview with Klein.

48   Not at all coincidentally, these same acts performed at Stony Brook more than once. Frank Mastroplo, "The Anderson Theater Forgotten Forerunner of the Fillmore East," Bedford & Bowery, January 22, 2018, https://bedfordandbowery .com/2018/01/the-anderson-theater-forgotten-forerunner-of-the-fillmore-east/.

49   "SAB Institutes New Program to Train Prospective Members," uncredited, The Statesman, March 8, 1968. "Student Activities Board Appointed, New Members Approved by Selection Committee," uncredited, The Statesman, May 14, 1968.

50   Interview with Howie Klein, November 8, 2020. Klein pointed out that while the industry had developed around "big bands," like The Four Tops, it hadn't developed for rock bands. Thus, while a big band, meaning an established, popular one, cost $3,000–$4,000, he routinely booked rock bands for half that or much less. He paid $400 for The Doors and $750 for Jefferson Airplane, for instance.

51   Interview with Howie Klein. That concert was also the occasion for Klein to meet Danny Fields, at the time publicist for Elektra Records, The Doors's label. This was his entrée into the music business.

52   Interview with Howie Klein. Jesse McKinley, "Howard Solomon, 75, Owner of Famed Village Nightclub," The New York Times, June 16, 2004, accessed August 16, 2021, https://www.nytimes.com/2004/06/16/us/howard-solomon-75 -owner-of-famed-village-nightclub.html. See also "Cafe AU Go Go, New York City 152 Bleecker Street Rock: Performance List July–October 1969," Rock Prosopography 101 (blog), January 8, 2010, accessed August 16, 2021, http:// rockprosopography101.blogspot.com/2010/01/cafe-au-go-go-new-york-city-152 _6672.html. Charles R. Cross, Room Full of Mirrors: A Biography of Jimi Hendrix (New York: Hyperion, 2005), 210–211. Howie Klein, "Condemned by the DAR: Jimi Hendrix," The Statesman, March 1, 1968.

53   Of course, for Graham, the Fillmore East came with its own East Coast complica-tions, like cops, unions, biker gangs, and, most seriously of all, East Village activist group the Motherf-ckers, who opposed Graham as an outsider and a capitalist. See Bill Graham and Robert Greenfield, Bill Graham Presents: My Life Inside Rock (New York: Doubleday, 1992), 253–257. Patrick Burke, "The Fugs, the Lower East Side, and the Slum Aesthetic of 60s Rock," Journal of the Society for American Music 8, no. 4 (2014): 538–566. Paul Nelson, "The Motherfuckers: Occupy Nightclub! A Blow-by-Blow Account of the Battle between the Owners of the Fillmore East and Hardcore Hippies," The Rolling Stone, February 15, 1969. Additionally, Graham very intentionally promoted a diverse and broad range of performances, from rock, folk, and blues to country and western, jazz, and even stand-up comedy. Michael Lydon, "Bill Graham: The Producer of the New Rock," The New York Times, December 15, 1968.

54   "Stations Playing Progressive Rock," uncredited, Billboard, March 2, 1968, 22. Claude Hall, "FM'ers Busting Out with Progressive Rock Airplay," Billboard, March 30, 1968, 35.

55   Granquist managed to hang on to various documents from this process and pass them along to me. These "scratch sheets" are from University Attractions, Inc., 200 West 57th Street, New York, NY, and College Entertainment Agency, Inc.,

300 West 55th Street, New York, NY, and range from 1966 to 1968. Originals in the author's possession. Also, interviews with Greg Granquist (June 27, 2018) and Barry Fenstermacher (May 8, 2018).

56 These commitments are also detailed in *The Acorn*. Indeed, coverage of both the Vietnam War and Civil Rights is robust throughout these years.

57 As far as I can tell, when these bands played in the state of New Jersey, with rare exceptions they played only Drew University. Exceptions include John Mayall, who played Jersey City on March 12 and 13, 1969, and Chuck Berry, who did South Mountain Arena, West Orange, NJ, on May 30, 1969.

58 Interview with Greg Granquist, April 2, 2018. "Drew Only School Stop for Who," *The Acorn*, January 22, 1968.

59 Interview with Greg Granquist, April 2, 2018. "Who Making Their First Tour of U.S.," uncredited, *Billboard*, March 2, 1968, 18.

60 Interview with Greg Granquist, June 27, 2018.

61 Interview with Greg Granquist, April 2, 2018.

62 Interview with Greg Granquist, June 27, 2018.

63 The Richie Havens show was profitable for a couple reasons. The students booked him for around $2,000 and, related to that lower price, tickets were $2, rather than the $3.50–$4.50 price for The Who. "Richie Havens in Concert Here for Spring Weekend," uncredited, *The Acorn*, April 19, 1968; "Folk Rock Artist Havens Here Spring Weekend," uncredited, *The Acorn*, April 26, 1968; and "Havens: 'Sing What We All Know,'" uncredited, *The Acorn*, May 3, 1968.

64 Although much anecdotal evidence exists for this story, I was unable to verify it with complete confidence. On April 7, 1968, at the club Generation, other musicians performing at King's wake included B. B. King, Big Brother & the Holding Company, Buddy Guy, Jimi Hendrix, Joni Mitchell, Paul Butterfield, and Al Kooper.

65 Conversation with Greg Granquist, Madison, New Jersey, August 24, 2018. Both Barry Fentsermacher and Greg Granquist were impressed with Havens's humility and earnestness. Both told me of the singer's arriving at the train station in Madison and walking alone with his guitar on his back (others arrived by limousine) the half mile to the campus. He left after the show the same way.

66 Interview with Greg Granquist, April 2, 2018.

67 In addition to individual trips to Fillmore East for concerts, groups of Drew students went numerous times, and *The Acorn* published reviews of the concerts held there. See, for example: Mark Ransom, "Traffic Show Off," *The Acorn*, September 27, 1968; Mark Ransom, "At the Fillmore: The Bluesmen, as Usual, Excel," *The Acorn*, November 8, 1968; David Marsden, "After Drew, What?," *The Acorn*, September 12, 1969; Clay Horsey, "At the Fillmore: C.S.N. & Y. show," *The Acorn*, September 26, 1969.

68 The *Life* article, in fact the entire issue, is expansive, covering Jefferson Airplane, Country Joe & the Fish, Cream, The Who, Frank Zappa & the Mothers of Invention, and others in some detail. The writing is also provocative and rhapsodic. To wit, "The *Jefferson Airplane* flies the runways of the mind and the airways of the imagination." "The New Rock: Music That's Hooked the Whole Vibrating World," *Life*, June 28, 1968.

69 Jeff Tamarkin, *Got a Revolution: The Turbulent Flight of the Jefferson Airplane* (New York: Atria Books, 2003), 173, 175–176.

70 Cathi Grumbine, "Social Committee Exposed—But Not Too Much," *The Acorn*, September 27, 1968. For a contemporary review of Earth Opera, see Paul Williams, "The Way We Are Today: Earth Opera & Joni Mitchell," *Crawdaddy*, August 30, 1968. "Airplane to Play for Packed House," uncredited, *The Acorn*, October 4, 1968.

71 One of the Drew students I interviewed recalled the importance of FM radio, and New York's WNEW in particular, in his own discovery of rock music in 1968, lauding the playing of "album rock," also known as Album Oriented Rock, or AOR. If you were listening to rock in the New York area, that was the station, according to Bob Johnson, at least "among the people who were serious about this new music that was emerging." Interview with Bob Johnson. Incidentally, the radio station adopted its rock format in October 1967, among the earliest in the nation to do so. See the New York Radio Archive, accessed August 31, 2018, http://www.nyradioarchive.com/index.html. See also Richard Neer, *FM: The Rise and Fall of Rock Radio* (New York: Villard, 2001), 52, 62.

72 Interview with Greg Granquist, April 2, 2018.

73 The show was reviewed as outstanding, in spite of the crowd's insufficient enthusiasm. Mark Ransom, "Airplane, Opera Excel," *The Acorn*, October 11, 1968, 6.

74 In addition to local and regional press coverage of these events, I interviewed several residents of the house, including Billy Shaw, Tom Wetzler, and, nominal leader of the communal living arrangement, Bob Courboin. I also interviewed Doug Chapman and Barbara North, both regular visitors at the house.

75 "Jefferson 'Airplane' Finds a Home in Madison," uncredited, *The Madison-Florham Park Eagle*, July 2, 1968.

76 Interview with Tom Wetzler, September 24, 2018.

77 Interview with Tom Wetzler.

78 Interview with Doug Chapman, October 14, 2019.

79 Interview with Barbara North, October 21, 2019. Barbara told me that the police had her and her mother go and speak separately with a detective. She believes the police did this with the other juveniles as well.

80 Interview with Tom Wetzler.

81 Interview with Tom Wetzler.

82 Tom Buckley, "Young Rebels Set Up Own Community in Jersey," *The New York Times*, August 26, 1968.

83 "Jefferson 'Airplane' Finds a Home in Madison," uncredited, *The Madison-Florham Eagle*, July 25, 1968.

84 "Jefferson 'Airplane' Finds a Home."

85 Interview with Bob Courboin, July 4, 2018. According to Courboin, employees at the Fillmore actually built the airplane themselves. Interview with Tom Wetzler and phone conversation with Billy Shaw. All three of these men resided in the house.

86 "Jefferson 'Airplane' Finds a Home."

87 "Madison Hippies Get Howe Warning," uncredited, *Madison-Florham Eagle*, August 15, 1968.

88 Gitlin, *The Sixties*, 216–217.

89 Interview with Bob Courboin.

90 "Hippie Haven: To Be or Not to Be," uncredited, *The Madison-Florham Park Eagle*, August 22, 1968.

91 "Complaints Sought," uncredited, *The Acorn*, October 18, 1968. Police cartoon in *The Acorn*, October 11, 1968. Mark Ransom, "Intolerance," *The Acorn*, October 18, 1968. "Townie Fined $85," uncredited, *The Acorn*, October 18, 1968. "On 'Greaser' Actions," uncredited, *The Acorn*, October 11, 1968. "Violence Against Drew People Looked Upon with Some Concern," uncredited, *The Acorn*, October 11, 1968. "Townies and Troubles," uncredited, *The Acorn Year End Supplement*, 1969.

92 The judge authorized the search warrant on July 29, 1968, to be carried out within ten days of issuance. Nevertheless, the raid was not conducted until September 27. Municipal Court of the Borough of Madison, County of Morris, The State of New Jersey vs. Robert Courboin Jr. and 47 Main Avenue, Madison, New Jersey, Search Warrant, Return, and Inventory, July 29, 1968. Courboin shared this document with me.

93 Buckley, "Young Rebels."

94 "Assault Charge Upheld in Court Special Session," *The Madison Eagle*, October 10, 1968. "Townie Fined $85," uncredited, *The Acorn*, October 11, 1968. "A Victory for Hate," uncredited, *The Acorn*, October 4, 1968. "Violence Against Drew People." David Hinckley, "Hippies Raided, Driven Out," *The Acorn*, October 4, 1968.

95 Hinckley, "Hippies Raided, Driven Out."

96 "A Victory for Hate," uncredited, *The Acorn*, October 4, 1968. The U.S. Census found Madison nearly 90 percent "white" as of 1970. See Campbell Gibson and Kay Jung, "Historical Census Statistics on Population Totals by Race, 1790 to 1990, and By Hispanic Origin, 1970 to 1990, for the United States, Regions, Divisions, and States," Population Division, U. S. Census Bureau, Washington, D.C., 20233, September 2002, Working Paper Series no. 56., accessed September 9, 2018, https://web.archive.org/web/20141224151538/http://www.census.gov/population/www/documentation/twps0056/twps0056.html.

97 Robert L. Way, "Police Arrest 120 at 'Hippie House,'" *The Daily Record*, September 28, 1968.

98 Hinckley, "Hippies Raided, Driven Out." Interview with Tom Wetzler.

99 *The Acorn* ran a front-page story on October 18, 1968, in a good example of the coverage. "Assault Charge Upheld in Court Special Session," uncredited, *Madison Eagle*, October 10, 1968.

100 Standing in front of St. Vincent's Church in Madison, police approached the students and told them to stop. The students did, and they walked back to campus. Back on campus, a police cruiser intercepted and arrested them there for handing out leaflets without a permit. "Two Students Picked Up for Leaflet Distribution," uncredited, *The Acorn*, February 2, 1968. John H. Fenton, "Dr. Spock Guilty with 3 Other Men in Antidraft Plot," *The New York Times*, June 15, 1968. "Complaints Sought," uncredited, *The Acorn*, October 18, 1968. Mark Ransom, "Intolerance," *The Acorn*, October 18, 1968, 8. "On 'Greaser' Actions," uncredited, *The Acorn*, October 11, 1968, 4. "Townie Fined $85," uncredited, *The Acorn*, October 11, 1968.

101 "Violence Against Drew People Looked Upon with Some Concern," uncredited, *The Acorn*, October 11, 1968, 4.

102 Ronald C. Eisele, "Objects to Harassment of Hippie," *Madison Eagle*, October 17, 1968.

103 Helen Meyers, "Neighbors Speak Out about 'Hippies,'" *The Daily Record*, October 3, 1968. "On Police 'Walk-In'," uncredited, *Madison Eagle*, October 10,

1968. Walter Berthold, "Police Book Juveniles for Associating with Hippies," *Madison Eagle*, October 3, 1968. "Raid on Hippies Deplored," editorial page, uncredited, *The Daily Record*, October 4, 1968. "Police Raid Hearings Set for Next Week," uncredited, *Madison-Florham Park Eagle*, October 24, 1968. Kenneth Haynes, "Question: Why Do They Hate Us So Much?," *Madison-Florham Park Eagle*, October 3, 1968. "Hippies Protest Madison Raid," uncredited, *The Daily Record*, September 30, 1968.

104   Interview with Barbara North, October 21, 2019.

105   Interview with Tom Wetzler, September 24, 2018.

106   Interview with Bob Courboin. Interview with Bob Johnson. Interview with Tom Wetzler. "Airplane Double Sell Out; Potential Audience Seen Large," uncredited, *The Acorn*, October 11, 1968.

107   A number of the attendees fled in various directions and got away. For some of the local press coverage of the "hippie house" issue and the police raid, see "Madison Hippies Get Howe Warning," uncredited, *The Madison-Florham Park Eagle*, August 15, 1968. Kenneth Haynes, "Question: 'Why Do They Hate Us So Much?'," *The Madison-Florham Park Eagle*, October 3, 1968. "Do You Really Need a House to Make a Home," uncredited, *The Madison-Florham Park Eagle*, October 17, 1968. Ronald Eisele, "Objects to Harassment of Hippies," *The Madison-Florham Park Eagle*, undated (but a response in the immediate aftermath of the raid). "Police Book Juveniles for Associating with Hippies," uncredited, *The Madison-Florham Park Eagle*, October 1, 1968.

108   "Court Kicks Out 'Hippie House,'" uncredited, *The Acorn*, October 18, 1968. Courboin told David Hinckley, "Our experiment in communal living has ended. It was not a failure, but to continue it here, in an atmosphere of hate, could have served no purpose." See Hinckley, "Hippies Raided, Driven Out."

109   See cover story, *The Acorn*, October 18, 1968.

110   "Iron Butterfly Flying In," uncredited, *The Acorn*, November 8, 1968. "Heavy Sound of Butterfly Comes Tomorrow Night," uncredited, *The Acorn*, November 15, 1968. "Butterfly Worthwhile," uncredited, *The Acorn*, November 15, 1968.

111   Interview with Greg Granquist, April 2, 2018.

112   "Heavy Sound of Butterfly."

113   Interview with Barry Fenstermacher.

114   Interview with Greg Granquist, April 2, 2018. The opening act is listed *The Acorn* as the King Biscuit Blues Band. The group shifted its name routinely, according to Granquist. Email from Greg Granquist, September 9, 2018.

115   Interview with Barry Fenstermacher.

116   Interview with Barry Fenstermacher.

117   Granquist continued, "It's fun to talk about now, but it was a horrific experience at the time." Interview with Greg Granquist, April 2, 2018, and June 27, 2018.

118   Ed Duzak, "Butterfly Worth the Wait," *The Acorn*, November 22, 1968, 6. The concert did lose money, and both Granquist and Fentstermacher viewed it as a disaster in terms of public relations. The social committee even went to the Dean and, together, Drew threatened to stop payment on the check of $1,500, a serious move. This might also mean the band would sue the university. In the end, none of this came to pass, and the story of what actually happened did not make it into *The Acorn* coverage. That story claims the delay resulted from a broken-down equipment truck not getting to Drew on time and the hotel manager driving the

one remaining band member to the show late—rather than Fentstermacher driving over to get him—and there is no mention of the drug use nor an ice bath. See "$1,500 Butterfly Payment Held," uncredited, *The Acorn*, November 22, 1968.

119 In addition to the acts and bands highlighted here, the Committee arranged for other performances, several per month, for dances and the like. Local bands, like The International Silver String Submarine Band and Clockwork Orange, as well as national acts such as The Shangri-Las and Sha Na Na performed.

120 Interview with Glenn Redbord, August 6, 2018; interview with Greg Granquist, June 27, 2018; interview with Barry Fentstermacher, May 8, 2018; interview with Don Orlando, June 25, 2018; interview with Jeff King, June 2, 2018.

121 Fred Kirby, "Collegians in the Forefront," *Billboard—Campus Attractions*, March 22, 1969, 4. See also Eliot Tiegel, "Student Power Leads to Campus Rock Revolution," *Billboard—Campus Attractions*, March 28, 1970, 16–22.

122 Richard Robinson, "Rock Group's Rocky Road to Campus," *Billboard—Campus Attractions*, March 22, 1969, 28. See also "The Built-In Audience," uncredited, *Cashbox*, November 9, 1968, 3.

123 Robinson, "Rock Group's Rocky Road to Campus."

124 Mark Ransom, "Hentoff Calls Legitimacy Key Issue," *The Acorn*, September 27, 1968, 5.

125 "Frank Barsalona: The Lisa Robinson Interview," *Billboard*, August 18, 1984, 11.

126 Chapple and Garofalo, *Rock 'n' Roll Is Here to Pay*, 137–147.

Chapter 5   The "Americanization of Rock"

1 Theodore Roszak, *The Making of a Counter Culture: Reflections on the Technocratic Society and Its Youthful Opposition* (New York: Anchor Books, 1969), quote on pp. 27–28. President Oxnam's comments are in *The Acorn*, September 19, 1969, 7.

2 Timothy Tyler, "The Cooling of America: Out of Tune and Lost in the Counter Culture," *Time*, February 22, 1971.

3 Michael Kramer, "Busted: Rethinking Columbia Records 'But the Man Can't Bust Our Music' Ad Campaign," June 14, 2019, accessed November 13, 2021, https://www.michaeljkramer.net/busted. Challenging Tom Frank's thesis of "the conquest of cool," Kramer argues the ad "is a testament to the power of uncertainty, flux, confusion, and weirdness itself surfacing in the everyday print culture of the historical moment of the late 1960s. We glimpse, perhaps, how countercultural ideas of something beyond corporate profit could oddly circulate precisely through the forces seeking that profit. They did so through absurdity, humor, and incongruity." Thomas Frank, *The Conquest of Cool: Business Culture, Counterculture, and the Rise of Hip Consumerism* (Chicago: University of Chicago Press, 1997), especially 7–9.

4 "Two Return from Spring Bust," uncredited, *The Acorn*, September 26, 1969, 2. Interview with Bob Smartt, August 17, 2018. In April, the head of the Morris County Narcotics Division gave a presentation on the campus in which he detailed the role of undercover agents—the division, he boasted, currently employed five—on college campuses. After providing much lurid and provocative detail to the students, he then declined to answer a student question about undercover agents at Drew. See Maxine Hattery, "Sgt. Mckenna: Marijuana Dangerous, Foolish," *The Acorn*, April 25, 1969, 4.

5 "18 Arrested on Drug Charges; Fires, Violence Plague Campus; Polity Calls for Student Strike," uncredited, *The Statesman*, May 13, 1969. See also, "Outbursts Occur Throughout the Night," uncredited, and "Violence Erupts in Tabler; SDS Member Beaten; Three Hurt in Retaliation," uncredited, both in *The Statesman*, May 13, 1969.

6 "The Bust and Its Aftermath," uncredited, *The Statesman*, May 13, 1969, 4. See also "Barry Urges Crackdown Against Campus Dissent," uncredited, *The Statesman*, February 28, 1969, 2.

7 "Gregory Emphasizes 'Youth' Job Big," uncredited, *The Acorn*, March 14, 1969, 9. Four of the editors for *The Statesman* spent a couple hours in a car ride with Gregory as they drove him from the annual United States Students Press Association Conference in Indiana to his home in Chicago on the eve of the Democratic National Convention held there. Stu Eber, "A Midnight Ride with Dick Gregory," *The Statesman*, September 27, 1968, 5. Philactos and Stanker, "Gregory Appeals for Students to Change American Society," *The Statesman*, September 27, 1968, 5. See also Federal Bureau of Investigation (FBI) on Richard C. Gregory, part 5 of 8, p. 158, accessed November 15, 2021, https://vault.fbi.gov /richard-c.-gregory.

8 Interview with Ken Schulman, July 3, 2018.

9 "The Times That Almost Were," editor, *The Statesman*, April 25, 1969, 17–23. "Barry Urges Crackdown Against Campus Dissent," uncredited, *The Statesman*, February 28, 1969, 2. Ned Steele, "8 Professors Subpoenaed to Testify on Drug Abuse," *The Statesman*, March 11, 1969, 3. "Campus Repression Spreads," uncredited, *The Statesman*, March 18, 1969, 3. Widespread coverage is in *The Statesman*, April 29, 1969. See also "A Statesman Wallposter," March 13, 1969. "21 Students to Be Freed on Friday," uncredited, *The Statesman*, March 27, 1969, 1. "3 Injured in 'G' Tabler Attacks," uncredited, *The Statesman*, April 29, 1969, 1. Ned Steele, "'Justice Above Law': Library Sit-Ins Granted Amnesty by Polity Judiciary," *The Statesman*, April 29, 1969, 1. "SB Faculty Jailed for Contempt of Court," uncredited, *The Statesman*, May 2, 1969, 1. "Student Strike and Picketing Continue; Present New Governance Proposal," uncredited, *The Statesman*, May 16, 1969, 1. "Senate Approves Pass-Fail; Censure of Suffolk Police," uncredited, *The Statesman*, May 16, 1969, 1.

10 "J. Bond of SNCC to Speak Here," uncredited, *The Statesman*, November 15, 1966. Interview with Howie Klein, May 23, 2021. The SAB had earlier invited former chancellor at UC Berkeley Clark Kerr to speak on October 30, 1968. The next day, the SAB presented Charlene Mitchell, U.S. Communist Party presidential candidate. See "S.A.B. Presents Two Speakers," uncredited announcement, *The Statesman*, October 25, 1968, 5.

11 Interview with Bob Smartt, August 17, 2018. Interview with Harry Litwack, June 1, 2019. "Students Heckle at Thurmond Lecture," uncredited, The Acorn, Year-End Review, May 1, 1970, 23.

12 At Drew these included: Martin Luther King Jr., Roy Wilkins (head of the NAACP), Seymour Melman (as part of a "think-in" on campus), Floyd McKissick, (leader of CORE, 1966), Andy Warhol, Ralph Nader, Allen Ginsberg, Ted Sorensen, Dick Gregory, Roy Innis, Strom Thurmond, Sydney Hook, Ralph Ellison, Abbie Hoffman, Nat Hentoff, Jerry Rubin, William Kunstler, Pete Seeger, Jane Fonda, Tom Hayden, Bobby Seale, and William F. Buckley.

13 "This Man Is Evil," uncredited, *The Acorn*, January 24, 1969. See also Chris Welch, "Frank Zappa & the Mothers of Invention: The Truth Is, They're Not as Ugly as Their Pictures," *Melody Maker*, June 7, 1969. Mike Jahn, "Frank Zappa & the Mothers of Invention: Fillmore East, NY," *The New York Times*, June 7, 1971.

14 Dr. Bruce Barrabee, "Nobody Got What They Expected, Not Even Frank & the Mothers," *The Acorn*, February 21, 1969, 7. "Zappa, Mothers, Consider Audience," uncredited, *The Acorn*, February 7, 1969, 3. "Mothers Are Music Too, Says the 'Non-image' Zappa," uncredited, *The Acorn*, January 31, 1969, 2.

15 Mike Jahn, "Blood, Sweat & Tears Rocks with the Music of Al Kooper, Hunter College, New York," *The New York Times*, November 10, 1968. Tellingly, Jahn wrote in his review, "Blood, Sweat & Tears occasionally forgets that while it is a great rock band, it is only a mediocre jazz group, and the audience has come to hear rock."

16 "S.A.B. Presents," uncredited announcement, *The Statesman*, October 22, 1968, 7. Fred Sternlicht, "B.S.&T. the Second Time," *The Statesman*, March 4, 1969, 9. See also Howie Klein, "From the Concert Chairman: The Truth about S.A.B.," *The Statesman*, October 29, 1968, 11. *Specula*, 1969, 45 (excellent photos of Blood, Sweat & Tears, Tim Hardin, and Joni Mitchell in this yearbook).

17 "Monte Carlo, Concert Highlight Weekend," uncredited, *The Acorn*, March 14, 1969, 2.

18 Interview with Greg Granquist, June 27, 2018. Interview with Barry Fenstermacher, May 8, 2018.

19 Interview with Barry Fenstermacher. Interview with Greg Granquist. Interview with Dave Marsden, May 5, 2021. "Concert More Up Than Down; Show Achieves Many 'Firsts,'" uncredited, *The Acorn*, March 27, 1969, 3. Penny Peterson, "The Incomparable Mr. Berry: Incomparable and Real Good," *The Acorn*, March 27, 1969, 7. Karen Westergard, "Berry: Another Perspective," *The Acorn*, March 27, 1969, 7. Barry Fenstermacher, "Concert Paradox," Letters to the Editor, *The Acorn*, February 28, 1969, 6.

20 Interview with Mary Beth Medley (née Olbrych), December 16, 2021. The fifty-mile rule is something of a legend. Everyone I spoke to mentioned it, but I never saw it written down, and it was certainly not enforced regarding colleges/universities. Barsalona and Olbrych carefully measured the distance and informed Graham that it was actually fifty-two miles.

21 Robert Glassenberg, "Campus: A Medium in Its Own Right," *Billboard*, Campus Attractions, March 28, 1970, 4.

22 Ian Dove, "UK Groups Maintain Campus Impetus," *Billboard*, Campus Attractions, March 28, 1970, 36.

23 Dove, "U.K. Groups Maintain Campus Impetus," *Billboard*, Campus Attractions, March 28, 1970, 36.

24 Michael Lydon, "Rock for Sale," *Ramparts*, June 1969.

25 Robert Christgau, *Any Old Way You Choose It: Rock and Other Pop Music* (New York: Cooper Square Press, 2000),194.

26 Eliot Tiegel, "Cost Sky Rocket in Cutting Hip Sound," *Billboard*, December 30, 1967, 1.

27 Ned Steele, "'Rock Inflation' Forces," *The Statesman*, October 14, 1969, 6.

28 Ned Steele, "'Unique' SAB—and the Budget," *The Statesman*, October 17, 1969, 3. Ned Steele, "SAB Planning Winter Schedule," *The Statesman*, October 21, 1969, 3.

29 "Stop the Rape of the Rock Industry," American Talent Associates (ATA), advertisement, *Billboard*, Rock Now, November 14, 1970, R-37.

30 Ed Ochs, "Rock Now!," *Billboard*, November 14, 1970, R-3.

31 Interview with Ed Ochs, December 5, 2021.

32 Interview with Ed Ochs. For other critiques and observations, see Paul Williams, "What Goes On," editorial, *Crawdaddy*, March/April 1968, in Paul Williams, ed., *The Crawdaddy Book: Writings (and Images) from the Magazine of Rock* (Milwaukee, WI: Hal Leonard Corporation, 2002), 252. Lydon, "Rock for Sale." Laura Deni, "Pop Heros as Con Artists," *Billboard*, Rock Now, November 14, 1970, R-49. Richard Robinson, "Rock Music—Consider the Alternative," *Billboard*, Rock Now, November 14, 1970, R-50. Greg Shaw, "Music Magazine: The Real Rock 'n' Roll Underground," *Creem*, June 1971. Marge Pettyjohn, "Talking about My Generation," *Billboard*, Rock Now, November 14, 1970, R-60.

33 Bill Graham, "An Open Letter to Managers and Agents," *Billboard*, June 27, 1970, 25.

34 George Knemeyer, "San Francisco Revisited—A State of Flux," *Billboard*, Rock Now, November 14, 1970, R-6. Deni, "Pop Heros as Con Artists," R-49.

35 Marge Pettyjohn and Jayne Ferguson, "Whatever Happened to That Love Generation," *Billboard*, Rock Now, November 14, 1970, R-54. Laura Deni, "The Great Rock Concert Controversy," *Billboard*, Rock Now, November 14, 1970, R-56. "Rock Fest: To Be or Not to Be Is the (Trade) Question," uncredited, *Billboard*, January 23, 1971, 1. "Do or Die Rock Concert Due for Las Vegas Feb 13," uncredited, *Billboard*, January 30, 1971, 8. Historians Steve Chapple and Reebee Garofalo wrote, "Woodstock was both a festival of youth culture and an example of its commercialization and control." See Chapple and Garofalo, *Rock 'n' Roll Is Here to Pay*, 145.

36 Bill Mankin, "We Can All Join In: How Rock Festivals Helped Change America," *Like the Dew: A Progressive Journal of Southern Culture & Politics*, March 4, 2012, accessed October 12, 2021, https://likethedew.com/2012/03/04/we-can-all-join-in-how-rock-festivals-helped-change-america/#.YWWMNtrMI2y. Many of the outdoor festivals were poorly managed and actually lost money. For details on the Watkins Glen show, see Chapple and Garofalo, *Rock 'n' Roll Is Here to Pay*, 147, 150.

37 "Something Must Happen," uncredited, *Billboard*, Rock Now, November 14, 1970, R-63.

38 Jayne Ferguson, "Rock-Ego Trips," *Billboard*, Rock Now, November 14, 1970, R-66.

39 Bill Graham, "The Americanization of Rock," *Cue*, October 10, 1970.

40 Graham, "The Americanization of Rock."

41 Lydon, "Rock for Sale," 19–24. Graham, "The Americanization of Rock." On Bill Graham, see also Deni, "Pop Heros as Con Artists," R-49.

42 "A Time for a Change," uncredited, *Billboard*, Campus Attraction, March 28, 1970, 24. Chapple and Garofalo's history of the industry makes this observation: "As college students joined hippies and sophisticated listeners in liking progressive rock, campuses became centers for record company promotions as well. Major companies established representatives (Warner Brothers had twenty-five), bought ads in campus papers and campus radio stations, and subsidized college concerts." *Rock 'n' Roll Is Here to Pay*, 75.

43 "A Time for a Change."

44 "A Time for a Change." Bob Glassenberg, "Group Price Inflation Must Stop Say Concert Managers," *Billboard*, Campus Attractions, March 28, 1970, 26. Bob

Glassenberg, "Student O & O Store on Campus Spurts," *Billboard*, January 23, 1971, 1. "Retailer Says Students Should Stick to Their Own Business," uncredited, *Billboard*, January 30, 1971, 26. Bob Glassenberg, "N.Y. Dealers in Dilemma on Price Hike: Absorb or Pass On," *Billboard*, January 30, 1971, 3. "Col Boosts Prices to Dealers—Capitol Does Same to Consumer," uncredited, *Billboard*, February 20, 1971, 1. Bob Glassenberg, "What's Happening," *Billboard*, February 20, 1971, 28. Deborah Spicehandler, "Mother Records Deficit May Force Reorganization, Closing," *The Brown Daily Herald*, October 17, 1973.

45 Mildred Hall, "Colleges Form Co-op to Bow, Back Low $, Peaceful Concerts," *Billboard*, February 20, 1971, 1.

46 Hall, "Colleges Form Co-op," 66.

47 On regional differences, see Eliot Tiegel, "Student Power Leads to Campus Revolution," *Billboard*, Campus Attractions, section 2, March 28, 1970, 16. For Stony Brook's confrontation with large, unruly crowds, see Ned Steele, "Mismanagement and Gatecrashing Add Up to Summer Concert Loss," *The Statesman*, September 16, 1970, 4. Tom Murnane, "Dead Concert Attracts Many; Campus Security Kept Busy," *The Statesman*, November 3, 1970, 1.

48 Claude Hall, "College Radio: Better Than Ever," *Billboard*, Campus Attractions, section 2, March 28, 1970, 28.

49 Email thread with David Hinckley, Glenn Redbord, and Greg Granquist, January 2020. Interview with Howie Klein, November 8, 2020. Interview with Bob Johnson, July 11, 2018. Claude Hall, "College Radio: Better Than Ever," 28. "Finally: WERD Covers the Campus," uncredited, *The Acorn*, January 30, 1970, 1.

50 Although numerous musical acts performed on campus, almost no other well-known, chart-topping band or act performed on the campus until REM in 1985.

51 Chapple and Garofalo, *Rock 'n' Roll Is Here to Pay*, 141.

52 Chapple and Garofalo, *Rock 'n' Roll Is Here to Pay*, 142, 147–154.

53 Jerry Resnick, "The Fall Concert Series: It's Not What It Used to Be," *The Statesman*, November 9, 1971, 8. Lonnie Bennett, "Managing the Concert Ordeal," *The Statesman*, February 1, 1972, 5. "No Curfew for Concert," uncredited, *The Statesman*, February 15, 1972, 16. Ruth Bonapace, "Major Concert Planned by SAB Despite Sizable Budget Cutback," *The Statesman*, February 9, 1973, 4. "SAB: It's Been Bad Weather," uncredited, *The Statesman*, February 20, 1973, 13.

54 "Orlando Releases Group Live Concerts," uncredited, *The Acorn*, November 6, 1970, 12. "Orlando Releases More Group Concert Costs," uncredited, *The Acorn*, November 20, 1970, 10. Interview with Don Orlando, June 25, 2018. Interview with Jeff King, June 2, 2018. "Social Committee Seeks More Money-Music," uncredited, *The Acorn*, November 1, 1974, 1.

55 Albert A. Logan Jr., "Colleges Weigh Banning Rock's 'Super Groups,'" *The Chronicle of Higher Education*, November 30, 1970, 4.

56 William A. Sievert, "Rock Superstars on the Campuses," *The Chronicle of Higher Education*, October 21, 1974, 11.

Conclusion

1 Bruce Rosen, "'Nice Jewish Boy' Bids Students to Vote, Steal," *The Acorn*, October 6, 1971, 6. The report from the FBI agent who sat, undercover, in the audience that day can be found in *Federal Bureau of Investigation: The Vault*,

Abbie Hoffman (Summary), 12 of 26, pp. 38–42, accessed June 6, 2018, https://vault.fbi.gov/abbie-hoffman (henceforth FBI, Abbie Hoffman). "Abbie Hoffman: Good PR for Drew," *The Acorn*, October 22, 1971, 2. Roger Vaughan, "The Straight Word on Abbie Hoffman's Hair," *Life*, October 22, 1971. Bob Smartt, "Abbie Stages a Second 'Final' Jersey Goodbye," *The Newark Star Ledger*, October 4, 1971, 3. Note this article was written by Bob Smartt, now graduated from Drew and working in journalism. Hoffman's impromptu haircut grabbed national attention, and coverage of the incident is widely available. Incidentally, a Drew student, Jeff King, hastily scooped up that lock of hair and still has it. Interview with Jeff King, class of '72, Drew University, June 2, 2018.

2   Several of the former students I interviewed I met at one of these summer reunions. They include Jeff King, Glenn Redbord, Harry Litwack, Barry Fenstermacher, and Tom McMullen. For a listing of all notable appearances at Drew, see https://uknow.drew.edu/confluence/display/DrewHistory/Concerts.

3   The Long Island Music Hall of Fame, https://www.limusichalloffame.org/our-history/. Glenn Jochum, "Stonybrook's Music Roots: Rock and Roll Revisited," *The Brook* 4, no. 3 (Spring 2003): 7. Alan H. Fallick, "A Moody Blues Fan, Then and Now," *Newsday*, April 27, 2012. Interview with Norm Prusslin, November 9, 2020.

4   Andrew Hunt, "When Did the Sixties Happen? Searching for New Directions," *Journal of Social History* 3, no. 1 (Autumn 1999).

5   Among others, see David T. Courtwright, *No Right Turn: Conservative Politics in a Liberal America* (Cambridge, MA: Harvard University Press, 2010).

6   Thelin, *Going to College in the Sixties*, 13–14.

7   Aaron Sternfield, "Nation's Colleges Offer Music Industry Lush Market of 5,900,000," *Billboard*, Music on Campus, March 19, 1966," 16. Chapple and Garofalo, *Rock 'n' Roll Is Here to Pay*, 146.

8   Sam Adams, "Why I Hate Forrest Gump," *BBC Culture*, September 3, 2015, accessed October 28, 2019, http://www.bbc.com/culture/story/20150903-forrest-gump-love-it-or-hate-it. Doyle and Braustein, *Imagine Nation*, especially the introduction. Michael William Doyle, "Debating the Counterculture: Ecstasy and Anxiety Over the Hip Alternative," in *The Columbia Guide to America in the 1960s*, ed. David Farber and Beth Bailey (New York: Columbia University Press, 2001), 143–156. Alice Echols, "Hope and Hype in Sixties Haight-Ashbury," in *Shaky Ground: The Sixties and Its Aftershocks* (New York: Columbia University Press, 2002), chapter 1.

Bibliography

Interviews:

Barbara North
Barry Fenstermacher
Bob Courboin
Bob Johnson
Bob Smartt
Charles Backfish
Dave Hinckley
Dave Marsden
Don Orlando
Doug Chapman
Ed Ochs
Glenn Redbord

Greg Granquist
Harry Litwack
Howie Klein
Jeff King
Ken Schulman
Mary Beth Medley (nee Olbrych)
Moyssi
Nancy Malagold
Norm Prusslin
Tom McMullen
Tom Wetzler

College Newspapers:

The Acorn (Drew University)
The Brown Daily Herald (Brown University)
The Colonial News (SUNY Binghamton)
The Concordiensis (Union College)
The Daily Californian (UC Berkeley)
The Daily Spectator (Columbia University)

The Herald (Hobart College)
Hunter Envoy (Hunter College)
The Justice (Brandeis University)
The Kenyon Collegian
The Octagon (Elmira College)
The Scarlet & Black (Grinnell College)
The Spectrum (SUNY Buffalo)
The Statesman (SUNY Stony Brook)

Newspapers:

The Adirondack Daily Enterprise
The Daily Record
The East Village Other
The Herald (Geneva)
Lake Shore News & Times
The Long Island Advance
The Madison Eagle
The Madison-Florham Park Eagle
The New York Times

The Ogdensburg Journal
Press-Republican
The Pulaski Democrat
The Sag Harbor Express
Sandy Creek News
The Suffolk County News
The Village Voice
The Williamson Son & Sentinel

Magazines:

Billboard
Cashbox
Crawdaddy!
Life
The Nation

Ramparts
Record World
Rolling Stone
Time
Variety

Books/articles:

Bangs, Lester. *Psychotic Reactions and Carburetor Dung.* Edited by Marcus Greil. New York: Anchor Books, 2003.

Beebe, Roger, Denise Fulbrook, and Ben Saunders, eds. *Rock Over the Edge: Transformations in Popular Music Culture.* Durham, NC: Duke University Pres, 2002.

Beidler, Philip D. *Late Thoughts on an Old War: The Legacy of Vietnam.* Athens: University of Georgia Press, 2004.

Brackett, David, ed. *The Pop, Rock, and Soul Reader: Histories and Debates.* 3rd ed. New York: Oxford University Press, 2014.

Bromell, Nick. *Tomorrow Never Knows: Rock and Psychedelics in the 1960s.* Chicago: University of Chicago Press, 2000.

Burke, Patrick. "Tear Down the Walls: Jefferson Airplane, Race, and Revolutionary Rhetoric in 1960s Rock." *Popular Music* 29, no. 1 (January 2010): 61–79.

Chapple, Steve, and Reebee Garofalo. *Rock 'n' Roll Is Here to Pay: The History and Politics of the Music Industry.* Chicago: Nelson Hall Inc., 1977.

Charters, Ann. *The Portable Sixties Reader.* New York: Penguin Books, 2003.

Davis, Joshua Clark. *From Head Shops to Whole Foods: The Rise and Fall of Activist Entrepreneurs.* New York: Columbia University Press, 2017.

Doggett, Peter. *There's a Riot Goin' On: Revolutionaries, Rock Stars, and the Rise and Fall of the '60s.* New York: Canongate Press, 2007.

Doyle, Michael William, and Peter Braustein, eds. *Imagine Nation: The American Counterculture of the 1960s and 70s.* New York: Routledge, 2002.

Eisen, Jonathan, ed. *The Age of Rock: Sounds of the American Cultural Revolution.* Vol. 1. New York: Vintage Books, 1969.

———. *The Age of Rock: Sounds of the American Cultural Revolution.* Vol. 2. New York: Vintage Books, 1971.

Farber, David. *The Sixties from Memory to History.* Chapel Hill: University of North Carolina Press, 1994.

———. "Building the Counterculture, Creating Right Livelihoods: The Counterculture at Work." *The Sixties* 6, no. 1 (2013): 1–24.

Foster, Julian, and Durward Long, eds. *Protest! Student Activism in America*. New York: William Morrow & Co., 1970.

Frank, Thomas. *The Conquest of Cool: Business Culture, Counterculture, and the Rise of Hip Consumerism*. Chicago: University of Chicago Press, 1997.

Frith, Simon, Will Straw, and John Street, eds. *The Cambridge Companion to Pop and Rock*. New York: Cambridge University Press, 2001.

Frith, Simon, Will Straw, John Street, and Andrew Goodwin, eds. *On Record: Rock, Pop, & the Written Word*. New York: Routledge, 1990.

Gitlin, Todd. *The Sixties: Years of Hope, Days of Rage*. New York: Bantam Books, 1987.

Goodman, Fred. *The Mansion on the Hill: Dylan, Young, Springsteen, and the Head-On Collision of Rock and Commerce*. New York: Times Books, 1997.

Graham, Bill, and Robert Greenfield. *Bill Graham Presents: My Life Inside Rock and Out*. New York: Doubleday, 1992.

Hajdu, David. *Love for Sale: Pop Music in America*. New York: Farrar, Straus and Giroux, 2016.

Isserman, Maurice, and Michael Kazin. *America Divided: The Civil War of the 1960s*. New York: Oxford University Press, 2000.

Jones, Steve, ed. *Pop Music and the Press*. Philadelphia, PA: Temple University Press, 2002.

Kramer, Michael J. "The Civics of Rock: Countercultural Music and the Transformation of the Public Sphere." PhD diss., University of North Carolina at Chapel Hill, 2006.

———. *The Republic of Rock: Music and Citizenship in Sixties Counterculture*. New York: Oxford University Press, 2013.

Lipsitz, George. "Who'll Stop the Rain: Youth Culture, Rock and Roll, and Social Crisis." In *The Sixties from Memory to History*, edited by David Farber, 157–178. Chapel Hill: University of North Carolina Press, 1994.

McLeod, Kimbrew. *The Downtown Pop Underground: New York City and the Literary Punks, Renegade Artists, DIY Filmmakers, Mad Playwrights, and Rock 'n' Roll Glitter Queens Who Revolutionized Culture*. New York: Abrams Press, 2018.

McMillian, John. *Smoking Typewriters: The Sixties Underground Press and the Rise of Alternative Media in America*. New York: Oxford University Press, 2011.

Mungo, Ray. *Famous Long Ago: My Life & Hard Times with the Liberation News Service*. New York: Citadel Press, 1970.

Neer, Richard. *FM: The Rise and Fall of Rock Radio*. New York: Villard, 2001.

Peck, Abe. *Uncovering the Sixties: The Life & Times of the Underground Press*. New York: Citadel Press, 1991.

Rips, Geoffrey. *Un-American Activities: The Campaign Against the Underground Press*. San Francisco: City Lights Books, 1981.

Rubin, Jerry. *We Are Everywhere*. New York: Harper & Row, 1971.

Tamarkin, Jeff. *Got a Revolution: The Turbulent Flight of Jefferson Airplane*. New York: Atria Books, 2003.

Thelin, John. *Going to College in the Sixties*. Baltimore, MD: Johns Hopkins University Press, 2018.

Wald, Elijah. *How the Beatles Destroyed Rock 'n' Roll: An Alternative History of American Popular Music*. New York: Oxford University Press, 2009.

Ward, Ed. *The History of Rock and Roll, Vol. I: 1920–1963*. New York: Flat Iron Books, 2016.

Williams, Paul. *The Crawdaddy! Book*. Milwaukee, WI: Hall-Leonard Corporation, 2002.

Index

About the Author

JAMES M. CARTER is an associate professor of history at Drew University in Madison, New Jersey, where his specializations include U.S. foreign policy, the Vietnam War, the Sixties and the rise of the counterculture. He is the author of *Inventing Vietnam: The United States and State Building, 1954–1968*.